Lifting the
Veil of Duality

How to be Free and Without Judgment

With Special, Channeled Messages from:
Lady Diana, Albert Einstein, Edgar Cayce, Mother Teresa,
Mahatma Gandhi, Abraham Lincoln, Apostle Paul, Merlin,
Aristotle, Oliver Wendell Holmes, and other luminaries

Andreas Moritz

Also by Andreas Moritz

. . .

The Amazing Liver and Gallbladder Flush

Timeless Secrets of Health and Rejuvenation

Cancer Is Not a Disease

It's Time to Come Alive

Simple Steps to Total Health

Heart Disease No More!

Diabetes – No More!

Ending The AIDS Myth

Heal Yourself With Sunlight

Feel Great, Lose Weight

Hear the Whispers, Live Your Dream

Sacred Santémony

Ener-Chi Art

Lifting the
Veil of Duality

How to be Free
and Without Judgment

Andreas Moritz

Ener-chi Wellness Press

For Reasons of Legality

The author of this book, Andreas Moritz, does not advocate the use of any particular form of health care but believes that the facts, figures, and knowledge presented herein should be available to every person concerned with improving his or her mental; and physical state of health.. Although the author has attempted to give a profound understanding of the topics discussed and to ensure accuracy and completeness of any information that originates from any other source than his own, he and the publisher assume no responsibility for errors, inaccuracies, omissions, or any inconsistency herein. Any slights of people or organizations are unintentional. This book is not intended to replace the advice and treatment of a physician who specializes in the treatment of diseases, including mental illness. Any use of the information set forth herein is entirely at the reader's discretion. The author and publisher are not responsible for any adverse effects or consequences resulting from the use of any of the procedures described in this book. The statements made herein are for educational and theoretical purposes only and are mainly based on Andreas Moritz's own opinion and theories. The author makes no warranty, expressed or implied, with respect advice or therapy, whatsoever. Except as otherwise noted, no statement in this book has been reviewed or approved by the United States Food & Drug Administration or the Federal Trade Commission. Readers should use their own judgment or consult a holistic medical expert or their personal physicians for specific applications to their individual problems.

ISBN-10: 0-9765715-3-6
ISBN-13: 978-09765715-3-7

1st Edition: March 2002
2nd Edition: Revised and updated: February 2005
3rd Edition: Improved and updated: April 2007
4th Edition: Improved and updated: May 2010

Published by Ener-Chi Wellness Press - Ener-chi.com, U.S.A. (May 2010)

Printed Cover Artwork: Oil on Canvas by Andreas Moritz

Acknowledgments

I would like to express my deep love and gratitude first and foremost to my longtime partner, best friend, companion and guide, Lillian Maresch, Ph.D. for her continuous and unending love and support and for channeling the ruminations (at the beginning and end of each chapter) of beings that have lived in human form on this Earth and now reside in higher dimensional realms.

I also dedicate this work to my ever-growing soul family and all those who have the courage to acknowledge, accept and express their divine nature and purpose.

May 15, 2010
Andreas Moritz

Table of Contents:

INTRODUCTION

You chose to open this book, maybe you are eager to begin reading or perhaps you are a bit puzzled as to why you made this choice. You may even be aware of an ache deep inside, a sense that there is more to life, a sense of "If only…" You may have been searching for that something for a long time, or have only just begun. Yet here you are, reading these words.

What drew you here, now, to this volume? Perhaps it was the title that so intrigued you. Perhaps it was the double spiral symbol on the cover. Perhaps the table of contents piqued your interest. Perhaps it was that ache inside that needs to find something more, something that brings a deeper meaning to this life. Perhaps it was all of this. Or perhaps none of it.

I can only say this: *there are no coincidences in life.* You were drawn here, to this book, at this time and this place, for a purpose: to learn, to grow, to become. You are here because you are ready; ready to 'lift the veil of duality' and begin your journey to Freedom.

Do you know that there is a place inside you - hidden beneath the appearance of thoughts, feelings and emotions - that does not know the difference between good and evil, right and wrong, light and dark? From that place, you embrace the opposite values of life as One, and you know that both are equally valuable and significant for your personal evolvement and for the evolution of humankind and planet Earth. Rumi, one of the most insightful poets that lived on Earth, strongly believed that we all had access to this place. He said: "Out beyond ideas of wrong doing and right doing, there is a field. I'll meet you there."

Although you have actually never been separate from that place of Oneness, this world of situations, conditions and circumstances has kept you from fully merging with the higher aspects of your self, commonly referred to as the 'Higher Self' or 'Silent Observer' (for simplicity sake, whenever you see the term 'Higher Self' it is meant to include all the various levels of Higher Self, such as Over-soul and Source-self). You have one 'foot' or part of your consciousness anchored in the *Lower Dimensions* (First, Second, and Third) of existence. The other 'foot' or part of your consciousness dwells in the *Higher Dimensions* (Fourth, Fifth and above). These two parts of your consciousness coexist, *at the same time.* Yet, strange as it is, m1ost of us are only aware of existing in the material reality of the Third Dimension. The ultimate goal here on Earth is for all of us to become fully aware of, and functional, in all our dimensional realities, without difficulty or conflict.

Existence here on this three-dimensional Earth gives us the opportunity to explore all the ins and outs of duality: the good and the bad, the right and the wrong, the light and the dark, abundance and poverty, love and fear. Experiencing these contrasts of duality enables us to see who we really are and to discover that the common Source of all opposites lies within us. As we come closer and closer to understanding who we really are, we find that judgment (seeing one thing, situation or person as better than another) actually prevents us from discovering and realizing our true essence. By identifying ourselves with the Source of duality rather than with its expression, we actively begin to create a new world, one based on *being* Love, not just on feeling it. At last, we are finding our way Home.

Before you can move into your new home you must free yourself from every limitation that you have imposed upon yourself during duality living. You become free by accepting who you are. This is what is known as *Awakening*. The awakening process allows you to start seeing yourself and every aspect of life in the world through a new lens - the lens of clarity, discernment and non-judgment. In order to fulfill your purpose on Earth you need only switch to another channel of perception, one we all are equipped with but have been afraid to use. If you are open to it, both the material contained in these pages and the double spiral symbol[1] on the cover will begin to create a reference of Universal Oneness within the depth of your being, a Oneness that will bring you to perfect acceptance of yourself and all there is.

We are all on the same journey of discovery, searching for that special place, the Divine Moment (known as the 'state of grace') where judgment has no value or meaning, where we are free of fear and resistance, beyond desire and its fulfillment. It is a quiet place: a unified state of silence where opposites meet and merge their differences. Untouched by the turbulence of thoughts and activity, it is here that you can truly be who you are, and be Love. The Divine Moment, which is a field of all possibilities, is not held back by the past and it is not plotted into the future. It is free and ever-present, at each segment of time. In this sacred place, you are at peace with yourself and at peace with your world. The very moment you enter the state of grace, (a state of non-separation) you are complete. Knowing your completeness, you feel fulfilled. There is nothing more to realize, understand or experience. You are still, you are Love, and you are full. You are Home.

---

[1] A more detailed explanation of the double spiral symbol is given at the end of the book.

This book will take you to many places and will test and perhaps uproot many of your beliefs. It explains why all that we believe in has its roots in some form of judgment, which is the awareness of duality. Our personal views and our worldviews are currently challenged by a crisis of identity. Some are being shattered altogether. The collapse of our current World Order forces humanity to deal with the most basic issues of existence. We can no longer avoid taking responsibility for the things that happen to us. When we do accept responsibility, we also empower ourselves.

The following pages show you how you create or subdue your ability to fulfill your desires and how you control the course of your personal and planetary destiny. Furthermore, you will find intriguing answers to the mystery of time. I have devoted several pages to the truth and illusion of reincarnation, the misleading value of prayer, what makes relationships work and why so often they do not work. It seems very important for us to know at this time why injustice is an illusion that has managed to haunt us throughout the ages. I have dedicated an entire chapter to this topic. Throughout the book, you will find ways to access and utilize your Spiritual Essence. You will learn about our original separation from the source of life and what it means with regard to the current waves of instability and fear so many of us are experiencing. Find out how to identify the angels living amongst us, what it really means to have past and future lives, and why we all have light-bodies. You will have the opportunity to identify the ultimate God within you and discover why a God seen as separate from yourself keeps you from being in your Divine power. In addition, you can find out how to heal yourself at a moment's notice. Read all about the 'New Medicine' and the destiny of the old medicine, the old economy, the old religion, and the old world. And much more...

Everything in this book ties in with the topic of judgment but nothing or nobody in this book is devalued, seen as useless or harmful. You are about to find out that mistakes, accidents, coincidences, negativity, deception, injustice, wars, crime and terrorism all have a deeper purpose and meaning in the larger picture of things. So naturally, much of what you are about to read may conflict with the beliefs you currently hold. I do not ask you to change your beliefs. All I ask is, when you run up against something that makes you groan or shake your head, that you *continue reading with an open mind*. An open mind does not have any belief systems. An open mind enjoys freedom from judgment. It is only by taking risks, by opening ourselves to new ideas, to new ways of looking at ourselves and at life, that we grow, expand, and become who we really are.

Try not to judge what you read as you read it; instead, *read with your heart and feel what the words mean to you* rather than trying to understand them rationally. Much of what is in this book will resonate with you immediately and much will need to be kept on the 'back burner' of your mind until it makes sense. Some of it may never make sense, and that is perfectly fine, for we all understand what we need to understand and precisely when we need to. There is no right or wrong here, only various levels of knowing and recognition. At any moment, we are exactly where we need to be.

In your truest essence, you are beyond all the images and beliefs of the mind. Now the time has come to honor, respect, and accept the opposing aspects of life, enter a state of willing acceptance and take your first steps into the field of non-judgment where freedom dawns, the freedom to be yourself with all your power and glory. You always knew you were special, didn't you, somewhere, some time, long ago? Do you remember when you were very young you had this feeling... this sense... this conviction... that you had a great destiny, that there was something magical about you? You just knew it. Then you grew up, and you spent much of your life ignoring and burying those 'magical' beliefs about yourself, though they have nagged at the back of your mind, now and then saying: "What if...?" Now the time has come to resurrect that knowing and claim your true heritage. All you need to do is - continue reading...

I wish you a wondrous journey to the place where you belong!

Chapter One

Where Judgments Come From

You are one with us; never doubt it for a moment. In a moment's notice or the blink of an eye you may have it all. The world is truly your pearlescent oyster. Hold it dearly and tenderly in your hands with outstretched arms, showing the goodness and the blessings and the oneness in gratitude of all. For we are here to serve each other, we are here to surrender our ego selves like shields on the battle fields, for in the laying down of arms we come back to the realization that all is nectar flowing from the source mother of love.

Lady (Princess) Diana
Channeled on January 7, 2001

Life Is Meaningless Unless You Give It Meaning

In our quest to move to mastery of self we seem to be stumbling upon many obstacles and adverse situations. The challenges we encounter in life occur in four major areas: relationships, health, abundance and self-worth. Although they are all interwoven with one another, each one appears to affect us in a unique way. A broken heart, a sudden illness, the loss of money, or being abused by someone may inevitably bring up the question: "Why did this happen to me?" The question is prompting a search that can never reach a satisfactory conclusion. Trying to figure out

1

why things go wrong in life takes you on a spiral of never-ending twists and turns. It leaves you with the disturbing discovery that for every cause there is yet another cause. However, when you finally stop searching for the answers to your problems, you begin to realize that there is no meaning to anything except the meaning you give to it.

Nothing in this world is the way it appears to be. There are no hidden meanings in our encounters and experiences, no secret agendas that influence us or have power over us. Quantum physics tells us that there are no real colors, shapes and forms in this universe except the ones we create in our minds at the time of observation. Likewise, there are no other meanings to life other than the ones we fabricate in our minds to confirm the existing beliefs we have acquired during the course of our lifetime. God doesn't exist, unless *you* decide so. Likewise, Satan assumes reality only if *you* choose to believe in his existence. There are no angels unless *you* feel and know they are around you. Love is a meaningless word that comes to life only if *you* give it life.

You are an endless sea of consciousness that somehow is compelled to decide whatever kinds of waves it wants to be. You may either choose to become high-riding waves that display great power and strength, or assume the shape of small and fragile waves that cruelly seem overtaken by the larger ones. In every case scenario, you are and remain the sea. Judgments arise when you begin to question your identity and look for answers as to why you are or behave a certain way. Once the perception of being a small wave begins to dominate your awareness, the knowingness of being the infinite sea of consciousness rapidly fades away. The knowingness of being the infinite sea also begins to fade if you choose to be a mighty wave. *Both* experiences of being powerful and weak forfeit the unbounded potential that you are. You forsake your real nature just to gain a little pleasure or to lose a little pain. Strength and weakness are finite expressions of us just as different waves are expressions of the sea, yet in no way do they represent who you truly are.

You Are What You Think You Are

Judgment is the attempt of the mind to attach some kind of meaning to your experiences in life. This meaning in turn defines who you are in relationship to certain events, circumstances or people you meet. In other words, the way the world represents itself to you is an exact replication of what or who you think you are. If you see yourself as a victim of abuse, you will see potential abusers everywhere and consequently manifest even more abuse in your life. Some day you may decide that

2

this low self-image is no longer an appropriate reflection of you and so you begin to feel more deserving and lovable. Because of this perceptual shift, your world has no other option but to accommodate and respond to the *new* meaning of yourself, thus, it brings more giving and kind people into your life and blesses you with greater abundance.

In any case, you are the master creator of your life, whether your creation appears to be positive or negative. This occurs in a mostly unconscious fashion, making the process very difficult to manipulate or control. You cannot be fully aware of and live your true potential unless you take conscious charge of creating meanings for all the things that happen in your life. Most people would want to know why, for example, they missed a train, forgot to pay their phone bill, or sprained an ankle just when they decided to go and visit a friend. One person may come up with only derogatory reasons for all these events, such as: "I just wasn't myself today", "I should have been more alert" or "How stupid of me!" A religious person may have a very different interpretation of these incidences: "God must have had his (good) reasons to make me miss that train, to receive no phone calls for a couple of days, or to prevent me from going out to visit my friend." Both kinds of responses are self-created and in no way reflect the true meanings of these occurrences. Absolute reasons simply do not exist. They are subjective projections only, with no objective or independent truths in them. No one else except *you* can give meaning to what occurs in your life. Such is the power of your existence. You can apply this power in any way you want. It is for you to choose and decide *why* things are happening the way they do. Their meanings are completely up to you.

A person with terminal brain cancer may argue that there is no other choice left but to die, that 'my time is up'. However, they are the only ones who can decide whether the tumor is going to kill them or not and they have that choice at every moment they are still alive. This is not to say the one decision is right and the other is wrong. It just means that it is up to them to direct their infinite power toward bringing about the destruction of their physical body, or restoring it back to health. Very few people realize that they are the ones who make the body self-destruct through an autoimmune disease such as cancer.

The majority of those falling ill do not feel they have the power to heal themselves, which may perhaps be the reason they become ill in the first place. The self-assessment of the lack of healing ability is by itself a powerful decree or judgment destined to become a self-fulfilling prophecy; it effectively blocks the healing process. This, however, does not mean these people have no capacity for self-healing. The very fact that they are able to live on this Earth plane and sustain a complex physical body proves that they are an unfathomable pool of creative intelligence. Yet, they have decided to funnel their energies toward fulfilling the unconscious decision that they cannot heal themselves. And the body merely carries out the instructions.

There *is* no deadly cancer as such. Some people decide that cancer cannot kill them and they live through it as if it were the flu. In fact, studies have shown that at least 85% of all cancers disappear on their own. Those who had them didn't even know they had them. Others fear cancer like a terrible monster or as an influence that is beyond their conscious control, and they die from it regardless of how effective and successful a particular treatment may be. Consequently, the cancer seems to take control of their body and their life. In truth, there are no other influences than the ones they create or attract toward them. Accidents, mistakes, failures, achievements, happiness, conflict, peace, and whatever else takes place in our personal world, are all our own making, not God's or anyone else's. You literally make up every single reason why something happens to you the way it does.

Your *intention* is what determines whether you deviate from or stay on the path of life. While unconscious of your own power, you are naturally afraid of outer influences that could upset you or throw you off balance. The projected fear becomes your decree, your intention, and your judgment. If you are afraid of disease, you are literally praying or asking to become sick. Why would you do that? Because you can learn from the pain it generates. Sickness can take you beyond fear and reclaim the power that you are. If you consciously choose to appreciate an illness or an accident as an opportunity to initiate a long overdue internal shift and transform your life, then that is what it will do for you. Basically, nothing that happens to you has a hidden or useless agenda.

Your future is in your hands, at every moment. The instant something happens to you (remember, you have attracted that situation), it is your intention and interpretation of this situation that determines how you feel about it and what it has brought into your life. The way you interpret things or expect them to be is, in turn, based on your previously acquired beliefs. These beliefs serve as crutches to help you feel more secure. You create expectations in your life because thinking you know what comes next helps pacify your old fears and insecurities. By expecting something bad to happen, you feel you can prepare for the worst if need be. This, however, is a catch-22 situation. These expectations actually manifest what you do NOT want to happen.

How You Create Your Reality

Your subconscious has its roots in the oneness or singularity of Self. There cannot be two of you. All thoughts originally come from this Higher Self, and as such, they are untainted by beliefs or fearful expectations. It is only as your thoughts emerge from your subconscious that you attach all sorts of meanings to them, all of which are based on previously gathered beliefs and experiences. But the Higher Self has no reference to negative duality, expressions such as: no... not... can't... won't... don't... etc. So when you are thinking: "I hope I am not getting cancer like my mother did" or "I wish I am not going to run out of money again this month", your subconscious mind will hear: "I hope I am getting cancer like my mother did" and "I wish I am running out of money again this month".

Fearful expectations put energy into exactly that which you *don't* want. Your Higher Self is made of one (not two) and has no limitations in its ability to fulfill desires, only infinite possibilities. It simply cannot recognize a negative (don't) versus a positive (do) instruction. It also perceives your doubts and fears as desires that need fulfilling. *All* desires 'return' to the pure consciousness of your Higher Self to become fulfilled; they do so *automatically* the moment after you have expressed them. So the universe has no other choice but to follow the instructions you are feeding into your subconscious mind which has access to infinite energy and intelligence.

If you had cancer and came to my office with the question: "How do I get rid of it?" you would hear me say this: "Honor it, and it will heal you." Attacking cancer in any way ignores its purpose and value. Cancer isn't out to destroy you; it is there to *free* you from your limited beliefs. Trying to get rid of it implies that you believe cancer is a terrible disease that somehow has got hold of you and that you need help to take it out of your body again. The truth of the matter is that the cancer would never have developed if you hadn't had such a belief system in you in the first place. The cancer, which on the physical level is just an imbalance manifested in the cells of the body, is your opportunity to bring balance into all aspects of your life and to trust in yourself. You chose cancer to assist you in doing that because it deals with balance issues most effectively. Once you have accepted and honored the cancer for its role and purpose you are ready to move on and heal from within yourself. This is how you create your own reality in life.

There are no limitations to the self *except those which you believe.* If you want to create a different reality for yourself, you need to under

5

first what your beliefs are. The reason you are equipped with a conscious mind is so you can examine those beliefs and give your inner self a different picture of reality. There is no power in the world that can take this ability away from you. If you are angry with someone, it is the idea or belief *you have* about this person that causes you to have this emotion, and not the other way around. The emotion is very dependent on what you believe. Therefore, based on your beliefs, you will first create certain emotions and, subsequently, the corresponding thoughts that reinforce your original beliefs. The thoughts may (or may not) drive you to action to manifest them in your life.

For example, your new friend promises you to take you out on a dinner date. You get all dressed up and expect to have a wonderful evening together, but he doesn't show up. One reaction finds you disappointed, then frustrated because of all the effort you put into getting ready, and eventually downright angry - angry because you believe that he let you down or forgot the dinner date he promised you. Another reaction to this scenario might be concern about your friend's well-being, thinking that perhaps he had a car accident. The idea that something bad could have happened to him causes you anxiety and nervousness. A third reaction could be taking the situation exactly as it is without creating a mental projection of what might be the reason for the delay. This version would not include an emotional response at all. However you react, and it is your ideas and beliefs which form the structure of your experience. All situations are fundamentally neutral. They possess no built-in meanings other than those you attach to them.

Tainted by your personal beliefs, neutral and unbiased energy translates into specific feelings, thoughts and emotions that, in turn, create your life experiences. The beliefs automatically cause you to feel and behave in a certain fashion. Trying to avoid, suppress, or change unwanted thoughts, feelings, or emotions is a hopeless undertaking because their roots (beliefs) are still in place. Being *with* these thoughts, feelings, and emotions allows you to get in touch with the beliefs that have caused them in the first place. Seeing them as neutral allows you to attach any given meaning to them. Instead of saying: "This is causing me a lot of problems", you can just as well ask: "In what way could this help me?" By mentally translating a seemingly negative situation into a useful one, you enliven and actualize the conscious ability to create a new reality for yourself and your world.

Your beliefs and the reasons for them are found in your conscious mind. Many people assume those beliefs are forever buried in the past of this life, either of this lifetime or perhaps even another. Unless they

6

change that belief, they will not be able to grow and expand. All the beliefs we could possibly have are right with us at every moment. It is time to examine all of them and let go of those that imply basic limitations, such as: "I can't do this job because I am not clever enough" or "You can't have everything in life" or even "We all must age and die". It is time for us to realize that any idea we accept as truth is a belief that we hold. That belief creates and shapes our personal reality.

Once you identify a belief, you can change it and create a new reality. If you feel angry or sad about something, ask what beliefs you must have in order to feel this way. Then acknowledge the beliefs you hold. You will discover that there is no real reason that could justify anger or sadness, except the illusion (belief) of separation. Accepting a broader, more unifying understanding of your situation will generate loving emotions that, in turn, will generate completely different thoughts than you had before. This will also change the way you behave and act.

All beliefs contain their own intrinsic self-perpetuating system of logic and evidence. Each belief has its rationale, its relative truth and perspective. If someone poor thinks it is rightful to steal from the rich because the rich exploit the poor, they are likely to become a thief and even feel good about it. They have actually created all the reasons to think this way. The basic principle here is that you will only be able to understand and create in your life what you believe is *your* truth. You see what you believe, not more, not less. There is no other reality out there than the one you create inside. Things don't just 'happen' to you, you *make* them happen. The ultimate truth of life is not based on an idea; it is the state of consciousness that creates from within itself anything it wants, without limitations. We are in human form to learn consciously the craft of creation.

Your Truth is what You Make It to Be

Searching for life's meaning is a dead-end road; it leads nowhere because there is no meaning other than the one you create at each new moment. Making conscious decisions of how you want your life to be determines how it is going to be. Instead of *searching* for the meaning of a particular event, or of life as such, *give* it meaning. You actually do that anyway, although unconsciously. So if you would like to see something affect you in a new and different way, *consciously choose* to give it a new meaning that supports your desire. Instead of deciding that the cancer is there to take your life (the old belief), you can just as well decide that the cancer is there to help you appreciate life more, awaken

7

you to a new purpose, or give yourself the love and attention you so deserve (the new belief). The old belief is limiting and destructive, the new one is liberating and enriching. The belief you focus your energy on will determine the outcome of the disease.

Judging a situation or a person is highly unrealistic because *nothing* in the physical world is real. You cannot attribute anything to the categories of good and bad, right or wrong, etc. Duality exists only in the minds of those who maintain a duality perception. Unity, on the other hand, exists only in the minds of those who see all as one. To become a medical doctor may feel right to one person but wrong to another. What is a dreadful experience for one person may be a relief for another. Many soldiers who fought at the frontline in World War II rejoiced greatly when they were injured by flying shrapnel or gunshots because this meant they would leave the battlefront and be released to go home. On the other hand, a person injured in the surroundings of their own home might suffer greatly because they may be taken away to a hospital.

Pain and suffering are a matter of interpretation and, therefore, are highly subjective. An earthquake may be seen as a terrible disaster that takes hundreds of lives, or it may be seen as the Earth's way of regenerating itself so that it can nourish and give life to millions more. Perception and knowledge are different in different states of consciousness. The consciousness of our Higher Self seeks no outer source to supply it with knowledge, whereas our human self depends on our senses and our mind to gather information and ideas. The Higher Self sees itself reflected in everything and seeks to unite opposites, whereas the lower self sees itself as separate from everything and seeks to divide things into isolated objects of time and space. Yet no one state of consciousness is right or wrong, better or worse. Each state has its own value; one is there to learn about duality and the other one is there to master it.

You are on a journey to mastery. The mastery is not about anything outside. It is the mastery of conscious creation that you are really after. You *already* create your own life situations, whatever you do. This book was conceived to help you *become aware of the power* you are already using. Once you are aware of your creative power, you can direct it in any way you like. Even as the words of this book enter the space of your mind, a restructuring is taking place in all the different dimensional parts of your being that is going to help you to create conscious mastery over every moment in your life. As this process unfolds, you will know that:

8

1. **The only meaning there is in anything is the meaning you give it.**
2. **Your experience is what you say it is. Nothing else and no one else can define it.**
3. **Since you are exactly who you say you are, then, at each new moment you are gifted with a life-altering choice.**

Judgment is the unconscious attempt to give meaning to things and thereby defines us as players of duality. Therefore, the ultimate choice in life is to gain freedom from judgment and become the doers of oneness. Attaining freedom from judgment is a process of peeling off the layers of meaning that we have given to everything that has occurred throughout the ages (what we refer to as our beliefs). When there is nothing left to find meaning in, when there is only the oneness of the ALL, we pass through the veil of ignorance and stand in our own power. So let us begin the peeling process.

The Mistaken Intellect

We have lived in a world of judgment throughout all human history. Every war and conflict the Earth has ever witnessed, and still experiences, comes from the inability of human beings to accept one another exactly the way they are, with all their unique differences, faults and assets. Whether it is the clashing of creeds, nationalities, races or beliefs, or the occurrence of disease, strife and/or poverty, any kind of problem the human race faces, can be traced back to an awareness of separation i.e. the sense of separation from our spirit self (our Higher Self), and from the laws of nature, the Earth and its inhabitants.

This seeming separation lies at the root of all misconception or judgment. Ayurveda, which is the most ancient and comprehensive healing system available to humanity to date, has chosen an almost simplistic explanation for the suffering and confusion that prevail in almost every area of life. The 6,000-year old records of Ayurveda, which means 'Science of Life', depict one single cause to be responsible for every ill that could possibly befall life on Earth. Ayurveda calls it *Pragya Bharat* or mistaken intellect. It means that we perceive the world as separate from us - an illusion created by the intellect.

Ironically, although this illusion is brought about by a misapprehension of what life really is, you cannot remove it just by creating the proper intellectual understanding of its essential nature. If that were so, then reading the holy scriptures such as the Bible, the

Vedas, the Koran or any other religious or spiritual books would have easily corrected this flaw of the mind and saved most of mankind from the pitfalls of ignorance and the perils of self-destruction. However, learning does not *begin* in the mind or intellect; it starts on the faintest level of *feeling* where the soul decides what is real and what is not. Indeed, we may only be able to overcome the mistaken belief of the intellect by walking the path of judgment first, by feeling what it means to judge and to be judged.

Judgment may take on any form and intensity but *in all cases, it implies separation*. For example, preferring to wear a red shirt today rather than a blue one basically means that for this moment you feel red is more suitable or better than blue. You accept red as the 'right' choice but reject blue as the 'wrong' one. These choices create segregation and occur on the level of feelings. Now, if you bring your rational mind into this situation you may in fact run into a conflict because, let us say, the red shirt doesn't go with the color of your pants. You may even become angry because the color of your pants doesn't match the color of your shirt. When you go to a party and see someone else wearing non-matching clothes like you, you may find that your previously experienced anger suddenly gets rekindled and you start judging that person for not knowing how to dress. Of course, if everyone in the world wore non-matching colors, we might find nothing 'wrong' with it.

You can see from this simple example that separation of anything into good and bad, right and wrong, etc. is based on a feeling of judgment, a feeling that lies at the core of most of life's discrepancies. It is because we *feel* that one thing is good and the other is bad that we carry this division (judgment) into our thoughts, emotions and actions and, thus, create our current world reality. If someone felt strongly enough that their financial problems would be more quickly resolved by investing their money at a poker game or at the roulette table in a casino, rather than utilizing it in a more reliable way, it is their *judgment* that will take them to the casino. If they win they will feel great about having made the 'right' decision and their world will suddenly look bright and propitious. However, if they lose their investment, their world will collapse further into disarray and hopelessness because of a 'wrong' decision. In either case, they carry the seeds of judgment within them, which become the lessons for further learning of the ins-and-outs of duality existence.

Once we have completely explored and emotionally captured the entire bandwidth of all the possible highs and lows of our existence in this dimensional reality, we can consciously merge with the ground we are standing on and perceive everything else that enters our field of experience with the wisdom of ultimate knowledge. This book is designed to take you through this path more consciously and swiftly while it also serves as a means to burst the bubble of illusion that you are in fact anything other than oneness of diversity. Once rooted in the oneness of your Higher Self, your perception of life is radically changed. Judgment, which belongs to the field of duality, is non-existent when Oneness shines forth. The mistaken judgment of the intellect, *Pragya Bharat,* dissolves in the fire of knowledge just as ice melts in the presence of heat.

Separation Consciousness

The word judgment implies that there is someone or something that is better or worse than someone or something else. We are indoctrinated to the belief that whatever is 'better' should be welcomed or accepted and whatever is 'worse' should be avoided or discarded. Racial discrimination, for example, isn't caused by differences intrinsic in the races but by the consciousness of separation that exists within the person who feels irrational and uncontrollable anger toward another fellow human being with a different skin color. Moreover, if we ourselves are judging those who are judgmental of others, all we do is repeat the same pattern of judgment that we so disapprove of in others. Racism, to use the above example, doesn't go away if we merely enforce laws that prohibit it at the working place or in public areas. Suppressed anger, which often is caused by previous traumatic separation issues, continues to be present and may even turn into further, more violent and uncontrollable reactions.

Later on, we shall explore how to resolve conflicts in life in a more natural and easy way than we currently are able to. First, we need to probe more deeply into our own consciousness to find out what really bothers us when we pass judgments. If oneness is our true nature, why do we suffer from separation consciousness? Why do we *not* feel one with everyone? The answers to these questions are essential to moving from duality back to Oneness.

Very young children usually don't have this separation consciousness. They behave as if the whole world belongs to them. The young ones have very few inhibitions and concerns about not being wanted or loved. They take it for granted that their parents, relatives, and even strangers, love them. Children display an irresistible charm and innocence that melts even hearts made of stone. So what happens to us as we grow up? Why do we lose that joyful spontaneity and openness to the world once

11

we interact with it for a certain length of time? Are we programmed to be judgmental or can we choose to regain the power of innocence we once had?

Learning Not To Be Good Enough

Contrary to the idea that we are born sinners, being judgmental of something or someone's behavior is not part of our essential nature. We have *learned* to be judgmental in order to navigate the ebbs and flows of life so we can discover who we really are. We have acquired this almost universal personality characteristic, first, to learn all about the worlds of opposites (duality) and, second, to detect our underlying oneness. If we cannot accept that we are here for a higher purpose - a viewpoint that agrees with the concept of existentialism - then going through the hardships of life seems totally senseless and atrocious. It would mean that the God who put us here has made a great mistake. This would go against the core of our instincts and beliefs.

Still, there are questions lurking in the back of our minds that remain unanswered, such as: "How could someone so innocent and beautiful as a new-born baby become someone who ends up hating and killing other people?" Take, for example, US school shootings. Psychologists may argue that the children must have been abused physically or emotionally to display such a level of violence in their lives. Or perhaps they were exposed to too much violence on television. Maybe easy access to guns tempts kids to shoot their classmates and teachers. All cogent arguments, yet without a higher perspective, none of these explanations completely suffice. This applies to all conflict situations in life. To get a better understanding of the ultimate root of judgment, and therefore suffering of any kind, we first need to take a closer look at the early stages of our lives.

From early childhood, many of us have *grown into* the shame of not being good enough. As toddlers, we may have sensed the warm and loving approval of our parents as we successfully took our first steps or managed to climb a staircase without falling down. But we may also have learned that when we weren't as 'successful' in our attempts to master the force of gravity as our parents would have liked us to be, their faces would look somewhat less satisfied, even disappointed. Although we were unconscious of the subtle differences in their reactions, we registered nevertheless that one reaction was preferable to another.

This basic pattern repeated itself many times over in different ways. For one action, we received our parents' consent and for the other we earned either no response or even outright disapproval. There is actually nothing wrong with falling down when learning how to walk. In fact, it is highly beneficial for the physical, emotional, and spiritual development of children to experience falling down and then getting up again through their own effort, similar to a young bird that learns to fly. We learn the truly important skills of life by mastering the difficulties that seem to prevent us from becoming who we want to be.

I have watched many children who, while playing, have injured their knees or elbows. In most cases, the child's first response was to look at their mother to check how she reacted to the fall. If she showed fear and concern or even anger in her face, the child started crying. In most of the cases where the mother smiled or laughed, the child showed no obvious signs of pain and even responded with a grin. In the first instance, the child interpreted the pain from the fall as something bad and fear instilling, whereas in the latter case, the child had no negative reference that could allow for an unhappy response.

Can I Really Trust Myself?

Children often fall 'accidentally on purpose' if their bodies require a boost of immunity. A wound that becomes infected due to dirt very often serves as a quick self-help method to stimulate the immune system and further increase the level of natural resistance to disease in a child's body. Many growth spurts are initiated in this way. We tend to think that children don't know what is happening, but their Higher Selves and spiritual guides are ever watchful to permit only what truly is in their highest interest, even if this means injury. However, what begins to happen is that this natural instinct or 'innocent knowingness' becomes gradually distorted through the varied responses the child receives from the surroundings. Basically, all reactions in life are ego-driven, which means they are rooted in the *fear of separation*. Without fear, there would be no reaction, only action. Since separation can only occur in the ego or consciousness of non-reality, none of what appears to be real is actually real. Separation appears so real because there is no perception of the underlying oneness.

How many of us remember having been scolded for not finishing what our mother had prepared for us? Maybe we weren't hungry or our body's natural instincts suppressed the urge to eat for other reasons, such as feeling unwell or upset about something. Or maybe we just didn't like the food she cooked. Our body's own normal and natural responses, however, were criticized with such words as: "You are a spoiled brat!" or "You don't value what God is giving to you."

Several years ago, I had a patient who complained to me about his eating disorder. "I can never sit at a table and eat a meal like everyone else does," he said. When I inquired about his childhood eating habits he reluctantly told me that his mother literally used to throw portions of food at him that he was unable to eat. Although his mother truly believed that this was the proper way to teach her son to appreciate the food she was preparing for him - because of her own unfulfilled needs for love and appreciation - such 'justified' methods of educating her son had led to his highly disturbed relationship to food and eating. Using food as an educational tool to teach the young ones the 'right manners' of adulthood has become very popular. The good intention of the parents, however, has turned out to be the most influential contributing factor causing a disproportionate part of the population to suffer from eating disorders and obesity. These people have learned from early in their lives that listening to the body is wrong. Thus, in later life, they have no way of knowing how to read or decipher the body's language. The communication link between the inner and the outer aspects of life becomes severely disrupted and so does the spiritual connection to the Source Self.

Consequences of Not Trusting Yourself

The link between one's Higher Self and the physical awareness of the body - the Ego Self - becomes further disturbed when the body shows signs of malfunctioning. Instead of trusting the body more and more as we grow older and cooperating with it when it falls ill, we are told that the body cannot be trusted because it makes mistakes. To correct our body's 'mistakes' we employ specialists (doctors) who have gone through many years of rigorous training and acquired the diagnostic skills to listen to the body and to decide what is wrong with it. Then *they* apply the appropriate procedures to rectify its 'misbehavior'.

Since doctors have been given the 'legal right' to treat disease, and you haven't, you may feel obliged to do whatever they tell you to do. Motivated by a strong desire to feel better again, you willingly hand over the power and responsibility for your body to a stranger, someone you may have met with for 15 minutes or less. The ready acceptance, on your part, of the idea that your body must be doing something wrong if it is not well, further heightens the feeling of failure or incompetence. Perhaps you even believe that your body is out to cause you trouble and

14

you feel angry at it for disrupting your life and your plans. This is where you start feeling powerless against your own body. It may not occur to you that *these thoughts* themselves may be the very instructions and self-fulfilling prophecies that render your body powerless against illness.

It doesn't make things any better that you are given a dozen or so immunization shots to prevent future illnesses. We begin to learn that there are 'horrible' germs out there, which have no purpose other than to make it difficult for humans to survive. Although everything in your body lets you know that you do not need these interventions - through such sensations as fear or the fight-or-flight response - the even greater fear of perhaps being wrong about this is stronger. You unconsciously admit that you are less powerful than a pill or a shot consisting of dead virus material.

What you may have gathered from all this is that illness is 'bad', and health is 'good'. Also that disease strikes indiscriminately and has to be 'cured' by whatever means. Consequently, we so often say or hear: "You are so lucky to be healthy." It seems, though, this luck changes with age. 75% of the people living in our block have or had cancer of various types and most of them are retired people. Does this mean that unlucky people are more likely to get cancer if they are retired? Can we really account bad luck for being a credible cause of disease? On the other hand, could there be something more sensible behind a heart attack or stroke than being an innocent victim of fate? Why does disease always seem to put a sudden brake on a person's life? All these questions may be served by one answer. Consider this: disease could be a fortunate thing because it *changes the course of your life* from a direction that no longer serves your highest interests to one that does. Disease may indeed be one of the most efficient healing responses the body has in order to return us to a condition of balance, health, and peace. But without seeing this larger picture and being open to receive the hidden opportunities that every moment of life has to offer to us, we are left with only the ability to judge what is 'good' and 'bad', and what is 'right' and 'wrong'.

Equipped with this learned ability to discern between right and wrong, we begin to divide the entire world into two categories, one favorable and the other unfavorable. Instance by instance, we begin to feel affirmed in our conclusion that we must be the victims of powers that are beyond our control. We learn that parents and teachers usually have the last say, even if their decisions seem biased and unjustified. Resisting the rules can cost you dearly. There are laws watching over everything, from how you ride your bike to how you address the judge in a courtroom. You learn that these laws must be obeyed or else you will

15

end up being in some kind of trouble. On the other hand, you also learn that being vulnerable and not being in control is not earning respect from others, and in some instances, they may even reject and despise you. So you begin to hide all those things within you that don't find approval by your friends and loved ones. You may be ashamed of not being smart enough and feel guilty if you cannot fulfill others' expectations of you, especially when they are close to you, like your parents, friends, teachers, and schoolmates. This sets the stage for a long and arduous fight for approval and recognition.

By now you have come to understand that the inability to meet other people's expectations in life is undesirable or 'bad'. It earns criticism and increases low self-worth. On the other hand, being 'good' at everything is honored and finds approval by others. The seeds of judgment that have been sown in the earlier stages of life are now beginning to sprout. The struggle of life begins, and you discover that you need to be competitive in order to 'make it' in this world. Of course, all this happens at an unconscious level, which allows you to enter the world of judgment with full impact. Later on, you will see why this is so necessary and important for your integration process.

Educated To Be Judgmental

Education plays one of the most crucial roles in a person's life. It can determine whether they are successful in their career or not. But it can also leave them disillusioned about life. One thing all students learn is that they have to 'prove' themselves to be considered 'worthy students'. You are told that only hard work will earn you a decent living. You must study with determination and discipline in order to compete in this 'selfish' world where nothing is given for free. It doesn't matter how you feel inside, the most important thing is how well you perform, how well you remember by rote what you have learned. You may have the best qualities of kindness, love and generosity, but none of these count when you have to take a test and show how 'good' you are. You are not valued for who you are but for how well your brain cells can assimilate and recall information, regardless of whether this information has anything to do with you and your life or not.

The division between your inner world and your outer world begins to widen further and you learn to put all your energy and emphasis on appearance. Since you are mostly judged by your performance and hardly at all by what you represent as an individual being, you also begin to judge yourself on this basis. You feel ashamed of yourself or guilty

16

when you fail a test, because you were programmed to believe that remembering well not only gets you to the top, but it also makes you a better person. Your teachers, parents and the school system do not approve of failure and if you fail too many tests, you are even forced to repeat a class. Having to repeat a class in school is a very embarrassing experience especially in a young person's life. I can attest to that.

The Beginnings of Self-Judgment

I grew up in a small town in Western Germany. Primary school wasn't a problem for me but when I enrolled in a gymnasium (high school) in the early sixties, my performance rates dropped sharply. I only felt free and joyful during the holiday season. My parents, like all 'good' parents, rewarded me with extra pocket money whenever I managed to bring home the occasional good grade. My elder brother, on the other hand, excelled in every subject and 'earned' a lot more money than I did. His astounding ability to memorize and recall anything he read or heard even just once gave him more free time for playing than I ever had.

Somehow, I drew the conclusion that I had become a failure in life because I was too dumb to keep information in my head. Since I wasn't as good a student as my brother, I assumed that my parents loved me less than they loved him. Although this was far from being the truth, it felt this way to me. As a result, I tried to prove to my brother and to my parents how good I was in other areas such as sports, music and friendships. I had so many friends that eventually my brother became jealous of me. We became very competitive, each in our own field.

This competitive streak became even more pronounced when I had to face the shame of repeating a class, especially because I wasn't able to memorize Latin vocabulary and the formulae of algebra, which I felt had no relevance to anything in my life. At the end of the term, my teachers praised the best students for their excellent performance but had nothing to say to me except that I hadn't been good enough to pass. I felt I was stupid because I wasn't as intelligent as most of my classmates. Like my teachers, I believed that intelligence was something you either had or you didn't have, and I certainly didn't seem to have it. This idea of not being 'good enough' became deeply engrained in my consciousness, especially when my jealous brother became somewhat triumphant over this, and my parents, especially my father, showed major disappointment upon my breaking the dreaded news. I felt guilty for not having worked hard enough and for having 'caused' grief to my parents. Self-judgment became a major part of my life from that day on. I was 'bad' because I wasn't 'good enough'.

Creating and Breaking the Facade of Worthiness

During my last seven years of high school, I spent most of my time studying and very little time playing. I wanted to make sure I would never have to repeat a class again. My father died when I was eighteen. Although I was very close to him and missed him very much, I also felt relief when he died because now there was no one in my life who had expectations of me.

Nevertheless, from then on, I made sure that I would reveal no weaknesses to anyone. I became an expert at everything I did in my life, except at showing who I was inside. For many years, I played the role of a spiritual teacher and healer, which earned me great respect and admiration by those I was able to help and assist in their healing. I played this role so well that I wasn't even aware I was playing it. I excelled in remembering what I learned and conveying it to others in a way that they could understand. Soon I became known for successfully treating hundreds of patients with diseases that defied conventional treatment; among them were even heads of state. I had created a façade of worthiness that I thought was the real me.

However, there was another side of me, the one living in the shadow and hidden from view. I only allowed the person closest to me, my former wife Maggie, to see what my 'dark' side was like, my weak spots, and then only after she 'pushed my buttons'. Since she didn't scold me but loved me even more when I showed my true feelings and emotions, I felt increasingly encouraged to reveal my sensitivity, vulnerability, and humanness to her and to others as well. The curse of self-judgment that I had put on myself started to release. It took me several more years, though, to unravel this deep form of self-judgment and source of resentment and conflict in life.

It is one thing to realize that much of the way you view yourself and the world around you is a result of all the messages and opinions that have been ingrained in your psyche right from the early days of your life. It is an entirely different thing to recognize that all these are there to actually serve you, in a way. To understand this, you must first sift through all the rules and beliefs that you have been fed about how you should behave, how you should look, what you should wear, how much you should weigh, where you should shop, what car you should drive, what you should do for a living, who you should be friends with, when

18

you should marry, or what you owe your parents. All these 'shoulds' have a stifling effect on your sense of freedom and inner knowledge.

Next, you need to open up to new worlds and different points of view. When you do so, you discover that there is more to life than just principles, a whole world outside the shoulds, the dos and the don'ts. You learn that when you give, you receive; when you love, you are loved; when you feel compassion, your heart opens; and when you are honest with others, you face no tension in your relationships. All of these experiences have a liberating effect. With *both* types of experiences, positive and negative, you learn that, for the most part, you get what you believe you deserve, and that *much of life is a self-fulfilling prophecy*. All the drama of life circles around one purpose, which is to face your true Self. The experiences you have in life are all reflections of how you view yourself. This means that by being in this world and interacting with other people we are constantly looking at mirrors in order to learn more about who we are. Losing ourselves and finding ourselves are expressions we use to define these experiences. But in truth, the Self is never lost and therefore does not need to be found.

The Self - Lost and Found

We have seen that the need to judge arises when we are feeling insecure, fearful, or dissatisfied. People who are in love feel as if they could embrace the whole world. Their sense of happiness transcends the barriers of division and allows them to perceive the underlying unity of all things. Even though this state of being in love may only be a fleeting moment of unity consciousness, it nevertheless shows that we are capable of bridging the gap of separation that exists between our world and us.

A mother who looks at her newborn child with utter affection feels no separation in her heart. She and her child are one unit, invisibly bonded by the uniting power of love. Where do the feelings of separation come from when months or years later she starts yelling at her child or criticizing them for their behavior? How do some mothers develop jealously and animosity towards their own children? Why do couples that have promised to love and care for each other for as long as they shall live feel they can no longer keep that promise? Where does the estrangement, distrust, and neglect that break us apart come from? Finally, why do we separate from the very people we once loved and felt at one with?

To answer these questions is both simple and complex. It is complex if we try to find the answers in single reasons since another precipitates every reason. It seems the reasons we cannot get along with one another or bring judgment into our lives are rooted in an unhappy childhood, abusive parents, unsupportive teachers, societal restrictions, adverse economic situations, etc. Yet, in truth, these factors represent only one link in the near-endless chain of events that underlie our problems in life. Whatever they are, the common thread that runs through them all is the experience of separation from our Higher Self or Spirit.

The age-old search for our true identity is caused by the age-old separation from our true identity. *Who am I?* and *Why am I here?* have almost become cliché expressions in the New Age movement, but they are nevertheless valid questions that nag everyone at some stage in life, even unconsciously. The reason for this is that we cannot become whole and fulfilled until we live the answers. An old saying tempts us to find the answer to what we are looking for in the question, and so it is with these two basic questions. The *Who am I?* question cannot be satisfied by substituting *who* with a name, a quality, or a physical appearance, for these can be changed in a moment. The only answer that makes sense is *I AM,* because that is all there is left when the body dies off and the world disappears with it. *What am I doing here?* has a similar answer: *TO BE THAT I AM.* In other words, we do not have to be *anything but ourselves* in order to be fulfilled and to make a difference in this world. We *are* everything because we *are one* with all there is, but the only way we can tap into that oneness and use it for the greater whole is by identifying with our Higher Self; nothing else will ever be sufficient to really satisfy us.

Still, most human beings tie themselves to, and describe themselves by, their career choice, their economic position, their religious preference, their political affiliation, their age, or even by their gender, but *no one describes themselves by the brilliance of their spiritual light.* The moment I use such words as I am an artist, I am intelligent, I am a failure, I am a success, I am your friend, I am a Light Worker, I love you, I love God, etc., I separate myself from that brilliant light of oneness that I am and instead identify with the limited ideas I have about myself, my personality, money, friendship, what love means to me, who I believe is God, etc.

Separation feels so real that is unnatural to feel any other way than this. To be one with the people walking down the street, the flowers blossoming in the field, the insects and birds soaring in the air, the clouds floating in the sky, and the Earth reverberating under our feet escapes all

20

concepts of imagination. It doesn't come from a thought or an idea but from the plane *before and beyond* thoughts and ideas. It is a state of being. Not even the greatest, most magnificent human form and achievement is able to describe the REAL YOU. A gold bracelet, a golden ring, and a gold filling each look very different and have different purposes but they are made of the same thing, namely gold. The appearance of a shape or form somehow conceals the true substance it is made of. Take the meaning or purpose away and you are left with what it really is: a piece of gold.

By letting go of the various meanings and roles we have given ourselves, or were given by others, we are left with nothing but ourselves. This process can be very scary at first, and it may cause a sense of great loss and loneliness. Nevertheless, when we face and thereby transcend, the fear of losing everything, when all associations cease, then we become aware of our fundamental connectedness with everything. When illusion of separation and the pain and judgments that uphold it fall away, we gain the ultimate freedom, the freedom TO BE. To regain our true identity we must undo all separations that have ever existed in all of our many lifetimes. All the false identities: "I am not good enough", "I am scared", "I am angry", "I am poor", "I am rich", "I am powerful" etc. serve their purpose only in the world of duality. They have no more meaning once we enter the world of oneness.

All these mistaken identities serve only one master, the primordial separation from our Source, often called the original sin. Sin is linked with guilt. We feel guilty for having separated ourselves from what many call God or Spirit. We fear we will be thrown out of Heaven because we aren't 'good enough' anymore. We have forgotten who we are and feel guilty about it. However, this emotion of guilt is based on the misconception that separating from our Higher Self or God Self was wrongful. We are now collectively dealing with this primordial guilt and fear of separation, and we are in the process of clearing it once and for all. We are clearing it in many different ways and it can feel very distressing at times but we are making great progress, both individually and collectively. In all this, we are both remembering and releasing the *Great Separation* that seeded all other separations we have ever experienced during our numerous lifetimes on Earth.

21

Judgment is a betrayal of the soul. The soul seeks not to define and decipher its merriments or foibles. Just to be. Let it be. Let it rise and fall like the midnight sun, the oil in the lamp at night, the tide at the shore. For it is eternal, the soul and its workings. Nothing more. Nothing less.

Ancient Chinese Wise One, 342 BC
Channeled on April 16, 2001

Chapter Two

The Great Separation

Oh great ones, your light shines ever brilliantly upon us. We see your greatness, your boldness, and your delicacy all at once. We praise you for every moment's breath we share in this lifetime. And we honor you for coming forth in your truth, in your beauty and your courageous dance. Spread your wings and follow your guiding light, for you are free to venture forth and fulfill your destiny.

Sister (Mother) Theresa
Channeled on December, 21, 2000

The Beginning of the End of Paradise

Before the *Great Separation* was the *First Creation*. This was a time (if you wish to choose use linear time as a means of understanding the occurrence of events) when we were highly evolved angelic beings who lived in the original creation, the first Circle of Life. This realm had no elements of duality in it, which made it impossible for us to perceive anything but oneness with everything and everyone. We were capable of creating new dimensions such as depth and width, and every idea and intention of ours turned into instant manifestation. There was nothing we could not accomplish. Since Oneness with the Supreme Source was our anchor, we had no fear and lived happily with our loved ones. All of us were endowed with the infinite knowledge and organizing power of the *Eternal Being* that sustained every aspect of the First Creation. In the simplicity of bliss, we could *be* the whole creation and all the beings participating in it, with no sense of separation.

Yet despite all the joy, passion and fulfillment we lacked one thing, if 'lack' is the right word to use. *We didn't know who we are.* To know who we are we needed to be able to 'see' ourselves - as if from the outside. So we moved to the 'edge' of creation, the original creation of oneness, in order to bring forth a parallel creation that allowed for the *experience* of knowing ourselves. This, of course, was only possible by creating the *illusion* of separating ourselves from our unbounded consciousness or God Self and entering what we now call the experience of duality because in actuality, we can never be separate.

We are one consciousness, but by creating the illusion of duality, (to become self-aware), we immediately projected that idea outward as a thought. Until this point, there had been no need for thought. However, as soon as our consciousness projected this thought of wanting to know itself, it believed that it *was* that thought. Moreover, when projected in thought, consciousness had no choice but to have a limited view of itself (and this is as true today as it was then).

Since the one consciousness is absolutely unlimited, then whatever it believes itself to be, it is. Therefore, in projecting itself out as a separate possibility, it chose to 'forget' it was an omnipresent being, the unlimited field of all possibilities. This separate possibility now became the new definition of itself.

Our very desire to know who we are brought on the Great Separation from our infinite self. The story of Adam and Eve in the Garden of Eden is an allegory. It is the story of infinite consciousness projecting itself as the desire of knowing and defining itself. Universal consciousness, in order to fathom greater aspects of itself, came to a point of wanting to know what it was like to *be*. It was looking for a mirror. First, the masculine aspect of infinite consciousness (often called Father God) projected itself into the physical plane as the energy Adam. Secondly, the feminine aspect of infinite consciousness (often called Mother God) projected itself as Divine Love into the masculine energy matrix of Adam.

24

The energy Adam was tempted to know and define himself (symbolized in the eating of the fruit of knowledge, which is also the fruit of life and death, good and evil, i.e. duality). The moment he projected his consciousness outward with the thought of wanting to know himself, he found himself in the world of limitation. Suddenly he became aware that he wasn't just one universal self, but two selves, a masculine self and a feminine self, yet still united as one. He longed to see his feminine self, but to know his feminine self, the masculine self had to fully part from it. Hence Eve, his feminine self, was (symbolically) born from his heart (not his rib). Eventually, the masculine and feminine selves started to see each other as separate beings (naked). The Garden of Oneness gradually became a garden of duality, where opposites ruled. This was the end of paradise and the beginning of a new world that would turn out to be our greatest challenge ever.

Discovering the Whys of Pain and Suffering

Although to some degree we were still consciously able to use our higher light-bodies at this stage, we began to notice very uncomfortable and unusual changes taking place inside of us. The further we disconnected from our God Self or Higher Self, the more challenging this became. We gradually felt sensations of fear and distrust occupying our heart centers, feelings that grew into anger and hate. This initial transition from oneness to duality traumatized us beyond anything we have experienced thereafter, at any lifetime in human form. We went through the worst kinds of pain and suffering that could have ever befallen anyone at any time on Earth, yet with much greater severity and intensity. The enormous energy that we previously held had to be dissipated, transformed and reduced to a miniscule level so that we could function in duality. This allowed us (our spirit form) to fully step into the matter density of the Third Dimension - the physical manifestations of the human body and the world, as we know it - to explore the ins and outs of creation.

To make it easier for us it was necessary to erase all memories of the journey, i.e. the battles and the pain we experienced that brought us to this point. But this also meant we *would not remember the source* from whence we came. By coming to Earth with no remembrance of who we are, we stood the best chance to gain a true understanding of duality. The preparation for allowing our higher dimensional beings (angels) to live in a dense physical body was very extensive. So before we actually took on a biological form we spent much time on Earth in our angelic forms in order to become acclimatized and set up the necessary energy grids. The shifting of our energies from high vibration to low vibration had to take place gradually until it was possible to function in a human body.

We have walked this Earth ever since, lifetime after lifetime, to explore every aspect of this dimension and integrate it with its Source. Everything we have done here on Earth to this very moment has all been an attempt to understand what happened to us when we left the original creation. We are setting up the *perfect* situations - through co-creation with our Higher Self or Spirit, spiritual guides and angels, ascended masters and fellow human beings - that allow us to relive and release the trauma of the Great Separation.

Every separation issue, such as being rejected or left by our parents, a lover, a friend, serves as a means for us to learn about, and deal with, our separation from Spirit. Each moment of pain and agony that we have ever experienced during any of our numerous lifetimes is only a result of our need to define and experience the original emotion of pain we felt during our first full experience of duality. The disharmony and conflict we have co-created with our fellow human beings has been the only way to bring out and solidify the original disharmony and conflict we went through while separating ourselves from who we were before the 'fall' into duality.

Every experience we have here on Earth is a precise reflection of the original experience while we were at the edge of creation. We needed to go through every kind of dualistic expression there could possibly be, such as love and hate, joy and sadness, fear and trust, right and wrong, good and bad, life and death, in order to learn about and undo the trauma that has enabled us to know, through experience, who we are and what this creation is like. All the great moments of joy and happiness that welled up in our hearts from time to time resulted from the release of these traumatic instances. Similarly, the periods of peace we experienced on Earth were the end phases of conflict, which gave rise to new opportunities for conflict and war, so that we could understand and release more of the original separation trauma experience at the edge of creation.

There Is No Wrong-Doing

Our all too common yearning for a place we can call home merely reflects our desire to return home to oneness. What we refer to as the incessant thirst for sensory pleasure and satisfaction, characterized by strong desire, greed, and lust, is just an expression of the deep loneliness that befell us when we separated from our higher nature.

Since all of our experiences on Earth are related to the experiences in the original Creation, all that we are doing is playing them out in duality, which is the ideal environment for learning and understanding. We are not guilty of any original wrongdoing then, and we are not guilty for any of our so-called bad actions ever since. Whatever we have done and are doing now is part of the reintegration process with Spirit. We are the integral part of a *Great Experiment* that has never been attempted before and we are using the physical aspects of duality, the mass, energy and our physical bodies, to help us and Spirit understand what happened when the Second Creation was formed.

Because of the need to expand and unfold the original Creation, some of the strongest and most courageous angels (beings of consciousness) volunteered to be the pioneers in this endeavor of separation. Because they had the most powerful energies and the deepest trust in their God Selves and in creation, they felt ready for the challenge to prepare the way for others less strong to follow. But they never anticipated that it would be so hard to enter the field of duality, for they had no previous experience of pain and separation whatsoever. The separation of one into two parts was so traumatic that they felt their essence was destroyed. They forgot what had been their inner connection to Spirit and the powers that were part of it. However, one thing they never forgot was the destruction.

Merits of the Lost Angels

The angels in the frontline were hit the hardest because, as pioneers of creating duality, they had to carry the most weight on their shoulders; i.e. they went the farthest away from their Divine nature and sank into the deepest sea of darkness and turmoil. Helpless and agonized to the core of their being, they desperately tried to unify the opposites, to love, to transform energies, but they failed. The 'lost' angels became outcasts among humans, killers of their fellow men, old people in lunatic asylums, beggars under bridges, witches burnt in medieval times. They were babies left to die because they were not wanted. They committed suicide out of loneliness and turned into angry savages due to unending guilt and fear.

Through these extremely painful experiences, those pioneering angels took it upon themselves to pave the way for those who entered the world of duality after them. They had ventured into realms and frequencies that were simply unbearable and this broke their hearts. Today they are tired and exhausted, lost in darkness, hopeless and without a spark of love, yet they made it possible for the rest of us to plough the field of life more easily and bring light into the dark, love and forgiveness to where it was absent, and transform duality back to oneness. We see them struggling now, trying to survive as homeless people in the streets of modern cities. We see them on televisions sets, starving to death. We see them killing others in modern concentration camps. We see them as terrorists who bring out the fear of death in the rest of the people. We see them as victims of genocide. We see them as murderers who themselves are executed by lethal injection or electrocution. We see them as addicts to alcohol and drugs and as those who are selling them to children. We see them as slaves in child labor camps and as those who keep slaves to enrich themselves out of an undying thirst for happiness.

It is only because we haven't understood death and dying that we have judged these angels and perhaps still do, calling them evil and destructive, or miserable wretches. Yet death is but rebirth. Death is the choice of those about to die, brought about by whoever's hand or for whatever reason, to start the cycle again and anew, equipped with more wisdom and knowing. Death is not something bad just because we are afraid of it. We are afraid of it because each death we witness or hear of is a reminder of the original death, which is our separation from Spirit. Although the separation never really took place, it felt like it did. So until now the illusion of death has persisted for most of us because we are determined to learn all about the deepest and most promising mysteries of life.

Death Isn't What It Appears to Be

For the majority of people on this planet, death still symbolizes the end of a life cycle, however short or long it might be. These angels who are currently living through the 'dark night of their soul' and are 'causing' death or harm to others and become known for this through the mass media, confront the rest of the people with their greatest of fears, the fear of death. Those souls who leave their physical form never actually 'die' against their will, although it may seem this way. Actually, it is the ego holding onto the cells of the body that triggers the fear of self-destruction. The ego holds the soul hostage within the body until a disease or injury caused by an accident or another person releases it and terminates the imprisonment.

The fear of loss of life makes the ego hang on to the body so desperately that it appears that dying is a struggle and worth fighting against, even if it means complete dependence on a life support machine for weeks and months. Those who opt for artificial life extension or allow others to make that decision for them are controlled by an attitude of 'life at all costs'.' Little do they realize that their brave souls are imprisoned by their physical vessel. Physicians who keep their patients alive against their wishes have a misguided sense of duty, which in turn originates from their own fear of death and ignorance of what death really means. *Death is never a punishment*, but most people take it to be one of the most awful things that could happen to them.

Therefore, when we hear about the murder of an innocent child we conclude that this must be something terrible for the child, shortcutting a life that could have had so much ahead of her/him. We do not realize that the soul had already accomplished all it needed and wanted to during its short stay in physical embodiment and was ready to move on to greater opportunities and accomplishments. In some cases, a child is born and will die from 'crib death' because it is a very young soul without any human experience and *not* yet ready to accept the challenges and trials of physical existence. Getting just a small taste of life is its soul's purpose during this first attempt.

The greatest learning that such situations offer is meant for those who are left behind and not for the one that has left. The bereaved ones experience genuine loss. The grief, once again, becomes an intimate reminder of the original loss of life, and is yet another opportunity to get closer to the realization that this loss is an illusion too. Children who died at birth or soon after will be conceived again within a short time, if this is their desire, and be born in a physical body that will support their purity, profound sensitivity and high-level energy. Death is the greatest teacher of all. As long as we fear death and don't know it for what it really is, we cannot truly live, and parts of us keep dying as life goes on. Yet every death is a blessing in disguise, for it brings us a little closer to immortality, our own immortality.

Those blessed people who work with the dying have much respect for, and very little fear, of death. When there is no more fear of loss, death loses its mystery altogether. It then reveals to us that the Great Separation or Great Death was the illusion we had to create in order to undo it again and recognize our immortality. Eventually, we will realize that we can live for as long as we choose. We are born with the vague recollection of this truth. There are already some humans upon this Earth whose bodies cannot be hurt or harmed in any way. Bullets would go right through them. Three-dimensional objects have no effect on their fourth and fifth dimensional light bodies. Their physical selves no longer vibrate on the third dimensional level and are, therefore, indestructible; yet they remain visible to the physical eye like every other object.

Fear of death or anything else exists only in the domain of duality of third dimensional existence. These fears make us vulnerable to what we fear. If we are afraid of anthrax, chemtrails or other destructive experiments by the governments, they are likely to affect us. Those who have no more fear, and therefore are truly of the light *and* the dark, can experience the world remaining unaffected and immune to any harmful influence. We tend to point fingers at those who destroy our natural environment and pollute our air and water because we are afraid that this will make us ill or kill us. In truth, it is the fear within which makes us susceptible to any sort of external assault. Without our (unconscious) permission, the radiation from a nuclear power plant or the carcinogens from a chemical factory could not touch or harm us in any way.

Collectively, we have created these realities of illusion in order to move into our indestructible light bodies. Our genetic material (DNA/RNA) is of a crystalline substance that has the power and ability to transmute anything we do not need or want, including deadly viruses. Pollutants, toxins and even super bugs all consist of molecular structures in various formations. The crystalline substance of our own light body can break down into base particles any molecular structure and reassemble it into crystalline purity, provided we have no fear or we trust and know that we can do this. Moreover, we all can do this, as has been documented, for example, by the Japanese molecular scientist Masaru Emoto. In his book *Messages from Water,* he demonstrates through illustrated research that mere thought or emotion affects the world around you in the most profound way. He showed that the dark and amorphous structure of polluted water with no crystalline structures could quickly become a highly organized white hexagonal crystal-within-a-crystal if exposed to positive human thoughts. A negative thought, on the other hand, can break up the crystalline structures of water, and distort and pollute it. The same principle applies to the food we eat, the blood that runs through our veins, the air we breathe, and all the things that come to us and touch us. What we believe or fear these influences will do to us, they *exactly* do to us, but not otherwise.

We are perfectly capable of blessing all things with our essence and thus lifting them up to vibrate on the same crystalline level as we are. By contrast, we can lower their vibration with our belief that they cause us harm. There is nothing outside us making this choice for us. We influence everything that comes near us and determine how it affects us. The belief of being a victim prevents us from using our indestructible light bodies. It robs us of the ability to use our endless, inherent powers. Instead of transmuting what we do not want in our lives, including physical death, we blame external influences, people, fate, the devil or even God for our suffering and eventual demise. Yet deep within we know that being a powerless victim doesn't make any sense at all.

Settling for a perspective in which death is a necessity is foreign to every human being on Earth. Instinctively we know that life doesn't *need* to end. This is especially true for babies and young people. When we grow older, our ego resists the notion that we can live forever. Much of this resistance is caused by guilt. We feel guilty for living because of having done so many 'wrong' things in life, and unconsciously we look for ways to terminate the guilt, through growing old and dying.

The Final Battle

The Beings of Light who live beyond the veil of duality have resolved the mystery of death and thereby pass no judgments on those who are on the Earth plane and do 'harm' to others. Those suffering in this world, regardless of whether they are playing the roles of the victim or the victimizer, are deeply honored instead, for what they have done and are still doing. Somebody had to jump into this vast pool of duality, explore its darkest and most filthy parts, and, for example, turn into a hopeless alcoholic or a serial killer (Dark Worker). Although it is not obvious to bystanders and even to the Dark Worker himself/herself, their actions do dismantle the collective pain of the Great Separation, bit by bit. Great credit goes to the Dark Worker for such total immersion. The Light Worker on the other hand only dips his/her toes into the pool and rejoices in the fact that they need no longer fully sink into the darkness of ignorance. Instead, they live in the light and work for the light. Both Workers were needed.

When Jesus pleaded with the people of his time to judge none, he spoke with the authority of a master who had seen behind the veil of duality. He saw that those who seem to be the last to enter the kingdom of heaven are actually the first ones. Those considered the least worthy, who have had the most challenges in life, are the most worthy of 'promotion' in the eyes of Spirit law.

We are at a stage now where the deepest darkness, rage and violence unite with the strongest light, love, and peace and are transformed into one whole. We are confronted with the fact, and this may be a difficult

31

lesson to swallow, that we carry no sin, no guilt, and no evil in us. We never did, none of us ever did. Like these pioneer angels, we did what we did out of love for each other and for the creation of a new universe, which combines the duality and density of the material world with the primordial Source of all life. To truly know what we experienced before our human existences, we had to relive the separation energy time and time again in a physical body, so that we could bring all our understandings into the new energy of unity, into the rising consciousness of a new world that has never been created before.

The very ability to judge each other and act upon our judgments is now. What is left for us to do is to clear the last memories of pain, sadness, and struggle. We are in the end stages of that final battle, Armageddon, where both duality and oneness are going to be the winners. For some time though, there will be two worlds, one that represents duality and the other that represent oneness of duality. There will be those who are still deeply entrenched in the world of separation, figuring out the lessons of duality. Yet in doing that, they form the basis for the new world to emerge more fully, serving like an anchor that holds a ship in place. The new world, which is already in existence, is for those who consciously reunite with their Higher Selves or God Selves. However, credit goes to everyone who has ever walked or still walks this Earth, and no one is better than another is. All of us need this process to continue and everyone plays a precious role in bringing it about.

Time is not an important factor in the evolution and growth of a soul; in truth, time is a non-existent factor in the realm of our higher nature. Since time is irrelevant in this respect, there *is* no being *more advanced* or *ahead* of another. This new perception of non-judgment, which dominates life in the new world, makes it possible for those living in unity consciousness to love and assist all those still in separation consciousness to also make the transition. This will eventually unite all dimensions of life into one integrated whole. This is the reason we are here.

Is it not the time to tell the tale of woe and reap the burden and the bounty that comes with such a message? It is from afar that we speak to you now and take this lamp-lit opportunity to surround you with our love and the glorious signals from the trumpets of harkening angels. We see you now ensconced within a great mist of hope and we salvage every opportunity to work with you to breathe in your essence and to breathe through our own vaporous mist of light and stardust. We enjoin with you at this time to say a prayer for the almighty ones who have gone before you and do continue on in their service to all of mankind and brotherhood alike. Amen.

Mikael
Channeled on January 7, 2001

Chapter Three

Self Worth -To Be or Not To Be

From the table of yore to the pillars of society, nothing can win the hearts of men so eloquently and fervently as a good fight for right and freedom. Be set on your way. Free yourself of shackles, self-imposed. Destroy the barriers that keep you from seeing yourself and your destiny with clear and vivid certainty. For as long as you hold on to the past, the future remains locked in your heart.

King Arthur
Channeled on April 14, 2001

Removing the Lens of Judgment

Judgment, which is a subjective compulsive need to categorize things or people to confirm, justify or validate our beliefs or opinions, seems to be a very meaningful and useful tool to navigate through the ups and downs of life. Yet there is hardly any basis to judgment other than feeling inadequate, unfulfilled, or empty inside. Putting people or things into higher or lower categories stems from not feeling worthy enough. The need to pass judgments on people to see them as anything but pure Love, reflects the state of unhappiness or lack of completeness in our hearts. This makes judgment a misdirected energy that lacks discernment. Judgmental energy is responsible for all the conflicts and disharmony the Earth has ever witnessed. Discernment, on the other hand, sees that every person and every situation in life plays an import part on the game-board of life.

Without being conscious of it, I had carried some deep sadness within me through most of my life. I wasn't aware, either, that I always categorized people, things and situations into good and bad. Once I began to feel, however, that my own flaws and discrepancies were a necessary part of my growth as a human being and actually served me very well, my urge to judge others began to crumble.

As I began to accept both my gifts and weaknesses, I no longer felt so compelled to hide my 'dark' side from anyone, including myself. As a result, I became more patient with myself and a sense of peace and serenity overcame me as I never experienced before. The inner drive to being a more important and better person than I really was felt less urgent and intense and I started to accept and even love the 'new' me. In due time, the chains of self-imprisonment broke to pieces and I felt truly free for the first time in my life. I suddenly saw why I had judged so many people and was grateful that I had played that role so well, for without it, I would not have tasted this freedom.

In spirit, I spontaneously began to thank everyone who had ever disapproved of me or judged me in any way. My parents, teachers and relationships had all helped me to experience how it feels to be judged and to become aware of my counter-reactions and defensiveness. Through the understanding and procedures described in this book I was able to 'rewire' my brain to support the new way of life I was dreaming about. Moreover, my experiences of this world began to change drastically. To whatever extent I can be aware of, my new brain has no more reference points for what is 'good or bad' and 'right or wrong'. My lens of judgment began to lift.

As I began to accept all parts of myself as equally important and good for me, I was also able to see that the same was true with regard to my relationship with others. My desire to change even those closest to me became less pronounced and eventually subsided once I let go of the expectations I had of myself. I rejoice now in the differences that exist between my partner or my friends and me. I can clearly see that their strengths and weaknesses are great assets for their own growth and learning, and that they benefit me too. In retrospect, the 'bad' experiences have helped me more on my path of learning than the good ones. Whenever someone hurt me, betrayed me, or even broke my heart, it has actually taught me how important it is to trust again. Things often seemed painful and unfair at the time, but in reflection, I know that without overcoming those obstacles I would never have been able to realize my potential, strength, willpower, and heart.

Once I accepted whatever I had rejected in myself before, I found very little reason to reject anyone or anything outside of me. I started to look right through my friends' critical comments, harshness, stubbornness, and inability to love and see the pain that prevented them from being the wonderful people they are. By extending my love to them, they too began to feel worthy of love once again and were able to heal their wounds of emotional hurt. I also understood why they came into my life.

Why We Meet People We Don't Like

How many times did I make critical comments about people who are unhealthy, fat or obese and shared these judgments with friends who I felt would have similar opinions? More often than I can think of. It was part of my training as a practitioner of Ayurvedic medicine, Iridology (eye interpretation), and Shiatsu, to look for and identify the physical and emotional causes of disease. So, whenever I met another person, regardless of whether it was a patient or an acquaintance of mine, I quite automatically 'checked them out' by reading and interpreting their eyes and/or using my intuitive diagnostic skills to find out what could possibly be wrong with their health. I got so good at this that I would know of any major or minor health issues a person had within a matter of seconds. Finding faults in others became my 'second nature'. And whenever I received confirmation of these health problems from these people, I became even more enthusiastic about my abilities.

The obsession of having to uncover what was wrong with everyone (by the way, I saw that almost everyone had some sort of health problem) soon turned into what I now know was a constant need to pass judgment. I not only discovered the causes of their illnesses or discomforts but I also blamed them for having these ailments. One type of person I disliked most was the overweight and obese. I found them aesthetically unattractive, to say the least, and I felt they deserved to look this way because they had no respect for their body and they overindulged in junk foods, sweets, meat, and alcohol. Many of them suffered heavy

36

perspiration and emitted an unpleasant body odor, which really turned me off.

I think my aversion toward obese people began during my early childhood when I was told that I was too thin. I felt very defensive about this, especially when the comments came from people who had put on extra weight, by pointing out that I was too thin they felt better about becoming too fat. But the true reason behind my reaction to them was because I didn't like myself being thin.

To help me balance the self-judgment of being too thin I had to meet people who were overweight or obese. In due course, some of my patients who were very overweight also became close friends of mine. This first step of tackling my judgments of fat people was still relatively easy for me because they were following the diet and regimen I had laid out for them and within several weeks and months, they had lost many pounds and felt and looked so much better.

The real challenge arose when circumstances put me together with obese people who weren't my patients or clients. At first, my old resistance came forward but after a while I realized the deep soul connection we shared. An undeniable love bond let me see directly into their hearts. Ironically, this occurred when I looked into their eyes. And my resistance broke down when I let them see into my heart. What was most humbling for me is that instead of seeing the problem areas of their body as reflected by the abnormal changes of color and structure of their iris, I only saw beauty, love, pain, sadness, joy, fear and loneliness in their eyes. They had opened their hearts to me, and all that I felt was a pouring of love and compassion for them. Since that time, I have really begun to see and appreciate the beauty of a person's soul, regardless of the body's shape, age, smell, color, etc. I suddenly was able to touch them, hug them, and be close with them, without any sense of discomfort or aversion.

Incidentally, whereas I never had an overweight friend before in my life, now almost half of my friends are overweight or obese. I feel no need to change them in any way because I see them for what they really are. In fact, I find that they have so much inner beauty in them that I cannot help but find them beautiful in their physical shape as well. I also began to understand why they needed to put on that extra weight. Some felt 'too exposed' to an emotionally harsh and cold environment and required a protective shield. The need to safeguard one's feelings against hurt and disappointment may arise from a previous incidence of pain from either this lifetime and/or other past lives. Thus, a deeply sensitive heart may have had no other choice but to build layers of protection around itself. Particular eating and lifestyle habits that become the supportive means for achieving weight gain are not coincidental; they are formed exactly around this need for protection. The deeper reason behind weight gain, however, is the increase of spiritual energy in the body. The density drop that accompanies the infusion of more spiritual light energy in the cells of the body may be too drastic or sudden for some. A symptom of that resistance is weight gain. To make the ascension process into spirit smoother and more bearable these highly sensitive people try to cope with these higher energies by becoming bigger. There is no reason for self-judgment in this.

Until recently, most of us were kept in the dark by the veil of forgetfulness. The veil made us forget who we are, where we came from, our connection with Mother Earth, the reason for the many roles we played in our lives, how we choose each life lesson, and most of all that we are part of the Oneness of Creation. The veil allowed us to grow and learn everything about the lower dimensional worlds. Had we not been enveloped by the darkness of forgetfulness, we would not have had the desire or motivation to learn about separation and duality, and the conscious experience of oneness would therefore have remained elusive to human life. Some people are so used to the veil of protection that they do not want to let it go, out of fear of stepping into their power and revealing their beautiful, gifted hearts to the world outside them. Once they let go of their resistance, they find ways to lose weight and return to what they may consider their natural physical condition.

Everyone IS Worthy

Whatever the relative cause of pain and suffering in life may be, the absolute cause is the Great Separation, which left many of us vulnerable to disappointment, abuse and abandonment. The more sensitive at heart one is or becomes, the larger a body one needs to have in order to feel protected. Those with sensitive hearts whose bodies are hyper-metabolic and very thin (Ayurveda calls them Vata body types) have little means for physical protection, and their nervous system can suffer great stress or breakdown under duress. To compensate for this, they usually seek others to protect them.

Neither situation, however, is seen as negative. *A large size body may be about the only thing that can keep a heart starved of love and self-worth from breaking.* The protective, dense body mass allows the heart to feel safe until such time that trust returns and defensiveness subsides. When it happens, love is naturally directed towards oneself. In the case of the overly thin person, a nervous breakdown may serve as an act of protection for the heart. With the breakdown comes the opportunity to break free of old fears and attachments that are no longer helpful or necessary.

Self-love not only dissolves guilt and judgments held inside but it also ends up as chemical messages that direct the body to improve its digestive and metabolic functions. At the same time, this self-directed love generates an increased desire for proper nourishment, cleansing of the organs, and a more natural lifestyle, all of which helps to melt away the layers of the protective shield. In the case of the Vata type, all of these things help him/her to grow more healthy tissue and to feel nourished and safe. A friend of mine lost 80 pounds in one year simply because she began to value herself more. When she saw the beauty in herself she introduced changes in her life that reflected her increased self-worth. Today she is a very attractive and desirable woman. She always was worthy and beautiful but *she* needed to know that, too.

When I Don't Like Myself...

It became very clear to me that obesity (or any other physical problem) isn't the result of a mistake the body makes, and it isn't *really* due to a harmful diet or lifestyle or a genetic error in the DNA. There will be more on this in Chapter Five *'The New Medicine'* but I would like to point out at this stage that none of these so-called 'causes' have sufficient power, if any at all, to override the authority of the self. Actually, we manifest them to facilitate the learning and understanding that is part of our journey home to oneness. Obesity and thinness are opposites, each of which serves a specific purpose in life. They help us see through the illusion of separation, each one through a different angle.

Each person may have a different major agenda to work through in life but the final one that is common to all is separation from self. An obese person may say: "I hate myself this way" or "I would do anything to lose weight". A very thin person may consider they look haggard and worn out. Both identify with the shapes of their bodies, send messages of dislike and even hate towards themselves. "I don't like myself", is the basic declaration you make when judging your own or another person's body.

I didn't like obese people because I didn't like myself being too thin. Why didn't I like myself being too thin? The answer isn't obvious. One of the 'reasons' comes from a past life of mine when my spouse who was after my possessions slowly poisoned me to death. The poison, which was mixed in my food, gradually destroyed my intestines and I died in agonizing pain. This lifetime, I suffered major digestive illness almost from the beginning of my life until I was 19 years old, unable to digest any food properly. I brought into this lifetime a suspicion of food, and because I *unconsciously expected* it to be poisonous, it became poisonous for me. As we have seen from the start of this book, we all give meaning and substance to whatever happens to us. My unconscious belief turned what is normally nourishing food for somebody into a cause of malnutrition and destructive processes in my body. Therefore, when someone pointed out to me that I was too thin, I unconsciously linked my weak physical state to the experience of being poisoned in a previous life. Nevertheless, this recall and subsequent re-enactment of being poisoned through food, even though it happened on an unconscious level, turned out to be to my great advantage.

Whenever we don't like parts of ourselves, something unpleasant happens to us that gives us the opportunity for further growth and learning. The difficult situation of having had a dysfunctional digestive system that defied any medical treatment forced me to study the digestive system by the time I was 12 years old. By testing out numerous diets and methods of self-treatment, I discovered some of the most simple yet extremely effective ways of curing such illnesses such as heart disease, arthritis, diabetes, cancer, etc.[2]

Ending All Struggles

In the course of my life, I began to see an underlying thread that connected all so-called negative events with positive ones. An untreatable disease revealed a hidden opportunity for a quantum leap in my personal development. An accident brought about a major turning point in my life. The loss of my beloved father changed the course of my life and allowed me to feel freedom for the first time. The separation from the person I loved most enabled me to overcome the fear of loneliness and attachment. The duality of life isn't to make us suffer for no reason, but at the very least, to recognize suffering as not harmful. Once embraced with fearless attention, suffering ceases to lose its pain and virtually becomes non-existent. How things affect us is purely determined by the meaning we give to them. The deep knowledge that there is nothing out there that is truly against us or is counterproductive

---

[2] See my books *The Amazing Liver & Gallbladder Flush, Timeless Secrets of Health and Rejuvenation,* and *It's Time to Come Alive!*

40

to our growth and learning serves like an impenetrable shield of protection. It is naturally present in the awareness of unity where the need to defend oneself simply does not arise.

We are all searching for the oneness of opposites in life. We look for the one thing that can make us feel complete and whole. Going through the extremes of duality makes us get there. Seeing ourselves as obese or too thin are just two examples of how deeply we may feel separated from who we really are, but eventually we need to let go of this illusion. By accepting that I am thin, fat or obese, I am no longer fighting it. I am really accepting myself regardless of the attributes I have attached to myself. Then I recognize that I am not thin, I am not fat, I am not this and I am not that, I just AM.

Whenever we criticize others or ourselves, all that we really do is point at our own worthiness issues. Criticism *always* implies that *we* feel unworthy or insignificant in some respect and have an inner urge to express it. We usually direct that expression toward other people. In the above situation of becoming fat, the lack of worthiness may come out as "I am fat and ugly" (being fat generally has a negative connotation in our society, in contrast to African societies where it is cherished as a sign of wealth and great beauty). If you truly feel unworthy in this respect, you may greatly benefit from telling yourself aloud:

"I am unworthy!"

This simple statement can bring about the following internal transformations:

As you are consciously giving in to the feeling of unworthiness, you are first exposing your shadow sides, your weaknesses and lacks. This is the first step of releasing them.

The complete acceptance that you are undeserving or not good/beautiful enough takes a huge weight off your shoulders as it relieves you of the burden of constantly needing to fight to be more deserving or lovable.

You will experience a profound shift within you, sometimes sensed as a loving energy or peacefulness that makes you feel good about yourself.

41

From this moment, your body will stop manifesting that fear of becoming fat and ugly, which you had carried in your subconscious for so long. Now there is no such image left because you have accepted yourself, in whatever form. This is love, love for yourself. Instantly, the body begins manifesting the newly developed acceptance of you. Self-acceptance, even if this includes accepting perceived 'negative' qualities, stirs the power of oneness in your life. In truth, negative things are actually disguised helpers on our path to completion. Accepting them reveals their true face and blesses them with purpose. Resistance to being unworthy warrants the building and maintenance of fat layers of protection; giving up this resistance melts them away. Within a short time your diet, lifestyle, and attitudes will undergo a major change and support the normalization of weight. At this point in life, being overweight serves no more purpose.

Now that I have accepted that I have a thin or slim body, I have noticed that nobody is telling me anymore that I am too thin; on the contrary, I receive only compliments. All aspects of myself play a particular role in my life and are essential for me to move forward in my spiral of evolution and growth. Since I am accepting myself as being thin, I am also accepting others being overweight. Everyone has a reason to be the way they are, no matter what it is. So, accepting what *is* then becomes the means for change and transformation.

We are on the verge of a great civil war both within and between ourselves. It is time to take up the lance and the sword to fight off bigotry, racism, and discrimination of any kind that is a detriment to our loving selves. We are here as mortals living an immortal existence. Let us share in our love and shed our differences.

Abraham Lincoln
Channeled on December 21, 2000

42

Chapter Four

God Become Real When Religion Ends

Platters of logic betray the human mind. Unwind the clock of honor and escape into the wilderness of your own space/time-thoughts. Never guide or direct these, for they will flow with the mother of Universal Life if left to their own accord. Be assured of this, Wise Ones.

Albert Einstein
Channeled on April 14, 2001

Crutches of Spiritual Poverty

Religious beliefs haven't always been a part of human life on Earth. In fact religious dogmas only began to emerge after we experienced ourselves as beings separate from our Higher Source Self or God. Instead of being mostly centered within and functioning primarily as light beings, we started to look outward and perceive ourselves predominantly as physical beings. As our soul began to increasingly identify with the physical self (ego), our Higher Self went as if to sleep like a caterpillar in its cocoon. Subsequently, we lost our ability to use our light bodies and

43

function in the quantum world, which had previously made living and creating so effortless and joyful. Identifying with our physical selves dropped our frequencies to a slower rate and made us denser, heavier and slower.

Before the soul 'distanced' itself from the Higher Self, physical matter offered no resistance to our bodies, allowing us to pass through objects like a butterfly moves through the air. With the increasing identification with the denser physical body, however, we began to bump into things and life became hard and difficult. Instead of living in accordance with the laws of nature that ruled over physical existence on this planet, we began to live against them, like swimming against a current rather than with it. The more we violated natural law the more we struggled and experienced wider and increasingly distressing extremes of duality. As we increasingly saw ourselves as 'body,' all emphasis, challenges and focus were on physical survival and reproduction.

From time to time, extraordinary souls incarnated in human form with full awareness of their Higher Self nature to remind us of our true heritage. They outlined for us the laws of nature and what happens when we violate them. They spoke of a Higher Being (God) that is the Source of the universe and all living beings, and told us that reconnecting with this being was our highest priority and purpose in life. Their words and teachings turned into guideposts of living and were recorded in books for others to read and follow.

Since we weren't aware of our own Divine Essence, we became fascinated by those who were. We began to worship them as Gods and built churches and temples where we could praise and revere them. They became the crutches for our spiritual poverty. We had no idea that by putting them above us we deepened the rift between us and our Higher Self or God. Instead of identifying with our God Self we distanced ourselves from It. God became an idol of worship, a supreme being we could never be, and we knew ourselves as ignorant sinners who needed to pray for mercy and forgiveness.

The gap between God and us widened so much we actually started to fear Him. Religion, which was meant to be a means of literally 'binding us back' to the Source of All and reuniting us with our origin, instead became a way of ending our relationship with God. Dogmas, rituals, and endless interpretations of the holy texts made us believe that we needed to slavishly follow them to 'secure ourselves a seat in Heaven by the side of God for all eternity'. We had replaced God, the ever-present substance of consciousness permeating every fiber of creation, with the *idea* of God. God became a fiction in our mind, a concept as big or small as a human thought. We gave our power away to a concept that others told us about, that books were written about, and *idolized the concept* as God. During this phase of human development, the collective focus moved from survival and reproduction as the basis of relationships to the exploration of emotions. This phase is characterized by the period of the Renaissance, which produced so much emotionally charged art and creativity.

The building of emotions as a way of knowing who we are was followed by another extension of ourselves: the development of the intellect. We began to explore our mind potential as a new way of defining ourselves. The information age is a product of this mind exploration, but at this point, it is coming to a closure. Now, we are beginning the process of discovering our true identity and the infinite creative power which that embodies.

As Is Above, So Is Below

During the earlier stages of human development, very few people realized that God wasn't someone outside us who wanted to be eulogized through our prayers and worship, but that He/She/It was the very essence of us, that everything was made of the very same essence, and that nothing and no one could ever exist without this essence. *'As is above, so is below,'* does not allow for a spiritual hierarchy because a separation of Spirit into lower and higher beings would make oneness, omnipresence, and omnipotence an impossibility and create segregation, duality, and conflict in the higher dimensional realities. Jesus, Buddha, Krishna, Allah, and other 'Higher Self-conscious' souls who have incarnated in human form knew they were here to spread the gospel of oneness. Most of their followers, however, looking through the lens of duality, turned it into a gospel of division. This division still persists today and can be seen in the actions of religious leaders, religious fundamentalists and even spiritual masters who try to gather followers and convert people to their belief systems. True masters do not want disciples. They do not like anyone to use them to spread fear-based, disempowering, religious or spiritual beliefs. They advise you to take self-responsibility for everything in your life and do not allow you to dump your sovereignty at their feet.

Praying to God implies that God and I are separate. Asking God a favor basically means that I concede to the (false) idea that *I am not God.* Prayers were appropriate only as long as our Higher Self was 'asleep' and the prayers helped us deal with the pain of separation. We required a

God 'above us' to carry on the illusion of separation from our Source in order to understand duality. Now that duality is ending, prayers are not only inappropriate, but they can also significantly interfere with our growth and learning. When we pray, we are begging for something to happen - but we are not here to beg. The sleeping giant in us is awakening. Allowing other Gods to come before or above us is counterproductive to our ascension process into the Oneness of All. The denial of our Divine nature lies at the basis of violating the laws of nature. This deep-rooted self-denial is the judgment that is known as the 'original sin'. It is also the cause of duality. However, without experiencing all of duality, we could not become conscious of our true heritage.

Religious institutions throughout the ages have indoctrinated the masses to believe that God is separate from us and above us, and they have succeeded. Their actual, yet obscure, purpose wasn't to bring us closer to God but in fact to increase the division further and thereby allow us to come into touch with the widest possible aspects of duality; everything that lies between Heaven and Hell (Heaven and Hell being the most contrasting states of human awareness).

Religious beliefs today are experiencing a radical shift. Those that cannot accommodate the principle of 'I see the Oneness of All in everyone' will become outdated soon because separation consciousness will be recognized as a fallacy that has lost its attraction, other than to stir up hatred and division. People will know from within who or what really God is. They will be their own guidance because they will know who they are. They will no longer need to ask for guidance from a spirit or entity they haven't even met before, for they will be the IS-ness that requires no guidance. All they need is to BE and radiate. Rules of behavior and doctrines dictating what God wants us to do will become increasingly obsolete.

Anti Effects of Prayer

The need to pray comes from lack. People pray to God because they want him/her to help them or others overcome difficulties that, in fact, they themselves have created for greater learning. Some pray for protection for their children, implying that God doesn't protect them in the first place. Others ask God to give them more abundance, not realizing that they have the power and creativity within them to provide for their own needs; instead, they choose to let God do that job. Letting

46

God do what they think they cannot do doesn't help them, it just enslaves them even further.

When there are natural disasters people begin to pray for those who have died, believing that events are 'wrong' (not appropriate). "How could God have let this happen?" we ask. But God didn't. *All things are always appropriate.* Those who die in earthquakes or floods or through other ways do not desire to receive anguished prayers from their beloved ones. They have decided to leave their Earthly existence and wish to be understood and honored for having chosen this particular way, at the appropriate time, to move forward in their evolution. They ask us to understand the cycles that they are going through in their own karma and lives. They are eager to come back as the new children and enjoy the new energy they and we have helped to create. Why try to interfere with their joy and their focus on what is so right for them?

Praying about or thinking of the departed souls with love and appreciation for who they are and what they have done here on Earth will have a much greater and more beneficial effect than asking God to help them overcome their grief and pain (they suffer no more worldly pains once they have passed to the other side or dimension). Many people pray to God to help others because they feel guilty for not having treated them right or helped them when they were in need. Primarily these prayers are an unconscious attempt to avoid or suppress their own fear and guilt, the guilt of not having done enough to help. At the very least, they believe that asking God to do what they failed to do themselves may alleviate their pangs of conscience.

Sending healing prayers to those who 'need' healing is another form of interference that merely reflects one's own need for healing. Wanting others to be spared the pain of going through an illness is a manifestation of *our own fear*, which causes us to become further enslaved to fear. If an illness occurs, it is appropriate for that person to experience it, for they have chosen so by decree of their Higher Self wisdom. Praying to God to take a person's illness away is not honoring that person's choice to learn. We are all here to learn to become masters of creation.

There are many lessons to be learned in life. Taking them away from others will merely lead to more intensified lessons. Praying for better crops, for peace in the Middle East, for the eradication of terrorists, for a better economy, etc. is based on 'lack consciousness' and often manifests even more lack, more conflict, and more turbulence. It is not in our or anyone else's best interest to pray to change anyone or anything, for this moves us *into* the limitations of what has already come to pass. We are moving outside our own power when we dwell on past or future events.

Not using our power and wisdom becomes a cause for further suffering and pain in life.

If our intention to help others is sincere, we must focus on us, rather than on them. Disease, war, conflicts, disasters, etc. are of a chaotic, lower vibration, not bad or good, just a lower vibration. They occur wherever people have a collective need to raise their vibration. When hundreds or thousands of people die as a result of an earthquake, a terrorist attack, or war, it is because they no longer choose to exist at that low vibration. They are ready to move on. We perceive this as death but, for them, it is liberating and uplifting. Why do we want to hold them back or interfere with what is in their highest good?

If someone is ill, it is for us to honor and respect that person's decision to choose illness as a means of raising their vibration and learning their life lessons. Trying to help them heal seems to be a selfless act but in fact, it reflects our own ego's fear of pain, loss, or death. To cover up these feelings, our ego tells us that this illness is a terrible thing and that it must be avoided or overcome at all costs. Of course, if a sick person *asks* us to heal them, we no longer interfere by assisting in their healing process. What they have done is to choose to forsake the opportunity to heal and empower *themselves*, at this time. There will be other, similar, opportunities (illnesses) to choose self-healing and self-empowerment, although they are often of higher intensity than before. If the person still decides to opt for external healing and the medicine or treatment is 'unsuccessful,' their body stops functioning and they die. This also happens out of choice, for the soul knows that the body is no longer suitable to serve in its quest to grow spiritually and move into a higher vibration.

Since nothing in the universe can happen by accident, on any level, trying to change something for the better only reflects our own inability to accept what is. It is our way of saying that what this moment presents is not 'perfect'. If something appears to be not right, it does not mean that we need to correct it. Change is inevitable, and it will happen of its own accord and in its own time. When we resist, change appears to be difficult because we see only one side of the equation. Due to past impressions and experiences, we associate change with pain, instead of seeing it for the glory it can bring. We are simply challenged to accept change for what it is, for if it wasn't meant to be, it wouldn't happen. Once we have surrendered to the moment we have accepted what it delivers to us. This then gives birth to another moment that provides an ever-greater opportunity for upliftment than would have been possible otherwise.

Praying for something that we do not have, or do not want to have, takes us out of the present moment and relinquishes our power and self-responsibility. The following is a very unusual 'prayer' from an author unknown. It points out so beautifully the futility of normal prayer and I feel it could add great insight to the understanding of the value or non-value of prayer. I present it with gratitude to the anonymous author, wherever and whoever he/she may be.

I asked God to take away my pain.
God said, No.
It is not for me to take away,
but for you to give it up.
I asked God to make my handicapped child whole.
God said, No.
Her spirit is whole,
her body is only temporary.
I asked God to grant me patience.
God said, No.
Patience is a byproduct of tribulations;
it isn't granted, it is learned.
I asked God to give me happiness.
God said, No.
I give you blessings.
Happiness is up to you.
I asked God to spare me pain.
God said, No.
Suffering draws you apart from
worldly cares and brings you closer to me.
I asked God to make my spirit grow.
God said, No.
You must grow on your own,
but I will prune you to make you fruitful.
I asked for all things that I might enjoy life.
God said, No.
I will give you life so that
you may enjoy all things.
I asked God to help me LOVE others,
as much as he loves me.
God said...Ahhhh, finally you get the idea.

True Prayer

The only prayer that may be appropriate is to *be yourself*. This kind of prayer stands in contrast to asking for change of some kind. It is the prayer of acceptance or BEING. *Being yourself* is all that is needed to benefit the ALL. Being love, compassion, peace, balance, harmony, happiness, etc. are the most effective 'prayers' there can be and inspires others to be the same. Knowing that you are an expression of Divinity radiates that expression out for the world to see. The beautiful sentiments and great feelings that accompany worship of someone perceived as greater than we are will eventually give way to the bliss of being one with our Higher Self.

Prayers as we know them will soon end because we will understand that everything is perfect just the way it is. Religions throughout history have laid much emphasis on the words and meaning of prayers, yet real communication with God or Spirit occurs not through words but through the vibration that emanates from you. It is not at all important what you say or how you say it when you confer with your Higher Self, an ascended master, or what you perceive as God; all that matters is *who you are*. And regardless of how good or bad you feel, or how right or wrong you assess your behavior, you are truly a Divine Being.

In the new era, there won't be any need to pray for a favorable outcome of one's activities or desires. Asking for something better than it already is would take us out of the Divine Moment. 'Being in the moment' serves as a constant prayer to our God within; it is our connection to our Highest Self. Gratitude for all that is, and the way it is, will become known as the best-guarded and most powerful secret of success. This cannot be manipulated, for that would take you outside the present moment, the moment of *being*. Everyone will be their own religion, for everyone *is* God. In reality, the thinker, the thought and the process of thinking are all one. God knows Himself/Herself/Itself as God, God knows Himself/Herself/Itself as you, and you know yourself as God. This Trinity of knowledge lies imbedded in consciousness, and within *IT* is everything that could possibly be. *You are That, I am That,* and *Everyone is That.* Looking outside us for something or someone greater than we are, instantly crushes our sense of Divinity and Oneness.

Many people still pray for others with inappropriate energy. They pray that others do not make mistakes or behave in a bad way. They pray that others may see the light of God and come to their senses. If their loved ones are ill, they pray that they get better. But true prayer honors people where they are, respects the lessons each one has chosen in order

50

to learn and grow, and supports them to become self-reliant regarding one's health and liberation. If they ask your guidance, which is the green light that indicates they have learned and are ready to heal and move on. Asking God or Mother Gaia to stop the earthquakes, hurricanes, fires, or flooding is similarly inappropriate, for these events are necessary for the evolution and regeneration of the planet.

When true prayer replaces these and similar requests and desires, and to a certain extent this is already happening, the world will be experienced as a spiritual world, one where our Highest Self or Spirit is known as the only reality, the only consciousness, the only God. We are fast moving beyond the need to pray because we are beginning to realize that we already *are* the balance needed to fulfill our destiny. To become fully aware of this, however, we may need to 'peel off some more onion layers' that are associated with the emotions and feelings of suppression and fear that have been co-generated by the religious institutions and the masses throughout human history.

As I describe my own experiences as part of my religious upbringing, you may consciously or subconsciously link into some of your own soul records from this or other lifetimes, and accept and heal any judgments that you may have had in this important area of life. In fact, this is very likely since most conflicts and suffering in the world have originated from some sort of religious fanaticism. Looking at the double spiral symbol on the cover of the book for about one minute when you finish this chapter will help clear possible misunderstandings and irritation linked with the area of religion.

In The Name of God

Religion played a major role during my childhood. Although I did not feel a particular affinity to God, which didn't surprise me since I had never really met Him or seen Him in person, my religious upbringing didn't leave me much of a choice but to at least acknowledge His existence. The church and its Christian teachings spoke of this God as a father who was even more important than my own father. I never heard His voice, yet I was expected to speak to Him every night before going to bed and thank Him for everything He did for me during each day. I was told that God lived up in heaven with millions of angels who watched over us and made sure that nothing bad would happen to us. When bad things did finally happen to me, my trust in God and His angels began to dwindle.

51

Coming from a strictly Catholic family, I was expected to adopt the same beliefs that my parents had. Going to church every Sunday and religious holiday became a normal ritual of life, so was confessing my 'sins' to a priest in a black robe once every month. I learned that we all carry in us an original, capital sin that can never go away no matter how 'good' we are. I had but little choice to accept that I was a born sinner, like everyone else. Fear crept into my heart when I was told that we human beings are at the mercy of an almighty God who may or may not forgive us if we strayed from the path of righteousness and committed 'sins' in our thoughts and deeds. The ultimate punishment that surely awaited the impious and wicked was burning forever in hell, another great fear that told me "don't mess with God".

By age 12, I already felt guilty about so many things I never thought were sinful before until I had read and heard about the rules of righteous conduct and the strict laws outlined by God. I was promised redemption from my sins at the time of death if, once every month, I kept confessing them with sincerity and honesty to one of God's designated representatives (the priests). Priests, so I was told, were the only ones in direct communion with God. God had chosen them to tell us what to do. The Pope, also called His Holiness, was the highest priest who knew God better than anyone else did. It felt strange, though, that God, who presumably loved all his children equally, would only want to communicate with His Holiness and his priests. Were they more worthy and holy than the rest of us? Knowing that I was sinner soon turned into a nightmare for me.

Before long, I developed a strong aversion to religion, which manifested in fainting spells during Sunday masses at church. Suddenly, and without prior warning, I would feel a weird tingling sensation emanating from my stomach and moving up towards my heart and respiratory tract. Quickly, the tingling would move into my limbs and my vision would be overcome by a black darkness. Everything around me would fade away and I would fall unconscious. Sometimes, while collapsing, I would emit a loud scream, which of course, attracted the attention of the entire congregation. Then I would hear a dull sound (of my head hitting the floor or the pew), as I passed out. The next thing I would be conscious of would be distant voices and the chanting tunes of a choir. As these became clearer, I would realize that I was lying outside the church on a bench or on the ground, with my father bent over me, and my shirt top opened so that I could breathe more easily. I saw the deep concern, worry on my father's face and knew that something bad had happened to me.

I fainted in a similar fashion about every four to five weeks and always during Sunday morning mass. A strange bout of illness would follow this, which lasted three to five days and then I would be fine for another few weeks. Soon I was terrified of going to church with my parents. Strangely, if I attended the evening mass alone, I never suffered a fainting spell. So I begged my parents to let me go to church service in the evenings instead. They gave their consent. A year later, however, instead of actually attending the hourly church service, I only pretended that I went, but instead spent an hour wandering around town. This, however, only added more guilt to what I had already gathered during the years when told I was a sinner. Now I also experienced fainting spells at other places. My already battered self-image dropped even further. Of course, I did not have the guts to confess either to my parents or to the priest that I no longer attended church services.

Replacing One God with another God

Once I left home at age 19, I never went into a church for another 15 years. I had developed a deep aversion to everything that had to do with religious doctrines or God. Religion had become a pretext for me to end a long and confusing relationship with a God who loved me all right, but who also judged me and punished me for my sins. As I began to sense a deeper spiritual meaning in my own life, I began to replace the concept of God with the concept of an omnipresent consciousness that was an essential part of everything yet didn't interfere with it. I began to look down on those who saw this as a person of some sort. It made no sense to me that God would be 'someone' with a voice, a body, and a beard who keeps track of all the bad things you do and counts them up at the end of your life on some 'judgment day'. It seemed inconceivable that I would then either be taken to Heaven by the angels or be dragged to Hell by the devil. However, the deep-seated fear that this could be true didn't leave me all at once; in fact it followed me for many years.

Immediately after leaving home, I took a seven-month training course to become a teacher of Transcendental Meditation (TM), which is a mental relaxation technique to develop higher states of consciousness and to find peace within. A few years later, I began working for, and with, the founder of TM, Maharishi Mahesh Yogi, to spread his meditation to the rest of the world. Little did I realize during the following ten years that I had become just as strong a fanatic in pursuing this mission as the early missionaries who tried to convert 'lost and ignorant souls' to become children of God.

53

In fact, I had become exactly what I dreaded seeing in others. The Maharishi told us that his meditation would solve every kind of problem in life, no matter of what origin. Therefore, as a teacher of this meditation, called 'Governor of the Age of Enlightenment', I believed I knew the answers to every difficulty. I would feel guilty if I missed a few minutes of meditation since I was supposed to meditate for a certain length of time twice daily in order to gain enlightenment and help create world peace. Being a very devoted and 'responsible' teacher, I was absolutely regular in my practice and spent whatever time and resources I had available in spreading TM to the world. I had no 'time' for personal relationships for over ten years and when I learned that not listening to the master's (Maharishi's) instructions or going against his wishes would incur such bad karma that not even God could save such a person, I became even more disciplined and meticulous about how I lived my life.

All I had done was replace the fear of God and the Catholic Church with the fear of a spiritual master, another God. I wanted to become spiritually enlightened so badly because I believed this would save me from hell. Thirty years of meditating twice a day, several years of which I would dedicate eight hours a day to the going-within practice, certainly helped me develop qualities of serenity and patience and other values, but it didn't bring me enlightenment. I had unsuccessfully searched for something I already was, but the search was necessary for me to get in touch with, and accept, my shadow side.

Once I had accepted, at least to some degree, all parts of me, I had no further desire to become enlightened. I then instantly knew that not being okay with myself, about my sinfulness, my fears of not being good enough for my parents, teachers, the church, God and the master Maharishi or anyone else, was the only obstacle on my path to self-realization. Once I embraced myself for who I was, regardless of my numerous faults, fears and egotistical forms of behavior, I began to recognize my own enlightenment. For me personally, enlightenment is not something you can reach or find and then you are there for the rest of eternity. In fact, the more you desire it, the less likely it is going to happen for you. If you can allow yourself to be carried on the wave, rather than trying to swim faster or against it, not only will you have a much easier time but also you will actually reach your goal.

Letting go of my relationship with my guru also helped me to let go of many other crutches I used to rely on. I realized that being a student following a spiritual master wasn't in my highest interest anymore. The master-student relationship we shared implied that my master was more evolved and therefore more blessed and worthy than I was. However, I discovered that I was no less loved, honored and evolved than he is.

If a master has a need to gather students, it is a personal issue that only he/she can resolve. The time for great spiritual teachers is ending now because the time for great spirits has come. Each one of us is a Great Spirit, no less and no more. There are only masters, no students. We are all masters, although we have managed to disguise ourselves as students, pretending that we are ignorant and in need of guidance. Now we are ready to show our true essences. There is not going to be a new master or a Messiah who will suddenly appear and take away all our troubles and pains. The Second Coming is not an external event. *We* are the Second Coming, every one of us is. It is not about being spiritual and doing spiritual things in life or gathering others around you who can learn from you how to live spiritual, meaningful lives. The only thing that counts now is *being* Spirit. Being Spirit is our essential nature and requires no special skills. Just being spirit also helps others to go through their own transformations and assists Earth to go through her birthing process without unnecessary pain or upheaval. We, each in our own way, have committed ourselves to transmute this planetary sphere, for otherwise we would not be here.

Ascending To One's Self

There is no use being concerned about where you are or where the planet is in the ascension process. Enlightenment or ascension to an exalted form of existence is the simple acceptance of each new moment as being perfect, with everything you are, whatever that may be. Ascension can occur on many levels. First and second dimensional life forms may ascend to third dimensional life forms. Humans, or third dimensional life forms, may 'move up' to either fourth dimensional worlds or fifth dimensional oneness depending on their level of evolution and their intent. No matter where we are at what level, we all are going through an ascension process. Those who are ready to ascend to the fifth dimension are now experiencing major changes in their body, for the merging of body and spirit into one being requires a pure, stress-free physiology. These beings will be perfected beings of light, in a physical body of light.

'Light Body' is a term that describes the transformed state of a physical body which has completely merged with the Higher Self. However, there are several levels of light body, each one reflecting the amount of light a person is holding within the cells of their body. The amount of light held by the cells is keyed to the level of light body. Therefore, the more light your body is capable of holding within its cells, the greater the degree of Higher Self awareness you can contain within it. Toward the end of this process, you will ascend to your own Self, to your Higher Self that resides in the sixth dimension.

Each time you move up one level of light-body, your perception of reality goes through major changes. For example, you may suddenly be interested in reading spiritually oriented literature, see other people's auras, or develop clairvoyance. However, before such shifts occur, you go through periods of emotional and physical clearing, which are often interpreted as disease, or a feeling that there is 'something wrong with me'. You may even go through an 'ego death', a feeling of major depression or a sense of nothingness or void, where life makes no sense and gives you no more joy. This void is a rest stop on your journey to the next level. The period of nothingness is necessary to allow your old reality to disintegrate and to leave its pains and beliefs behind so that you can create a new picture of yourself and your life.

I had to create a life for myself, filled with difficulties so that I eventually would see them as blessings. Enlightenment is the awakening to the light of one's Self, the completion of a cycle that ends and begins in wholeness and fulfillment. Life becomes meaningful, every detail of it, even having judgments. The insights contained in this book are the result of discovering the purpose and value of judgment.

Before moving on, I really do recommend that you now spend the next 60 seconds or so looking at the double spiral symbol on the front cover, as this will facilitate significant and deep healing for you.

We are but one mind united in thought and heart. Our brethren are us indeed. We are all children of God. Therefore, we are the most speakable oneness that has ever praised and walked upon the land. We are all lambs flocking and herding together in the comfort of one another's gaze. Let us not forget the beauty, the dignity, and the comforting caresses that we receive from another or from the herd-like masses that constitute our planet.

Apostle Paul
Channeled on December 21, 2000

Chapter Five

The Purpose of Judgment

The sword Excalibur harkens. On the wings of angels it seeks to traverse all time and space and settle into the land of Nan where all is right and righteous. There is no headstone at the table; there is no tribal leader. We are all as one in this army of life. Take flight on this magic wand for it serves as a carpet of wishes waling delight and torment, all intertwined in a crystalline structure so brilliant, so wondrous, so everlasting. See the sign of the Excalibur and rejoice, for it holds a great and mighty sword, which cuts through the confusion, ends the blurred vision and carves out a clarity, an unspeakable justice. Be well my saints and sinners, for we are all one, of the same cloth, of the same herd, of the same love.

Merlin
Channeled on January 11, 2001

There Are Only Points of View

I now honor all my past experiences throughout all lifetimes for they help me to see the unity and perfection of all things. I learned that it is not bad to be judgmental because in truth there is no one who is judged and no one who seeks to judge. There is only one great quest of the soul, which is to recognize itself as:

- An individualized expression of infinite Spirit
- Being one and undivided and yet expressing itself in infinite different ways
- The ecstatic joy of being intrinsically involved in every creative process that takes place in all of time and all of space
- The unbounded love that makes living on Earth so worthwhile

In order to be all of this, we are somehow required to bring to the forefront or expose everything that reminds us of not having fulfilled this quest yet. To return to my religious upbringing as an example, I needed to feel how it is to be a sinner in order to realize that I am not a sinner. Likewise, I had to feel lonely and helpless so early in my life so I could understand that this was just a notion I had created to discover that I was never alone, and that nobody else is, either. Only the ego can feel lonely. It creates isolation by favoring some things and rejecting others. In reality, I am just as loved by the universe today as I was before the Great Separation. Even in our darkest hours when we feel deserted, vulnerable and helpless, we are still one with our Source. The only thing that can possibly leave us is our ego identity, which is just an idea of what we think we are. Because we don't love or appreciate ourselves enough, we have learned to play certain roles in life that help us become a 'somebody' who is respected or admired, or we try to make those around us appreciate or love us instead. When the attention from others fades or the love and appreciation for us discontinues, we (as our ego selves) start to feel lonely.

The idea or judgment that we are lonely, however, is only related to the loss that the physical awareness or ego feels. The Higher Self (the 'I' in the thought "I am lonely") knows it is never alone; it is only the external physical self (the ego) grieving over its loss of attachment to others that makes us feel lonely. Therefore, our egos then become so busy trying to get our old identities and attachments back that we rarely get to feel the oneness we share with everything. There are people who are put in jail for crimes they haven't committed. They become separated from their families and become bitter and angry. Their enforced loneliness, however, gives them the opportunity to spend a lot of time alone and to become more aware of the dialogue within. Intimacy is the complete opposite of loneliness. Becoming more aware of one's feelings and emotions, the dialogue within, and accepting them for what they are without trying to avoid them, lifts the loneliness and replaces it with intimacy. Once they begin to see the bigger picture - the reason they have created these events in their life - they are no longer bitter and angry, and are no longer lonely. If only we accepted the loneliness, the deserted feeling or the loss the ego feels, and focused instead on our connectedness with everything, we would then be filled with the intimacy and love of oneness, and pure joy.

Viewed from the perspective of oneness, there is no lower or higher, better, worse, right or wrong, good or bad. In other words, there is no thing and no situation, which is not of the same ONE SOURCE of life. Placing any other value on this is contrived and merely reflects our inner urge to reconnect with this Source.

Although nobody is really weak and no situation is really bad, we may need to perceive these as such until we are ready to enter a state of grace where 'weakness' and 'strength', or 'good' and 'bad', are just viewpoints of the same thing. The perception we have of a particular thing, person or situation varies according to the angle from which choose to look at it. A particular flower may bring you joy, yet for another it may bring up pain and sadness. Every coin has two sides but some people may prefer one side to the other. This, however, does not reduce the value of the coin. Having two completely different sides, it nevertheless always remains one single coin. Likewise, good and bad, low and high, right and wrong are attributes we attach to things in order to understand them on our particular level of existence. There comes a time in our growth of consciousness when we have no more preferences, only acceptance. The third Zen Patriarch Hsin Hsin Ming declared: "The great way is not difficult for those who have no preferences. Make the slightest distinction, however, and Heaven and Earth are set infinitely apart." From a coin's point of view, both the head and the tail are essential parts of it. There is no question of one side being better, more useful or more beautiful than the other. The question of 'right' being better than 'wrong' arises only when our perception is divided and not rooted in the oneness of all things. Weakness can be just as important and precious as strength. All great writers, artists, or athletes built their achievements on the foundation of their disappointments and failures in life.

A coin remains the same regardless of who is looking at it and from what side it is perceived. If you feel that one side of the coin is better or more valuable than the other then this is your choice and preference *at*

60

that time. Nevertheless, this does not diminish or enrich the value of the coin nor does it eliminate the possibility that someone else sees the same coin in quite the opposite way. Similarly, if you don't like what I say or you feel that what I am saying doesn't make any sense, it is but your truth and has no independent credence because someone else might feel very differently about the same thing.

Whatever we like or dislike in another is colored by the perspective that we have of ourselves. We love in others what we really have within us as well, but we haven't become aware of it and so seek to discover or find it in or through others. Likewise, if you pass judgment on another person or situation, this merely reflects the judgment you pass on yourself. Since this process occurs unconsciously, we seek to express it through the act of judgment. Passing judgment is a healthy process of learning and when the learning is completed, the judgment is no longer relevant or necessary. What remains is innocence. When innocence dominates perception, everything comes alive and is as precious and valuable as one's self.

We are here to recognize our true nature regardless of what roles we play in our lives. Saints and sinners merely play out different aspects of themselves; both are equally precious and worthy. We are just as connected with our Divinity when we judge another, as we are when we do not. In truth, we cannot harm anyone, although on the surface level it may seem this way. All that we do transforms, bit by bit, the trauma of the Great Separation into celebrations of love and unity, and assist other souls to do the same.

Fulfilling Our Soul Contracts

Every time we reincarnate in physical form we make new soul contracts with souls whom we have met during previous lifetimes, or still need to meet, so that together we can become aware of our God Selves and merge the higher dimensional realities of Heaven with the lower dimensional realities of Earth. Prior to each new incarnation, every soul is aware of the requirements, conditions, and circumstances that he/she needs to manifest during the coming Earth years to bring about this integration of perception or transformation of consciousness.

We can liken this to a movie. There may be 30 actors involved in a particular production. They all have consented to play a certain role, and to seal their agreement they have signed a contract. Each of them learns all about the character they have agreed to play and every scene of interaction with others, and the actors draw out different aspects of these

61

personalities. The movie script may include a murderer, a murder victim, a detective, a judge, etc.; one actor plays the villain, another one plays the victim, a third imitates the role of a detective, and so on. Although the audience watching the film sees great injustice done, there is neither a real victimizer nor a real victim. All the actors simply fulfill their contract, which entails that they act out their respective roles to make this movie possible. Once the shooting of the movie is completed, the actors detach themselves from these roles and get on with their lives, moving on to other roles in other productions. Nobody blames them or sympathizes with them for having played these characters; instead, they might even receive an award for best actor.

Lose Your Self-Identity But Gain...

On the Stage of Life, things are not much different. Life's learning process is about letting go of one identity after another, similar to peeling off the different layers of an onion. Eventually, there comes a point when you can no longer identify with anything anymore.

What remains is you, the 'I AM.' We go through the various stages of life i.e. infancy, youth, adulthood and old age, not only in this life but in lifetime after lifetime and at each stage in each lifetime we take on various roles, such as being a toddler, a playmate, a student, a doctor, a father/mother, an athlete, a friend, a thief, a patient, a retiree, etc. Playing these various roles, however, is not who I am, it only is what I identify with. My identity of being a doctor would go through a drastic change if I suddenly decided to become a lawyer or a priest. Each new identity serves a particular purpose, helping me to learn and master life's lessons and develop more and more trust in myself. Yet none of these can serve as my ultimate, never-changing self-identity.

When we use such words as *I am wealthy, I am poor, I am worthy, I don't like myself, I am angry, I am happy, I am a failure*, etc., we merely refer to the identities that our ego creates in order to know or define itself at that moment. For the ego to be comfortable and feel safe, for example, while under threat, it may refer to being wealthy, powerful, and strong as its preferable identities. If the ego receives a lot of love, praise and good intentions from others it may see itself as a worthy and generous human being. An ego deprived of love and achievement, on the other hand, is likely to see itself as unworthy and a failure. The movie of life is about creating and playing all possible roles of our complex natures.

Although none of the roles we play has anything to do with our true identity, we must play them so well that we get lost in them, just like a

62

good actor who becomes one with the character he/she tries to imitate or personify. Once we have explored each role sufficiently we are compelled to let it go again. This causes pain because the ego is so used to or attached to its identity. It can really throw the ego to pieces when at one moment it is used to being a wife and at the next moment, it is a widow. The pain itself, however, can become the motivating force to assume another role, which furthers the growth towards completion and full self-identity even more.

It is important for human life to experience the full range of duality, all the opposites of life, and it is of lesser or no importance whether they are painted in a positive or negative light. For example, even if we are rich we may, in fact, feel and act as if we are very poor if our belief is that we are not making enough money or fear that, at any moment, we may lose everything. Conversely, many poor people feel fortunate and rich just making enough money to feed the family and have nothing left to save. Every situation in life brings out a different, mostly opposite, value in us, and step-by-step we learn everything about mastery in this physical world.

After having duly exercised our ability to live through duality and its challenges, we begin to develop a new awareness, the awareness of 'I AM,' without the need of being something or someone else. Torn no more between right and wrong or good and bad, we find a middle point of balance where we are neither one nor the other. There are no more roles to be played, no more identities to be assumed. We can then ascend to the throne of selfhood where the soul no longer identifies with the ego awareness of the body but with the consciousness of its Higher Self. There is now only oneness and a complete circle of the Self, which contains all: the ego, the body and the Higher Self. There is nothing else needed in order to know oneself but *being*. The 'I AM' is the final destination, the ultimate home.

At this stage of consciousness development, the reference to the dualistic aspects of life, such as love and fear, joy and pain, positive and negative, loses all relevance. It vanishes altogether. We also begin to realize that the whole journey of life has been an illusion and that we never came home because we never left home. I am today the same 'I Am' I have always been and will always be. There is no self-realization. Since the Self was never lost, it cannot be found. All that happens in the journey of life is the gradual letting go of trying to find our identity. A person who searches for their glasses, not knowing they are already wearing them, will eventually discover that they don't need to look for them in order to see properly. They are already equipped with the right

63

tools of sight. The journey of self-discovery ends when we realize that we don't need to do or accomplish anything in order to be who we truly are.

The cycle of life may continue but having stepped into the field of oneness of duality we are free to once again assume the various roles of life, with the main difference that we are centered in the oneness of Self. Suddenly, the extreme ends of dualism, such as right and wrong, dark and light, up and down, etc., make perfect sense and can no longer affect us in any way.

You Are Your Own Creation

It is difficult to define reality since there is no experience that is independent of the experiencer. There are just as many different realities as there are people on this planet. There may however be some global realities wherever there is a group consensus on some basic points. Apart from that, each one of us is, creates and lives his/her reality. There is basically only one law in life: Your life is the way it is because you (the *total you* consisting of a higher and a lower self) decided that that is the way you wanted it to be. There is a larger picture to everything in life, and therefore every detail, both positive and negative, plays an important role for you. However, if you cannot see or trust in a larger purpose or meaning, the larger picture is irrelevant and of little use to you. Once you see it, you can nevertheless make sense of absolutely everything in life.

Whatever you put your attention on becomes your reality. This law is inviolatable. You get exactly that on which you concentrate. The old proverb 'As a man thinketh, so is he' is not a judgment of any sort, it is just a law. It doesn't mean that you and your thoughts are two separate things, one causing the other. Rather, it means you are exactly the way you think. You are your own creation. If you think the world is beautiful, it is because you are beautiful. You cannot divide your perception of the world and yourself because, in truth, there is no division, it just appears that way. If you believe the world is a depressing place, this perception is yours only; it is how you see yourself. You receive on the outside precisely what your consciousness focuses on inside. In addition, thoughts/feelings are the most intimate tools you use to construct your reality.

If you love something, you are focusing on it. The loving energies that you direct toward the object of affection such as a pet or a car make it a lovable thing. It is no longer lovable to you if you withdraw those

64

energies from it, perhaps because you consider yourself unhappy or unworthy. When you are in love with somebody, all that you are really doing is expressing the love you have for yourself to that person. Once you withdraw your love from yourself, you can no longer love the other person. Suddenly, he/she no longer seems lovable to you. Similarly, if you hate something or someone, you are actually focusing on what you hate within yourself, and projecting that inner hate on a particular situation, thing or person.

We often hear people complain: "This person drives me nuts." What they are really expressing is their own impatience and intolerance, and they cannot stand it if someone else is that way, too. No one 'makes' you feel anything, ever. *You choose your feelings* just as you choose everything else in your life. Nobody but you is responsible for how you live and what comes your way. This law is eloquently stated in Job 22-28, "Thou shalt decree a thing and it shall be established unto thee and light shall shine upon thy way." Through your own will, you hold the key to every situation in your life. The problems and complicated situations you may be facing are dependent on what goes on within you; therefore, they cannot be resolved in a satisfying way unless you resolve them within yourself, too. There is no transformative or regenerative agency other than the one controlled by your own will.

It is up to you how you wish to use the powerful tool of attention. If you direct your attention to beautiful and uplifting things, you will feel joyful and uplifted. Conversely, giving your energy to things or situations you consider harmful manifests those exact difficulties in your life. This principle applies also to collective calamities such as drug abuse. Drug trafficking would never have escalated to the catastrophic self-destruction of millions of young people had we not declared war on drugs. There is no better way to increase drug abuse than have everyone's attention focused on it. Acts of terrorism are fuelled, encouraged and strengthened by giving them publicity and by retaliating against them. Everything you oppose becomes stronger by virtue of providing it with your energy. Since the universe assumes that whatever you put your attention on is what you want, it 'graciously' provides you with more of the same.

If enough people are fascinated with war, it is likely to become a reality. Opposing war is accomplishing just the same. Both are reflections of how people view themselves. Unless we alter our sense of self-identity and our attention, the universe, which is just a massive field of energy and information, will dispassionately and readily respond by fulfilling everyone's obvious and hidden desires and create whatever we then call reality. It is time for all of us to begin using our powers wisely and create realities that are worthy of who we are.

When Opposites Meet

If you hold the north pole of a strong magnet near the south pole of another, they pull toward each other. If you turn one of the magnets around, they are mutually repelled. We, too, act like magnets. We pull things or people toward us and we repel others, forcing them away from us. The moment we feel good about ourselves, we expose our attractive side and the moment we feel bad inside, we expose our repulsive side. We are constantly shifting our polarity, day-to-day, hour-to-hour or sometimes even moment-to-moment. The measurement of energy emanating from each side of polarity is usually about two thirds on one side and one third on the other. The duality experience and the ability to pass judgment are only possible when one side is more dominant. Sickness occurs when the balance between health and sickness has shifted in favor of sickness i.e. feeling two thirds ill and one third healthy. Since feeling ill dominates at that time, feeling healthy is not apparent; hence the experience will be that of sickness.

We may have had entire lifetimes, based two thirds in darkness (ignorance of ourselves) and one third in light (knowledge of ourselves). It is the vibrational friction between the dark and the light which exists specifically for us to experience and understand the game of duality. During the 'happier' lifetimes, we expressed more of the features of light, love and peace in order to learn more about this aspect of duality. In both cases, life was unbalanced, like two musical instruments that play the same music but are not tuned in the same way. They do not resonate on the same frequency level. On the level of our physiology, the double strands that form the helix of our DNA have been operating at frequencies that are disharmonious with each other. One strand represents the negative or dark and the other strand the positive or light forces of nature. As long as we continue to experience the unbalanced proportions of duality, the DNA of our cells will also remain unbalanced. Such imbalance favors susceptibility to viruses, illness and aging. When we are in the Divine Moment, the peacefulness of non-judgment or non-preference, our DNA strands become attuned to one another and operate on the same frequency level or vibrational harmony. This effectively stops the aging process, heals any physical and emotional scars, and renders the body immune to any type of disease. Yet without having gone through and fully explored and experienced the opposite ends of duality, we would not be eligible to enter this coming phase in our journey. It was necessary for us to go through all these phases, health and sickness, love and hate, wealth and poverty, etc. and finally to recognize that they are merely reflecting the opposite characteristics of our ego's self-perception.

If the ego perceives itself as sick, it repels everything that is healthy or has a healing effect on the body. If it changes its perception to one of being healthy again, the body's healing powers spontaneously mobilize and it returns to a healthy condition on its own. Opposing values such as health and sickness have no independent basis, and they lose all sense of realness once we stop identifying with either of them. Health is a fiction of the ego's imagination just as sickness is; all they do is define each other. There are as many levels of health as there are levels of disease. Ultimate health however (if this is a good enough term to use), goes beyond the two. It is the mastery over the elements, or physical immortality, achieved so far only by a few adepts who live in some of the most remote places on Earth. They have transcended the illusion of duality and are able to sustain Higher Self awareness while in physical embodiment. Their super-refined bodies now once again obey the laws of consciousness and thus defy aging or destruction. We all are destined to achieve this state through the integration of our physical body with our higher dimensional self.

Each time we fight against one thing to gain another, or grasp one thing to avoid the other, we move a little further into full awareness. Preferring one thing to another seems to disturb the balance of self but is appropriate for exposing and removing the illusion of separation. The experience of opposites such as pain at one moment and joy at the next occurs in alternating waves or cycles. There are no such cycles when we are anchored in the center of being or, to say it differently, the waves of high and low are not experienced as fearful anymore. Being poor or wealthy doesn't enrich or diminish the bliss of life. Regardless of which end of duality one experiences, the self radiates through both of them. The negative pole of a magnet is just as important as the positive one. Likewise, there is no one person better, or more important, than another. Each situation in life is perfect as it is, *for that moment*. In the next moment, the tides may have turned and presented a new scenario and that too is also perfectly suited.

The two opposite forces of a magnet are found united only in the central part of the magnet. It is there that the magnet has its true power. Although both the negative and positive poles are present in the center, they remain unexpressed or virtual. The center knows that it can both repel and attract but is not disturbed or concerned whether it does or not. It always stays the same. It knows its own power and is not overshadowed, or defined by, what it attracts or repels. By remaining centered within ourselves, we can clearly see the importance of all aspects of our personality, our relationships, and our actions. This is where judgment, or the need to define oneself, ends. When both the extremes of duality make perfect sense to us, there is no more preference of one over another. Anchoring in the center of opposites puts us into a state of fearlessness, which dissolves the basis for all judgment.

Each aspect of duality is essential to develop and maintain the other. Sadness and joy are always coupled and never exist alone. The moment joy ends, sadness begins. The moment sadness ends, it makes way for joy. Opposites will always remain opposites and there is no use in trying to avoid or favor one over the other. Problems of every kind are caused by the play of opposites, of one thing seeming to be better or stronger than the other. A problem can never be solved *on its own level* for this reason. If the leaves of a plant begin to wither due to lack of water, it is no use watering the leaves. A good gardener who is not deceived by the appearance of the problem (dying leaves) waters the root instead and thereby helps to revive the plant. Likewise, a good physician does not attend to the symptoms of a disease but to its root cause.

We are gradually learning, through experiencing the multiple problems that exist in almost every area of life, that there is a common ground to them all. *We* are that common ground. Division creates contrast for a true expression of unity. We have created all this division to discover that, by attending to our Higher Self, we will not only be able to solve every existing problem with ease and grace but create anything new with the same ease and grace. Our Higher Self, the I AM, is the permanent Source of duality. When we consciously identify only with the I AM, the dark and light sides of life are seen as equally useful and important. Then we are able to accept all our human characteristics, including the shadow parts, without judgment. All self-denial falls away and judgment has fulfilled its purpose, which is to make us see the world in the light of oneness, love and unity. And *Seeing* it this way will *create* it this way.

Relationships Bring Out the Best and Worst In You

We cannot stay on one part of the polarity for very long without feeling uncomfortable or unfulfilled, even if it is a pleasant situation. Even paradise can become boring if we remain there for too long. Thus, during a wonderful romantic holiday there may come a point where you feel the urge to go home and do something else. A person who is accustomed to living in luxury and wealth may one day find that being rich is not enough anymore. Having reached one end of duality we tend to move toward the other. The cycles of change are unstoppable, which is good, because otherwise there would not be any growth or progression in life. This is especially true with regard to learning through human relationships.

If you meet someone who represents all those things that you are looking for in your life (because you think you do not have them yourself), you naturally desire to have him or her near you all the time. Let us assume that your new friend or partner feels the same about you, and finds you attractive because your personality or skills fill a specific need in his/her life. So long as both of you meet those needs, the relationship thrives with happiness and excitement. But perhaps one day your partner begins to discover he is not so satisfied anymore with what he is getting from you, which generates an inner lack of some sort. To overcome this feeling of lack, he starts demanding more attention from you. Yet if you cannot meet his increased expectations, your partner may become frustrated and angry. As a result, you may feel pressured and even suffocated. In response, you may withdraw from him and pull back your energy to protect yourself.

Eventually, giving whatever you were able to give to your partner before with love and joy now becomes more and more contrived and unnatural. You begin to avoid him when he becomes too demanding of you. You do this because it feels as if he is draining your energies. This, however, is an illusion. Your energy level drops not because your partner 'zaps' it by demanding that you satisfy his expectations and needs, but because you shut down your heart center. This temporarily 'disconnects' your ego awareness from your Higher Self (which can never suffer a shortage of love or energy for any reason). You feel lonely, taken advantage of, disconnected and/or depressed.

Unless you decide to end this relationship, you yourself might now assume the role of the needy one. Since your heart feels empty, you look to your partner to fill it for you. This is often seen as a sign for both that the relationship is working again, and in fact, on one level it is. The reversed roles now create a new balance. In the dance of relationships, one partner tends to lead and the other is led, until the roles are reversed. The dance of give-and-take and take-and-give keeps challenging the relationship until at least one of you reaches a place of non-judgment. Once you know how to fill your own needs of wanting to be loved, and enjoy the freedom to love without condition, you are no longer disconnecting from your Higher Self and thus remain in your heart center. It is then that your partner also spontaneously stops putting demands on you.

You begin to see right through the neediness of your partner or friend, and what you see is his fear of not being good enough. So instead of pulling back from him and shutting down your heart center, you feel compassion and forgiveness and you open your heart to him even more. Because you connect more deeply with your own essence, you also notice his true essence and consequently you are able to accept him into your life without condition and without judgment. You no longer feel suffocated but instead you have the freedom to love without condition. In the same way, your partner will stop pursuing you in order to derive satisfaction and comfort for he will find peace within his own heart space.

The old pattern of pulling back and cutting ourselves off from each other merely serves to cause separation in life; it hinders love from flowing freely. Since separation isn't part of our natural makeup and it causes pain, we keep looking for the 'ideal' relationship that is magical, fun and forever lasting. This search ends and true relationships begin when we no more shut down our heart connection within.

Many relationships have been tested in this way during the past decades of global spiritual awakening. Many people have become very interested in the pursuit of spiritual practices and/or a metaphysical understanding of life, whereas their partners remain entrenched in the old, purely materialistic outlook on life. This has more often than not become a reason for estrangement and problems in the relationship. Yet, for example, a husband who has chosen to remain in the old energy or way of life is doing this (although unconsciously) in order to be a balance for his wife to hold the opposite energy. This anchoring effect created by the husband is very much needed for the wife to be able to explore and experience these new areas safely and without too much hurry. In reality, the husband is against all that 'spiritual stuff' out of love and affection so that his spouse can become more strongly determined to move on in her life. If the wife could see the role her husband is playing for her, allowing her to move into the energies of the new world, she would be able to honor him for that and enjoy a truly fulfilling relationship. If she cannot see it, she might decide to leave him and find an anchor elsewhere.

It seems most of us need to play all the roles when it comes to relationships. In one, we play the needy one, and in another we need to be needed. One commonly hears, in human relationships, the words "I need you" or "I cannot live without you". Such need-based relationships cannot last simply because needs are highly changeable. Yet when neediness shifts towards an opening of the heart, the relationship experiences a renaissance based on the mutual outpouring of love. Once you are able to keep your heart open to the one who needs you, be it lover, parent, or friend, you will experience a diminishing of your own need-demands, too. Unless we fully love ourselves, we play both these needy roles. They serve as our guideposts in learning about the duality nature of life. The frequent and sometimes intense oscillations from wanting our needs fulfilled by others to being needed by others, gradually become balanced and end altogether.

Every relationship of ours is a great blessing for everyone involved because it allows us to experience these dualistic aspects of life in a concrete and tangible way. Like the arms of a cross merging into a central singular point, all opposing values find their common basis in the heart consciousness of the person who experiences them, regardless of whether he is aware of this or not. Once we have learned enough about the opposing parts of life (the dualistic nature of separation) we are ready to see them as unified. This creates a new type of relationship with others and the world, one that accepts everyone and everything just as they are.

No Need to Change Yourself

There is no need to change other people if we can simply accept ourselves the way we are. When we judge another person, it is not because we dislike or disprove of them, but because their behavior, opinions, or actions reflect *our own feeling* of not being 'good' enough. Likewise, when our perceived or expressed expectations of others do not meet, we criticize them in order to make the reflection of our own pain more acceptable and bearable. In truth, judgment is not real. It is never directed against anyone or anything but our own feelings of guilt and inadequacy. And that is an illusion, too.

The challenge at this time is to claim your power and hold it dear, for you are the only one who can determine your reality, now that the new energy is permeating life on Earth. It is no longer helpful to look for others to make a difference in your life. Changing yourself to please someone else is only dispersing your power for no gain. The days of spiritual and political leaders who will tell you which way to turn are gone. Unless you choose to become a spiritual slave who believes there are others greater or more spiritually advanced than you, there are simply no more Gurus or leaders to follow.

Judgment loses its grip and power when the need to be a better person than we are subsides. Does this mean that a person who is without judgment has no more desire to learn and grow? No, it means quite the opposite. It implies that the non-judgmental person perceives each moment, regardless of whether it seems to be supportive or adverse, as equally fortunate, as a Divine blessing. They don't even question whether it is good or bad, they feel no guilt for having done something that others consider to be bad. They know that even the darkness will end, so they fear it not. They learn that there is always light at the end of the tunnel and that the tunnel actually serves as a path to the light. Each one of us is, at every moment, guided by our Higher Self, driven by an intrinsic power to complete ourselves and to master one of the most important lessons in life - being without judgment. Gaining freedom from judgment is the gateway to effortless living, unconditional love, continual abundance and unlimited potential.

All the 'good' and 'bad' things we experience happen to us for an important reason, that is, to rise above the illusion of good and bad and to perceive them both as Divine blessings. There are no bad things happening to us, and no good ones, either. It is we who attract and create everything we experience and then we give each thing a meaning. When we call it a bad thing, we create something that seems to hurt or harm us. If we see it as something good, we make it useful and beneficial for us. Either way, we learn to become masters of our human destinies. The way we judge things reflects how we are within. We ourselves have orchestrated this learning tool to once again become aware of our ultimate selfhood.

Being, and living without judgment places you in the eternal presence of the 'now.' You naturally accept whatever *is* at every moment as ideal. Without judgment in your heart, there is nothing that warrants comparison, nothing that is better and nothing that is worse. Everything is seen as unique and rightful. It is what it is. And it is perfect, otherwise it would not be. This of course requires trust in a Higher Intelligence, *your* Higher Intelligence, for it knows what is best for you, and what you need at every moment to move towards fulfilling your aspirations in life. And when you honestly ask yourself whether you can trust in this, you will find that you do. It is important to feel this trust.

The Great Sage Shankara, who lived in India about 500 years before Jesus Christ was born, exemplified throughout his life what it means to be without judgment. One day, as he walked the land with a group of his followers he came to a narrow passage, blocked by a beggar. One of Shankara's disciples asked the beggar to move out of the way to clear the path for the saint but the beggar did not budge an inch. Furious over this matter, the disciples tried to move the beggar with force but could not. When they reported to Shankara that the dirty beggar, who was from the lowest class, was creating a problem, the saint walked toward him and prostrated himself in front of his feet, kissing them with reverence. Shocked with disbelief, the disciples gathered around and wondered why the greatest sage on Earth would bow down to a Shudra, the Sanskrit word for an outcast.

When Shankara fell to the feet of the beggar, the beggar transformed into a Divine form of God and showered its Divine blessings and gifts unto Shankara, much to the amazement of the surrounding crowd. Shankara saw God in every creature and so had no ability to differentiate between a sinner and a saint. An ordinary person has all their energies locked up in stored emotions, beliefs, thoughts and memories, and has little or no energy to spare for a higher perception beyond what the mind presents. Shankara, on the other hand, had an 'empty' mind that had nothing with which to be entangled. His mind was free from any mental or emotional clutter, unattached to the limiting effects of memories. Since all his energies were held within his spiritual body, all he was able to do was to see God in himself. Naturally, he experienced God as non-separate from his own being. So he felt one with all of Creation, and the deep love he had for God within him was naturally extended to all there was without. He had no way of seeing anyone as inferior to himself, or being made of a different stuff than he was. Shankara was beyond judgment and all he did was to accept everything that he himself represented in life as an expression of the Divine.

We are all Shankaras. We move on the tracks of duality until we hit an obstacle or a problem. It is then our choice as to whether we want to see the problem as a source of misery or as a Divine opportunity to recognize who we really are. We can look at a beggar as a poor wretch and focus on all the imperfections that life has to offer, or we can search for the face behind the mask of appearance and discover that everything is in Divine order and good for everyone. To arrive at such a state of perception, all that is required of us is to accept and allow what is, *as it is*, and the obstacle will turn into a golden opportunity.

Any problem in a relationship serves as its own solution, provided we are willing to see it that way. Problems remain problems for as long we separate ourselves from a person or situation. Fighting them or struggling to avoid them keeps them strong and alive. Although this has been our

73

way of conducting our life's affairs throughout the ages, it hasn't been a very successful one in the sense of generating freedom and happiness. Problems, as such, are not responsible for causing us discomfort and limitation. Our reaction to them makes the difference. If our response to seeing struggle and evil is one of fear and anger, then struggle and evil seem very real to us and stay with us. All we really want is to get rid of the fear, which is the true cause of whatever we do not want in our lives. Yet we cannot escape the clutches of fear unless we renounce our striving against the odds of life and accept them for whatever they are.

Choose Your Choices

It is only possible to consciously play the game of choice making while behind the veil of forgetfulness and confusion. However, to get to the point where we can begin to enjoy true freedom we need to go through a state of confusion first. The pendulum of life swings, sweeping up to one side, but before it turns and swings the other way there is a pause, that magical moment where everything is possible, where problems reveal their hidden solutions. This magical space is what we call chaos. It is natural at first to feel anxiety in this space when familiar movement stops and nothing seems to happen. Feeling stuck in a void, there seems to be no guidance, no help, no assurance or assistance. We can feel very much out of touch, frustrated, ungrounded and/or stressed while being in this state of uncertainty. Yet this shows that we are, indeed, in the magical moment where something new is about to be birthed.

Life is such that we cannot effectively control what enters our head. We also seem to have little choice about what we fear, like or dislike because we are all part of the universal flow of the subconscious mind. The collective mind, which is what we *are* even if we feel we are not, delivers to us the mail of individual and collective karma like an echo that returns to the one who created it. When karma returns it isn't out to punish us or restore justice of some kind, but to direct our attention to the clues it contains. To understand the clues we need to be alert. When we are alert, we are able to deal with it. You can choose to see the struggles that occur in the field of duality either as a threat or as a blessing. We will never be able to undo polarity and why should we? The only thing that really matters is how we perceive it. Although the North and South Poles seem so different and disconnected from each other, they act as a power that holds the planet together as one whole and constantly evolving organism. This would not be possible if one of the two was

74

missing. Likewise, all the other opposites of life serve an indispensable purpose, provided we choose to see it this way.

It occurs to me personally that the reason for experiencing the duality of life is to discover, or become aware of, the underlying unity of things. The opposites of life cannot exist without one another. A wave of the sea that has reached its utmost level of height is bound to move to its lowest level in order to make it a complete wave. This is what gives the wave its power. In fact, the low level of the wave *defines* the high level just as shadow defines light. Without shadows, this world would not have a three dimensional appearance at all. It would be flat and terribly boring to look at. The relationship between the light and the dark, the high and the low of the wave, the positive and negative aspects of the Earth's poles, etc. are only possible because of the common basis shared by all opposites. There is nothing in this universe that is so opposed to something else that the two couldn't be reconciled or harmonized on a more fundamental level.

The End of Conflict

As human beings, we have done what are considered horrific things to each other throughout the ages, and yet many of us have come together again in this life as lovers, brothers, sisters, or friends, recreating situations that teach us the lessons of compassion, forgiveness and unconditional love. We have co-created the negative situations of war and hate so that we would be able to manifest and develop the corresponding opposite, positive values of kindness and peace. It wasn't wrong back then to go to war and kill our fellow human beings, just as it isn't wrong today to be loved by the same ones we killed on the battlefields. Peace would have no practical value, or, in other words, we would not appreciate what peace truly means, if it were not for the wars and conflicts we have had to endure. This is not to glorify war by any means. All it shows is that everything exists as a dynamic dance of opposing values that move through alternating cycles. These cycles are greatly helpful to our individual and collective growth toward unity consciousness.

Many soldiers have regained a sense of living, of appreciating what life is, when they fought at the frontlines. Killing others, who were fathers, brothers, or friends like themselves made so little sense, yet they felt trapped between killing the supposed enemies in order to survive and sparing their lives only to risk dying at their opponents' hands. Many are shaken to the core of their being by such conflicts. How could it be right to be forced to kill your fellow humans against your will and desire?

Deep, irresolvable conflicts often take us into these moments of total confusion, which in turn awakens us to our own inner sense of oneness with the all. By moving often enough through the cycles of extremes, such as war and peace, hate and affection, fear and love, we begin to enter the state of singularity where opposites unite. And it is not finding a solution to the conflict that is important. What matters most is the conscious experience of the pain and fear until it dissolves into the state of singularity where the conflicting parts or situations are naturally accepted and embraced.

Consciousness is the only field where differences are harmonized. Only when we step outside the field of duality and into the field of singularity or oneness can conflict cease to exist. If oneness penetrates the arena of war, the warring parties would find it no longer important to define the boundaries of land that belong to one side or the other, simply because sharing rather than owning them becomes the priority. While in duality awareness, territorial rights have to be defended, sometimes even at the cost of sacrificing thousands of people, in unity consciousness there is nothing to defend because boundaries don't exist. You cannot be attacked if you are sharing everything you have with everyone. This prevents the birth of an enemy altogether. Likewise, if you are able to accept yourself exactly the way you are, you have no need to defend yourself, either. If you have nothing to lose or defend yourself for, there won't be anyone around who would want to attack or hurt you in any way. This point deserves closer investigation because it will help us understand why each one of us is the sole creator of all our life experiences. Moreover, it will shed light on the mystery that surrounds human relationships.

It is with great fanfare and lively interest that we come to you today, wishing upon you baskets of goodness and plenty to adorn your table and enhance your feast of nations. Let us sit down with each other, hand in hand, and feel the words of goodness and holy ordinance onto each other. For without our brethren, we see and speaketh nothing but the truth from within. Our hearts play a mighty game of chance, as we dance around the tables of delight. But it is only in the company of others, the true companionship of friends, strangers, and loved ones, that we can, in earnest, love and understand ourselves very fully. That is so. And it has been done for eons.

Jeremiah
Channeled on April 14, 2001

Chapter Six

Demystifying Relationships

Is it not time to lay down our swords and speak peaceably with one another, salvaging the goodness, the kind words and the honor left remaining between us and amongst us? Let our humility reign freely and take us to a new and higher plane of self-awareness. May the doors to our psyches and to justice be ever opened so we may freely come and go as citizens of peace and enchantment. Once we are in harmony with our soul selves we are forever at home and may delight in our unity. May the horn of plenty shimmer upon your plate and fulfill your dreams with abundance of such magnitude that you are forever quenched.

Mahatma Gandhi
Channeled on December 21, 2000

Living with Two Selves

Every person on this planet is a spiritual being in human form, although this may not be a conscious experience for many and does not seem true when we think of the aggression, greed and hate prevailing in so many parts of the world. However, we all share the same Spirit at the core of our being. This, our essence self or Higher Self, is beyond duality and remains an eternal Love force regardless of how 'bad' we may seem in our human form. On this higher level of existence, we harmonize with each other and love each other for who we are, while in our incarnated forms we may assume the roles of being competitors or adversaries. It seems a paradox that on one level we love each other, whereas on another level we hate each other. But physical life is not quite what it seems.

Prior to incarnating as human beings, our individual souls make agreement with a number of other beings for the purpose of helping each other to balance the effects that the Great Separation has caused in us, and to manifest love as the principle force of creation on planet Earth and in the rest of the universe. There are numerous other ways to achieve this but none of them has anything to do with love directly.

The reason for learning about love through painful experiences lies in the very setup of duality as played out in the three dimensional (3D) world. To be able to live and function in this world we had to deny our Divine origin or love force. This we have done throughout most of our Earth lives. Being without a spiritual anchor permits us to learn the ins and outs of duality until we could see the entire range of duality as being rooted in the same Source with which we are eternally one.

One of the quickest ways of reaching the point of Oneness with the All is to experience duality in its most extreme expressions. Although the opposing aspects of duality emerge from one common origin, they certainly don't seem to. A thick veil separates duality from oneness. Our Higher Self operates beyond this veil in the field of oneness, whereas our ego nature plays in the field of duality. The two selves, the higher and lower, play their game perfectly. That they cooperate with each other at every moment may be hard to 'digest'. Why would the love-motivated Higher Self support or approve of the ego's strive for power, dominance, possessions, and useless sensory gratification if spiritual evolvement is one of the main purposes of our stay here on Earth? What possible good could there be in crime, hate, suppression, greed and rage? Yet, if we are essentially spiritual beings in human form, then we must at least consider the possibility that there may be some sort of purpose in suffering, negativity and destruction.

Seen on their own, negative personality characteristics make very little sense, if any, but when taken into the context of a larger picture, they suddenly become meaningful. Every single particle that constitutes our body, the world and this entire universe can only exist because it has an anti-particle somewhere. Although billions of light years may separate a particle and its anti-particle, they are attached to each other by a force that cannot be broken or destroyed. Regardless of the distance that may lie between them, if one particle rotates in one direction, let us assume it takes a left spin, its anti-particle spins to the right. The most astonishing thing in this mysterious event is that the exact opposite movements of the two particles are precisely synchronized. That is truly astounding! How does the one particle know when its opposite twin is about to rotate?

The only sensible answer to this question lies in the invisible field that is home to both particles and any other pair of duality, like light and dark, high and low, right and wrong, good and bad. This invisible field is *consciousness*. It unites opposites, keeps them together. This unified field of consciousness underlies all of duality. It is the central point where opposites meet and become one. The poles of a magnet, like the poles of the Earth's magnetic field, have opposite characteristics; one is negative and the other positive, yet both of them need one another to exist. The Earth wouldn't be here in this form if either the South Pole or the North Pole vanished. Since these polar points give rise to a huge magnetic field that polarizes everything, including our human bodies and minds, we cannot help but have to deal with the duality of life.

The poles of the Earth magnet exert no power at the exact middle point between them, yet this point in the inner Earth is the great power that keeps them both in balance. This power is silent and unifying; without it, the Earth would disintegrate like a rotten apple that could no longer hold on to its substance. And to some extent the Earth is now behaving like a rotten apple. The presence and activities of the human race on this planet have gradually thrown the Earth's magnetic field out of balance. The polarity is uneven. The bloodshed, conflicts, wars, fear, exploitation of resources, construction of large cities, the building of railways and asphalted roads, the chemical pollution of the soil, water and air, etc. have all contributed to the derangement and degradation of the Earth's magnetic field. We have reached a point where many species of animals are leaving the planet due to sickness, lack of living space and starvation.

Our human lives are polarized like the energy field generated by the poles of a magnet or the poles of the Earth. If our body's magnetic field was in complete alignment with the Earth's magnetic field, and the Earth's magnetic field were intact according to its original design, we would enjoy perfect, unending health and youthfulness in both body and mind. At the same time, the Earth would be a paradise. We would literally enjoy heavenly life on Earth. We are heading this way but we are certainly not there yet. We are in the process of leaving behind the confusion and chaos that occurs in the period of pause before the pendulum of time takes a new direction. Although chaos and confusion are more pronounced now than ever before, love, hope and compassion have never been so deep and widespread, either. These intensified experiences in duality allow us to get into something even deeper than we have ever experienced before, that is, 'spiritual passion,' the passion of spirit itself, the passion of Divine Love.

This is the time of the greatest spiritual renaissance the Earth has ever witnessed. The Earth herself is realigning with her original purpose and therefore with the central power point that keeps her poles balanced. The Earth is able to go through this major transformation because we humans are increasingly shifting our awareness from duality-based to singularity-based living. We are gently, or not so gently, motivated to become aware of the central point of unity that, in the field of duality, holds life together and makes it truly meaningful and passionate. We have reached the final chapter in the long history of life on Earth where everything that has ever disturbed our alignment with our Spirit Source is forced to the surface. This is not bad, though it may seem so at first. Many of the imbalances from the past are returning now for us to honor and bless them. Only when we do that will the imbalances leave us altogether.

Before we, in the role of our Higher Self, volunteered to make Love the principle keynote of personal and universal interaction on this planet, we didn't expect it would be so hard. Little did we know that incarnating in human form and acting out duality would also mean forgetting our Source and soul purpose. In order to create something more than there was before this great experiment, of which the Great Separation played a major role, we had to incarnate here many times. Each new life allowed us to experiment with and understand a new facet of duality. We were to infuse the highest form of love frequency into the lowest form of matter and energy that exists on this planet. This would raise the density of matter, which is so prevalent in the lower dimensions, and merge it with the higher energies of the fourth and fifth dimensions. To do this successfully we needed to *completely* immerse ourselves in the ignorance that is so typical for any perception in the third dimensional reality. This meant we had to experience, and feel every aspect of duality, both the positive and the negative.

Roller Coaster Life

Living in the world of duality is like a roller coaster ride; at one moment, you are moving up, and at the next you are moving down. In the many lifetimes we have spent on this planet we have sown the seeds of Karma (karma is a Sanskrit word meaning 'action' and implies that every action causes a reaction). Some of this sprouted and began to bear fruit during the same lifetime but much of this remained for other lifetimes that followed. We already know that in order to hold the universe together, every particle has an anti-particle. This same principle applies to karma; every action has its anti-action or reaction. This is universal law. Since we are currently living in the realm of three-dimensional space-time reality, time seems to move in a linear fashion. It is our perception that things occur in sequence, one after another. An action here causes a reaction there, after a certain time has elapsed. Although this is just an illusion created by our 3D-oriented senses, most of us live by this notion of time. This allows us to perceive cause and effect as two separate events in time and space. Based on this delusional perception we experience duality as a concrete reality, and this delusion runs through every event in our lives and is part of every relationship of ours.

We have purposely sown the seeds of happiness, joy, forgiveness, compassion, justice, friendship, caring, giving, saving life, health, strength, etc. many times over during our many existences on Earth. But we have also sown the seeds of fear, anger, depression, sadness, revenge, harshness, injustice, enmity, insensitivity, selfishness, destroying life, sickness, weakness, etc. What could possibly motivate us to cause harm to others and ourselves other than the conviction that we are essentially evil by nature? The answer is found in the fact that love cannot assume its role in life unless we feel how it is not to have loved. So we had to co-create, together with the members of our soul family, the ideal scenarios that would allow us to experience hateful relationships, feeling rejected, being lonely and/or isolated, etc.

All the players of the drama of duality here on Earth have known beforehand which role would benefit them most to bring them closer to conscious alignment with Spirit. We have all chosen to play the roles both of the victim *and* the victimizer innumerable times. I personally killed scores of people during my lifetimes as a warrior in the battlefields of the Middle Ages. I had been instrumental in bringing hardship and torment to many. Yet I could not have done that if other souls had not agreed and volunteered to play the victims, which then paved the way for me to sow the seeds of healing, love and understanding in other lifetimes, such as this one. In return, I offered to help others in mastering their life lessons by playing the victim in a similar fashion and according to the principles of karma.

There is no judgment in the law 'as you sow, so shall you reap'. It is merely a self-evolving, perpetual principle of life that sustains our perception of duality until we are able to transcend it and perceive it for what it is. We are not being judged by God or anyone else, except perhaps by ourselves, for taking duality to its extremes i.e.for being a saint in one lifetime and a sinner in another. On the contrary, we are praised by the angels and masters on the other side of the veil for doing such painful work. It takes a saintly vision and a lot of compassion to see God in a murderer.

The Love in Evilness

To see the love force behind the display of evil and lift the mask of duality is one of the greatest challenges we face in this world. This challenge is often met by experiencing what it is like to be a killer. We can only develop compassion for a murderer when we ourselves know how it feels to take another person's life. Our soul records are full of such memories, albeit we have little conscious access to them. The main question is, are we really capable of loving our enemies? Did Jesus live in a dream world when he suggested only seeing what is good in everyone and ignoring whatever bad they have done? Would we not incur greater injustice if we simply forgave those who have harmed us or others and leave them unpunished?

From the viewpoint of duality, there does not appear to be a satisfactory solution to these questions. In truth, though, all viewpoints have their validity and are reconcilable. When Jesus spoke, he spoke from the level of his kingdom, which is the consciousness of oneness, a place where all relationships make sense. He demonstrated at the cross that even murderers are eligible to enter this kingdom if they desire to. Jesus asked his own Higher Self - the Father above - to forgive his perpetrators, for "they know not what they do". With this statement Jesus pointed out that even his own killers were worthy of compassion and forgiveness because, engulfed by the illusion of duality (called ignorance), they could not have any real clarity about what was right or wrong.

Even murderers believe they are doing the right thing. Otherwise, they wouldn't kill. It is only *our* judgment that makes a murderer a 'bad' person. A killer, like everyone else in this world, has a Higher Self with only love as its basic motivating intention. When someone kills somebody else for whatever reason, the two agreed to play these roles prior to incarnating, out of love and mutual desire to help one another. One part of their consciousness actually may telepathically communicate with each other, while the other part of their consciousness acts out their specific roles. It matters not that their personalities are not aware of their cooperation and agreement. In fact, not knowing it helps both of them to be pushed to the extremes of duality life, and thereby prepare the way for going beyond the illusion of cause and effect. Life and learning don't end with physical death.

All Things Make Sense

The law of karma is so complex that even the wisest of men could not make any sense of it. The web of karma has far too many strands, each one connected with every other one. It is not possible to untangle them intellectually. Yet at the same time, karma has only one origin i.e. the separation of oneness into two. Karma rules the world of duality but it is powerless in the world of oneness. Karma's sole purpose is to restore the 'lost' awareness of oneness. Each time we re-experience the pain aspects of the Great Separation, as for example during moments of loneliness, fear or anger, we actually move a little closer towards rediscovering our true essence. Both the alternating currents of 'good' and 'bad' experiences in life are mixed up and make very little sense on their own level but in the context of the whole, which is *Oneness Of The All*, they can be truly enlightening.

A good deed, like helping a blind person cross a busy street or giving food to the homeless, seems to be more natural and in line with who we want to be rather than ignoring them and not doing anything about their plight. Yet how many times do we look away when we see the suffering around us, pretending we haven't seen it? I used to do that, and it brought up in me feelings of both compassion and guilt. I really wanted to help, but I didn't. And because I didn't do what I wanted to do, I felt ashamed of my own failure to help those in need. However, this guilt, if it becomes strong enough, can help build a bridge to one's compassionate nature.

One day while walking the busy streets of London on a cold, rainy afternoon, I passed a young man lying on cardboard at the entrance to a subway station. He was obviously hungry and cold. I tried to avoid looking into his eyes and seeing his pain because it would remind me of my own pain, and I quickly walked by, just as I had done so many times before. This time, however, the guilt of always ignoring people like him had reached a climax and something forced me to stop. I turned around and spontaneously, without thinking, I slipped out of my winter coat and handed it to him, saying something like: "I think you could use something to get you warm!" The young man looked at me with disbelief and said with genuine concern in his voice: "But what will *you* do without a coat in this cold?" I told him that I would buy a new one. After a few moments of trying to convince him that I would be just fine, he accepted the coat and put it on. Obviously pleased by this gift, he gave me a beautiful smile that warmed my heart. I felt extremely good about myself for days. His suffering and my accumulated guilt combined to open my heart in a way I had not allowed to happen for a long time. We both gained from this, tremendously, just for the price of a coat. In one short moment I had released years of pent-up feelings of guilt, or rather, my guilt had magically transformed into the joy of love. Psychology may see guilt as a useless emotion. What I have learned from this experience, though, is that guilt, if it reaches an intensified enough level, is just another means of putting us in touch with the ever-present love inside us.

One of the most crucial insights that will strike the seeker of truth is that all opposites are not just connected; they are, in fact, *dependent* on each other. Most people tend to separate the right from the wrong, and prefer the good to the bad, or suppress failures in order to feel successful. Yet this separation exists *only in the mind*. In truth, *both* are part of our growth process. Positiveness never stands alone; it is sustainable by negativity, and vice versa. There can be no electric current if one of the two potentials is missing. Likewise, there can be no progress or evolvement in life without experiencing both of them. The challenge comes when one is dominating the other. In one lifetime, we may be predominantly a 'good' person, one who is of service to others and who brings love and joy to the world. During another lifetime, we may exhibit mostly 'bad' qualities, harming others and adding stress and tension to the world. We may even shift from being a good or bad person to being a bad or good person within one lifetime.

Why do we do this? There are two main principles at work here, which, superficially, seem to contradict each other. The first one is the principle of 'like attracts like.' Birds of a feather flock together. If you are a happy, loving person, you naturally attract happy people around you. Smile at someone and you receive a smile back. When you give something to someone with all your heart, without conditions or expectations, you draw to yourself abundance in many forms. Similarly, your fears will magnetize situations in your life that make you feel even more afraid. Being distrustful or dishonest with others will draw to you people who do not trust you either. Holding on to money and possessions will reinforce your need to hoard wealth. And so on.

The second principle claims that 'opposites attract each other'. We have seen many examples in our history where good people have been ridiculed, tortured and even nailed to a cross for showing their goodness to the world. Martyrs are willing victims whose extreme goodness magnetizes extreme evilness. There cannot be martyrs without tyrants; they are merely representing the opposite roles of duality. The question is: do tyrants make martyrs or do martyrs make tyrants? It is my assumption that they manifest together. A tyrant may have the need to display and prove their power over the helpless, and a martyr has the need to prove their ability to defy such a power by facing death with courage and even a smile. In a way, both need each other to act out their respective roles. To make this possible they attract one another with perfect timing and precision. Many of the now so-called 'confirmed saints' were often mistaken for witches or servants of Satan during their lives, and they suffered greatly for disclosing their love for God. What is most amazing in all this is how ill-meaning dictators like Hitler or Stalin became almost irresistible magnets for millions of ordinary, good-natured family men, turning them into 'beasts' who felt rightful satisfaction from killing millions of people in concentration camps and battle grounds.

Being good to others is often misconstrued as being clever or manipulative. You may offer help to someone in need and, instead of reaping gratitude in return for your kindness, you are robbed by them. Or you give food to a beggar in the street who asks for change, and instead of being grateful for the meal they spit at you. Of course, you may not know that the food you gave cannot buy the booze or cigarettes they crave. People often wonder why it seems like only the most kindhearted people get cancer, those who live to help others. All these situations show that opposites do attract each other and on the surface, this seems very odd. But by looking deeper we can see the hidden mechanisms that control and coordinate all random events in life according to a master plan.

Your Master Plan

Each one of us has a master plan. This master plan is not the kind that tells you how to get from A to B or how you can be a better person than you already are. It is a Divine Plan that helps you see that there is nothing bad in evilness and nothing good in goodness. It is a script that we are all writing in each moment. The script guides us through the seemingly complicated and intricate experiences that dominate the unfathomable world of opposites, until we arrive at the point 'Be still and know that you are God'. Only when oneness finally clicks in do we know that the world of duality was an illusion the mind had created in order to help us identify with our true Source. This grand plan is built within the core of our being and it is the purpose of life to bring it to fulfillment.

Life and death, joy and sorrow, right and wrong, light and dark, all these are opposites and are blessings. But we only recognize them as blessings when we are in stillness, which is our only link to our infinite Source self, when we are in full acceptance of the moment. As soon as we move to prefer one thing to another, we are no longer still and thus display non-acceptance. Accepting one as good or right and rejecting the other as bad or wrong places us in the arena of struggle, the battlefield of judgment.

Holy people, when put to death in the past, often died with a blissful smile on their faces, much to the annoyance of their killers. These saints experienced no conflict within themselves for they had surpassed the limitations of life and death, right or wrong, joy and sorrow. For them joy was as equally confining as sadness, for one was bound to become the other. Physical death had little meaning to them because they had already identified with their higher, Divine Self as the one and only life there is. And what we consider life had value for them only as long as they had not ascended to their Higher Self. After ascending, acquiring a physical body does not add any benefits (although reincarnation may be an option, many incarnating souls have taken to assist others who are going through the same process of ascension). The rest of us are following in their footsteps. They have made it easier for us by showing us the way; a path more traveled is easier to walk on. They are guiding us safely through the jungle of duality. Whichever turns we take, none of them is right or wrong, all of them have the potential to liberate us from the pangs of separation.

Every choice of ours creates a new world of possibilities that would not exist for us if we hadn't made that choice. We alter our future destiny with every thought and feeling we choose to have, and each possible destiny or probable future is as good for us as it can be. With the help of duality, our master plan finds its fulfillment. Holy people know this and do not favor one thing over another. They have gained freedom from judgment.

Beyond the Veil

Some of the most challenging situations in the pursuit of completing our life lessons arise in the area of personal relationships. It is through our relationships that we are able to delve into the sea of love, but they also dig up the mud of struggle and pain. Relationships are rarely perfect, and *from the perspective of duality* perhaps they can never be. If they were always loving and beautiful, personal growth in this dimension would come to a halt. So while we are going through our birthing process to become beings of the unified field of consciousness, we need to play out our dual roles of being kind and unkind to one another. Even if we have no more personal 'issues' to go through ourselves, we are still here to help others to go through theirs.

It would be of little use to the mission project we signed up for on this planet prior to incarnating in human form, if we ascended to the Light of God or Spirit just for our own sake. We must take the journey together in order to make it worthwhile for all life in the Universe. To fulfill our collective purpose here on Earth, our Higher Self is always ready to assist our lower self (ego) in recognizing its roots. When the soul surrenders to the Higher Self, the ego self becomes a clear channel of Spirit and begins to see everyone as being of the same Source of infinite love and light. The veil that separates the Higher Self is lifted from the lower self (ego) and human access to the spirit world becomes unrestricted. We can achieve this most effectively when we help each other act out our polarity issues. Many of these exist on the personal level, the day-to-day stuff that makes us laugh, cry, get upset, become anxious or depressed. Other triggers that make us aware of these issues include economic problems, political conflicts, wars, acts of terrorism, public health scares, natural disasters, etc. Whatever they are, if they move us emotionally in some way, then they are useful opportunities for us to get closer to our goal.

Jesus Christ spoke from beyond the veil of duality, from the kingdom of the Higher Self, when he recommended that we love our enemies. He pointed out that having enemies or adversaries in life has a lot to do with how we see and treat ourselves. His advice "Love thy neighbor as thou lovest thyself" is not an impossible thing to achieve because from the higher perspective we are *already* one, we are all equals. But of course we can only love our neighbors or enemies if we love ourselves. Every relationship we have in life reflects the relationship we have with ourselves.

In the ultimate analysis, whether we are saint, martyr, tyrant, terrorist or just an ordinary person, no one is better or worse, more or less advanced, than another. We all are of the same Source and we are never separate from it; all we are here to do is to become conscious of this. Jesus Christ, or Joshua Ben Joseph as he is known on the other side of the veil, taught mankind that coming into human incarnation is not a punishment nor is it something that is to our disadvantage, no matter what happens. We are all saints or angels in disguise, yet on the human level, we may take on the roles of thieves and killers. Even saints can have enemies in life, or so it seems to the undiscerning eye. Although saints do not perceive those who persecute them as enemies, others do. Holy people - those who have become whole - can no longer see duality as real. Instead, they see friends and foes as equal and one, each fulfilling their self-assigned duties. Jesus knew ahead of time what calamity would befall him, yet he took it as being part of a Divine plan that would benefit the whole. Despised and ridiculed by many, he played the role of a button pusher, bringing to the forefront the false dogmas and beliefs people had of God and of themselves. Healing others or raising the dead may be a compassionate thing in itself, but it also challenges everyone's limited belief systems. Moreover, this can trigger massive reactions releasing excessive fear and rage.

Therefore, where there is good, bad is not far away. Likewise, in being crucified for helping those in need, Jesus initiated a wave of gradual awakening which has lasted for two thousand years, and has prepared the way for the ascension of humanity to its higher nature. As Jesus did during his Earth time, we are now beginning to see behind the veil of duality. Any interaction between people on the human level, including the 'negative' ones, also takes place on the higher planes, where love is the principle force behind it. We are about to recognize that we *are* beyond the veil.

Seeing with the Heart

There is a love-bound agreement between two souls who have decided to play opposing roles during their lives. The two sides are eager to fulfill this voluntary contract in order to unfold and bring to the forefront that which has remained hidden and undeveloped. Although this rarely feels joyful on the human level of experience, these souls do everything humanly possible to stick to their contract they have made with one another. This may explain why so often a battered wife stays with her husband just to be battered repeatedly, or an abused child cannot forgive an abusive parent even after decades have passed. The 'negative' bond remains and is often transferred to new relationships. Old patterns are repeated so that each party can deal with and learn from such experiences. Ultimately, the battered wife, the abused child, or the self-sacrificing martyr will realize that they played the victim for a reason.

Can anyone honestly claim today that if someone slapped them on the one cheek they would be prepared to offer the other? I have seen Christians and non-Christians alike who respond to a verbal or physical attack with a counterattack. Such reactions occur spontaneously and lie beyond the conscious control of one's mind or intellect, whether one follows a particular religious faith or not. Understanding what the holy scriptures say, and applying their teachings spontaneously in one's life, are two entirely separate things and have actually very little to do with each other. The Holy Scriptures offer book knowledge that can be used to verify or mirror one's progress and growth in life. However, they were not meant to replace taking self-responsibility for our thoughts and actions, both positive and negative ones. Letting scriptures guide your life causes separation from your Higher Self or God, for you then trust written words more than you do yourself. Your Truth becomes something delivered to you from outside rather than from within and you lack confidence in yourself. On the other hand, *living* by the 'Word' is wisdom that originates in the Source of life beyond dogma, words or interpretations of the Truth. In oneness, we don't feel offended if someone slaps our cheek, and therefore we have no need to defend ourselves. In fact, we wouldn't even get into a situation where we would feel attacked.

To get to the point where another person's action becomes transparent to us, we need to see with our heart instead of with our mind. Looking with the heart allows us to see that behind every evil deed there is an impulse of love, overshadowed by fear and frustration. Such perception, however, is only possible when we feel that love within us. By becoming aware of someone's true intentions, those that are behind the veil of appearance, we naturally recognize ourselves as love and we begin to build bridges of love. Then, forgiving someone for their 'wrongful' doings becomes irrelevant because there is nothing to forgive. If you are able to love and appreciate a human who sexually abused you at very young age, or broke your bones, or beat you enough to leave you

90

unconscious for two days, you are beyond judgment. No unfair treatment, rudeness, or criticism directed against you could trigger a counteraction after that. The illusion that harm comes from outside of me dissolves in the realization that any external animosity I face merely a reflection of my seeming inability to love and to be loved.

We cannot see this, however, unless we have experienced, to the point of saturation, what it means to offend and to be offended, to act and to react, to feel attacked and to take revenge. Until then, if we are slapped on the face, we may need to return the offence in order to know what it feels like to attack somebody. Of course, both hitting someone and being hit don't feel good to us, because we link into previous similar occasions in our lives when we acted and reacted in similar ways and felt angry, hurt or violated. Whenever in this lifetime or former lives we have caused pain and distress to someone, we developed feelings of guilt, even though these feelings remained unconscious if we felt that what we did was justified. The degree of guilt you feel in connection with the pain inflicted on others is exactly equal to the amount of judgment you still carry for your own past pain. *Guilt is a form of self-directed judgment.* How many times have you told yourself: "I know I shouldn't have done this!" or "What I did was wrong!"

Despite being aware of our 'mistakes' from the past, we find ourselves trapped in similar situations repeatedly. Why? It is because our feelings of guilt pull people into our lives who 'deserve' our attack or criticism. By 'rightly' hurting them, we are unconsciously trying to hurt ourselves so that we don't need to feel guilty anymore. Nevertheless, this strategy is a vicious circle in which we recreate the same scenarios time after time until we eventually grasp the purpose of the game. The game is actually a treasure hunt where the treasure hides within the painful experiences with others. If we can see beyond the appearance of attack or abuse, we find there are beautiful jewels of love behind every apparently negative action.

Of course, if we can't locate the treasure, then it is perfectly normal that we see nothing positive in painful experiences. Therefore, we either trample on them or dismiss them as useless trash. We may become afraid or even paranoid about not allowing pain in our lives. The strategy of avoiding, stopping or changing things that are unpleasant or painful for us (versus accepting them and finding the treasure they carry) isn't in our best interest and is therefore bound to fail. To take us out of that self-devised trap, we are offered help. The people we meet have all volunteered to play their respective roles and we have in turn agreed to

91

play the opposite roles. Moreover, we may even switch roles frequently to get a taste of the whole range of dualistic existence.

Either You Contract or You Expand

On the Earth plane, relationships are primarily experienced as physical. The emotional sensations of happiness, sadness, guilt, jealously, anger, fear and love are physical phenomena that require the secretion of specific hormones. For example, there is *adrenaline* to express fear, *cortisol* to produce anger, and *serotonin* to make you happy. Without these chemicals these emotions cannot occur. The cells of the body speak to us through the language of emotions. It is through emotions that the body tells us how we are dealing with certain situations, with others and ourselves. There are only two basic responses that our emotional and physical bodies can have to any given experience. [Although the physical body and the body of emotions are inseparable I have made this distinction to clarify the effect that emotions have on the body.] The two responses are contraction and expansion.

Contraction is the physical response to not feeling safe. Most human beings constantly assess the area around them and ask: "How safe am I here?" Just being with a person who appears superior or more powerful than you are can have a strong impact on you and your behavior. Your whole being knows this. You must have noticed that whenever you feel insecure in some way your body pulls inward, breathing becomes shallow, or you become cold. This contraction takes place in every cell of the body. Your cellular structure contracts if you feel judged or criticized by someone and thereby lets you know that it doesn't feel safe. Because you don't feel safe, you are not likely to open up to that person in fear of being hurt or put down.

Expansion, on the other hand, takes place when you feel safe and accepted. In a peaceful, beautiful environment, such as the top of a mountain, near a fresh water stream, or by the sea, you become naturally relaxed. The cells of your body don't need to 'hold their breath' and be tight to protect themselves. They can breathe fully and give up their light, their energies. They will tell you that you are safe in this environment. Here nobody dislikes you or sees you in a negative way. You feel expanded and free, free to be yourself without pretense and without having to play a specific role. All the masks you are used to wearing to hide or protect yourself are removed and you show your real you. You feel alive. Yet you know you cannot stay in this world of expansion

92

forever and must return to what you call the real world, back to contraction.

Human relationships can bring out our worst fears and insecurities. We are afraid of each other because we have spent lifetimes making each other afraid. Your world can be very scary if you perceive it this way. This point was once beautifully described by Albert Einstein in response to a journalist who asked something to this effect: "Dr. Einstein, you are recognized around the world as one of the most bonafide geniuses of our century, maybe of human history. Your scope of thinking has covered the workings of the universe from the tiny atom to the cosmos. You have seen your discoveries both evolve and enrich, and also mutilate and destroy the human life you so highly value. What, in your opinion, is the most important question facing humanity today?"

Characteristically, Einstein stared off into space for a moment, and then looked down at the ground in front of him. Finally, he looked back at the reporter and replied: "I think the most important question facing humanity is: 'Is the universe a friendly place?' This is the first and most basic question all people must answer for themselves."

"For if we decide that the universe is an unfriendly place, then we will use our technology, our scientific discoveries and our natural resources to achieve safety and power by creating bigger walls to keep out the unfriendliness and bigger weapons to destroy all that which is unfriendly - and I believe that we are getting to a place where technology is powerful enough that we may either completely isolate or destroy ourselves as well in this process. If we decide that the universe is neither friendly nor unfriendly and that God is essentially 'playing dice with the universe', then we are simply victims to the random toss of the dice and our lives have no real purpose or meaning. But if we decide that the universe is a friendly place, then we will use our technology, our scientific discoveries and our natural resources to create tools and models for understanding that universe. Because power and safety will come through understanding its workings and its motives."

In response to this challenge, each day it is up to you whether you withdraw your energies from the world and pretend that, in such a mode of contraction, you are safe, or alternatively, expand and extend your energy into all of life. The first choice leaves you with jittery, nervous cells that are ever vigilant to a possible assault; the other choice allows you to feel safe regardless of what happens around you. When you withdraw your energies from others, you do this only because of pain and fear of pain. Your body's cells contract and none of the cellular energies of love and light are available to you. For example, heart cells that have contracted cause physical and emotional pain, love is absent at such times.

A closed, contracted heart is the true reason for heart trouble. An aching heart is a purely physical phenomenon, not a psychological one. Whereas fear can grip the body, it cannot touch consciousness. It is important to remind ourselves that the emotional body is not separate from the physical body. Emotions are merely there to inform us what the cells are going through. A broken heart is one that believes it cannot feel safe again, and thus remains closed and contracted. Heart disease is the body's attempt to mend the broken heart by throwing the withdrawn and contracted feelings out in the open. Some people understand what is happening and begin to open their hearts; others don't and die from a broken, contracted heart. The latter ones remained stuck in their belief that others had hurt them and that this had caused them to withdraw their love. Those, however, who see beyond the illusion of pain, can move on and discover that they are responsible for creating their own reality and can therefore change it.

It is time to create a new cellular message, one that allows the cells of your body to extend to an area they don't need to be afraid of. There is no real safety in contraction. All that it can offer you is a false sense of security. You can easily change your body's response by replacing this outdated belief system (of feeling safe through contraction) with the belief that expansion will make you safe. Whenever you feel frightened or insecure, instead of holding your breath, you can decide to breathe more fully. This allows you to expand with your breath. Your whole body expands when you expand with your breath. Your chest extends with each intake of breath and your spine straightens. Even your heart expands. An expanded heart is an open heart, one that is capable of sharing love. Giving love can never hurt you, only withdrawing it does. The only reason we contract when we confront difficult situations or challenging people is because we are not conscious of our contraction. If you become conscious of your tendency toward contraction, you are highly unlikely to continue falling into this trap repeatedly.

You can practice expansion with all your relationships. If your partner, for example, walks in and tells you: "Sit down, we have to talk", do you expand or contract? Or, if you hear that you haven't been accepted for the job you applied for, do you expand or contract? Does being stuck in a traffic jam make you expand or contract? It is not in your hands to change anything about these situations but you certainly can do something about your response to them. Know that safety cannot come from outside, it is an inside job. You are always safe because you

94

are God, the universe; you are one with everything, so there is nothing you need to be afraid of and nothing that can harm you. You have agreed to everything that happens to you, for your own good. If it doesn't feel that way, it is only because deep down you want to give yourself the opportunity to change your (false) belief that safety lies in contraction. There will be threats to your sense of safety only for as long as you believe you need to safeguard yourself. Once you expand into the difficult moments of your life, they become less threatening and they vanish altogether.

One thing that can help you in the practice of expansion is regular meditation. Sitting in a quite place with your eyes closed produces a feeling of safety, which allows your cells to relax and be at ease and to open their energies to you. Knowing that every day there is a time of safety helps them to be open and free. This will make it easier for you to extend into those situations that you cannot change. Extension always brings love whereas contraction adds to your fear.

Relationships - A Two-Way Process

Sometimes our greatest insights come from simple life situations. On one occasion, after my partner and I had enjoyed an especially peaceful and joyful morning together, we both felt the strong love bond between us that brought us together a few years before, and all was well. But by late afternoon she told me that she didn't want to live with someone (that is, me) who had such contrary ideas and understandings of life and relationships than her. Basically, she felt that my views on relationships weren't realistic.

Frequently criticized during a previous fifteen-year relationship and marriage for having my own opinions about various aspects of life, I felt hurt once again. I interpreted my partner's critical comments as an ultimatum that said: "Unless you change your views we cannot have a relationship anymore". But this interpretation was faulty because I couldn't see behind the veil of appearance. What she really did was to bring to the surface of my awareness the old hurt of not being accepted for what I believed in. This felt very much like being rejected, not loved, once again. Of course, my partner wasn't aware of her role in this, otherwise she wouldn't have triggered this feeling rejected response in me.

As fate had it, we couldn't continue our exchange and complete this 'dance' due to a dinner engagement with friends of ours. Subsequently, feeling hurt and rejected I pulled back my energies from her. This, however, only attracted further criticisms over the dinner table, which I counteracted by pointing out what I considered a 'weakness' in her relationship with others. And to make a point, I did this in front of our friends, in a seemingly polite but piercing manner. By the time we arrived home, we could no longer tolerate the extreme discomfort between us and within ourselves. So we sat down and stated exactly how we each felt without trying to justify it or even try to understand it. We merely expressed our feelings, which quickly released the discomfort. We suddenly realized that both of us, not just me, were put down in the past for what we believed in, and wanted to be, in our lives. It became obvious that because of our close relationship and our eagerness to free ourselves from any form of limitation that we felt had been forced onto us in the past, we were now ready to release it altogether.

Communication is perhaps the most thorough therapeutic method in all personal relationships. We usually find something in the other person that mirrors back to us our own discomfort, weakness, or self-judgment. When my partner told me that she could no longer live with someone having such a different value system, she was really expressing her deep dissonance with her own value system. In this particular situation, I acted as the mirror that related back to her about why she really felt so unhappy.

Everything that happens in a personal relationship is a two-way process. Each person contributes 50% of the share of learning and teaching. However, it rarely feels that way because both sides believe that the other person's issue has 'nothing to do with me'. I too, had to look into the mirror my partner was holding up for me. She helped me see my defensiveness in response to what I had considered a personal rejection. As I used to do in the past, I had withdrawn my love energies from her and closed down my heart center so that I wouldn't get hurt again. What I experienced was a mirror image of my (unfulfilled) expectations.

Of course, my partner didn't reject me at all, she only needed to free herself from her own outdated belief system. But because rejection or abandonment is one of my issues, I needed an outlet for the anguish that stemmed from being abandoned by my parents and other loved ones during several of my lifetimes. To voice my pent-up frustrations about the string of rejections, I 'retaliated' by pointing out my perceived weakness in her which, of course, has been my own weakness. Since closing down my heart didn't make me feel any better, I had to tell my partner how I felt. As we both shared what we were feeling, our hearts flew wide open again and the issues, which we thought just moments

96

before were serious and insurmountable problems that threatened our relationship, evaporated into thin air, and they never came up again.

This simple experience once again showed me that we never really hold grudges against someone else. Others merely reflect to us what we do not like *in ourselves*. An old French adage says it so well: "If you are mad, you are really mad with yourself." In these situations, the ego 'I' identifies with 'mad' and therefore becomes mad. But since this is hard for it to accept, we tend to look for a scapegoat or an external trigger that can bring out the anger or frustration that lies hidden beneath our conscious awareness. While assuming the various roles of polarity, such as being a good and lovable or a bad and unlovable person, we are presented with the opportunity to become aware of everything that leads us to play these roles. So pointing out somebody else's shortcomings, faults and failures may often be the only possible route to detecting, within us, those same things in different variations and intensities. It may also bring to the surface of our awareness all the feelings we have ever had when we too were criticized for our own mistakes and inadequacies.

If we hadn't stored away such feelings within our subconscious, then no matter how badly someone treats us, they could not arouse negative sentiments within us. We would immediately see past the appearance of the behavior, and love and appreciate the person for who they truly are, a Divine being acting out their role in the arena of duality, both for their own benefit and for everyone else involved. This is the true meaning of 'Love thy enemy'. When we let the heart rule in our relationships, all animosity disappears. The love we have for ourselves translates into the love we have for others, regardless of who they are or what they do.

Your Enemies are Your Best Friends

Some might argue at this point that for peace to reign and hostility to cease, it requires the cooperation of the enemy. How could you possibly prevent a person or an entire nation, filled with wrath and feelings of aggression and hatefulness from doing you harm? Can a nation like America protect itself against 'senseless' acts of terrorism? The answers to these questions are not obvious; in fact, they lie hidden deep in the mechanism that controls the obvious. An enemy ceases to act like an enemy once we see who they really are, beyond the veil of appearance. In actuality, it is something within us that causes someone else to wish us harm. This principle applies both to societies as it does to individuals, because a group of individuals forms a group consciousness which acts like one. In either case, we merely project onto others whatever we do not like to see or acknowledge in ourselves. Although it may be hard to believe, the bottom line is that there is nobody out there who can possibly cause harm to another. We create our own enemies in order to learn from them.

We literally ask other people, via the flawless and instant telepathic links that exist between our Higher Selves, to come into our physical lives and put up mirrors for us so that we can see our own suppressed and unacknowledged feelings reflected by their behavior toward us. These feelings may harbor unfulfilled desires of ours that have turned into fear, shame, guilt, frustration and anger. When they surface through human interaction, we see them first in other people. Only in time do we realize that they are our own. We trapped these negative energies deep within us through denial. When we begin to acknowledge them, which is a process of self-acceptance, they lose their negative sting.

These feelings are living mirrors that never lie. They give us an exact account of our progress and development at each moment. They force us to deal with the judgments we have unconsciously imposed on ourselves and still do. In reality, nobody can put us down or turn us down for anything. Nobody can even physically kill us unless we have agreed on the higher levels to leave the physical form. Since the duality game is played out only on the level of physical awareness, which is the ego, we have no idea of this arrangement with other souls, and nor have they, unless of course they or we are consciously living and acting in alignment with Spirit.

Despite our ignorance about what is really going on during a conflict situation between two people or groups of people, we only draw to us what is necessary and needed in order to complete our journey back home, or, to say it better, to create a new world that is free of the binding influence of duality. To be able to enter the world of unconditional love, freedom, and non-judgment (the kingdom of heaven) we first needed to go through everything that could feel fearful and restrictive. We all needed to judge others so that we would know how it feels to be judged in turn, according to the laws of karma. Not liking someone is painful to our heart and a restriction to the oneness that we are. Our Higher Self has no such notions of dislike or separation; it naturally feels one with the person with which our ego has difficulties. Through karma, we are attached to one another, positively 'stuck' with this person until our human resistance melts down and disappears. Karma's only role is to bring back to us the awareness of oneness. That is why far-reaching events such as the World Trade Center bombings are important markers of self-reflection for all humankind. Many of those American Indians who died at the hands of the White People or in Vietnam are now back to 'balance the account' and to give us the opportunity to return what we have taken from them.

After having judged and been judged enough, we eventually find it in ourselves to forgive and be grateful to anyone who has ever been an instrument of turmoil in our lives. We learn that those who have put obstacles on our path actually made us stronger. They have taught us that we could remove these obstacles, if we choose to. Even if we are not there yet, the memories of what they 'did to us' remain strong and alive to serve as our guiding posts on the road to self-empowerment and self-love.

Once you arrive at the place of loving acceptance of all differences, enmity ceases to exist for you, no matter how hostile an environment you may live in. Those elements around you that were harsh, cold, resistant or aggressive now begin to soften and become part of a wider you. When your heart opens up, you are greatly extending your field of influence. You begin to sense the underlying unity of all things. In order to recognize unity, one must first have a clear reference on duality. Since unity of diversity is what makes up the Uni-verse, nothing in it is devoid of the 'Oneness with the All'. The one Source of the infinite diversity of nature supports even the extreme ends of duality, from the most creative processes to the destructive ones. In fact, destruction is as important and useful as construction is. Both are integral to any evolving thing, including human life.

While in human incarnation, we are challenged to embody more and more of the universal law of acceptance, which denies nothing that exists or takes place. It has no preferences; every detail of expression is precious and plays an important role in the creation and evolution of life in the universe. We can become just as accepting of the dualities as these are the very source of life itself, simply because we *are* that Source. We are that Oneness which is capable of accommodating all opposites and differences without even a trace of conflict.

Life is a Jigsaw Puzzle

By first learning all about separation, right and wrong, friendship and enmity, wealth and poverty, emptiness and fullness, sadness and joy, darkness and light, etc., we become familiar with the duality aspect of life and nature. As a second step, we learn to integrate the diversities and contrasting differences into the harmonious whole that we are. The old saying 'The whole is more than the sum of its parts' reflects a truth that glorifies the parts but puts the oneness above them all. The pieces of a jigsaw puzzle make very little sense when seen on their own in their separateness from all the other pieces, but once they have each found their designated place and formed a picture, their individual value suddenly seems to have risen to a collective value of wholeness. Before assembly, each piece is unique and different from every other piece. In fact, the emphasis of the game is in finding out how each piece *is* different from all the others. However, once the picture has been completed, the differences that make up each piece become irrelevant. Although the individual pieces haven't disappeared, they have joined to become one with the rest of the pieces and formed a picture that is much greater than being a separate piece which makes no sense at all.

We are these little pieces of life's jigsaw puzzle. While being strewn in every direction, we feel lost and lonely at first. As we search for our purpose and value in life, we begin to look for other pieces that fit our piece. We try to connect and sometimes we fail, but in the failing we learn more about why we don't fit other pieces, or why they reject us. In time, we succeed in forming lasting bonds, friendships that remind us about the purpose of the game, uniting with others until the picture is complete. Little do we know what might become of us when we all find our respective place in the jigsaw puzzle of life, but the rule of the game says that completeness is our destiny.

We may be envious of others who we believe have found a better position in the game, but that sentiment is only temporary. Eventually, once the larger picture is revealed, we will value each other as equally important. Some of the pieces of the picture may be dark and dull-looking, for they represent the shadow sides of life. Nobody likes them, but somehow they cannot be avoided or ignored, especially by the light-colored pieces. Since shadows define the light, the light and dark pieces need to make friends and be beside each other in order to bring out their unique contributions to the picture.

One of the most critical moments in this game of life is accepting everything about us, i.e. our particular shape and form, our color, our qualities of 'good' and 'bad', how we behave with others and ourselves. Once we embrace our particular role as useful and perfect for this very moment, we are ready to find our true place in the larger picture of things. We begin to realize that we *are* the larger picture, along with everyone else. We belong to everyone and everyone belongs to us. Although we maintain our individuality, we become universal too. Everything out there becomes as important as everything in here does.

Our struggles on the battlegrounds of differences have not been in vain or without purpose. Each difficulty has served as a milestone on our path to fulfillment. Every person you have ever met in any of your lives has been instrumental in creating this very moment in your life. Like the separate pieces of the jigsaw puzzle, the different events and the numerous relationships and experiences in your lives may have no obvious connection with each other. Yet the closer you get to becoming the larger picture - the Oneness of the All - the more clearly you begin to see that no drop of love and no tear was ever wasted. All of this was necessary and still is to this moment in order to get you where you are destined to be. There are nearly innumerable ways to complete a jigsaw puzzle, just as there are an almost infinite number of choices you can make to become aware of your essential nature. How and when you get there is of no real importance. That you do get there is what counts.

There is a mighty force behind all 'good' and 'bad' thoughts and actions, the uniting power of love that brings together the most controversial issues and standpoints, and it allows us to perceive their underlying oneness. We are all heading in the same direction, although we often fall prey to the illusion that others are not, especially when they seem to do us harm. Every person we have ever had personal contact with didn't just bump into us accidentally. All relationships are based on a mutual agreement reached by incarnated souls to help one another on their life journeys. This is regardless of what mirror image he or she may reflect back to us and the kind of mirror image we assume for them. All mirror images serve as opportunities to grow. While other people show us what we are like, we show others what they are like. The true motivation behind all this is unadulterated love.

Cracking the Code of Ignorance

Having said that, the time may have come for us to now honor each and every one of our suppressors, critics, abusers, unfair competitors and adversaries for the really helpful roles they played, and may still be playing, in our lives, for they are some of our best teachers. None of them are what they appear to be. All are mirrors of different aspects of us. They are doing and have done the job you have asked them to do. They helped you to grow stronger by pointing out your presumed weaknesses, even painfully exposing them until you started to wake up to your true strength and power. This, in turn, has set the course to remove the veil of duality that has kept this planet and her inhabitants engulfed in

101

darkness for eons. This is what we have come here for, to create something hugely significant not accomplished in all the worlds.

As simple as it sounds, there is no other more effective way to remove the veil of ignorance and be the infinite power that we are and share, than to accept every facet of our various relationships as Divine Gifts of the Moment. As difficult as it may seem while being in our duality mode (versus unity mode) of thinking and acting, we are perfectly capable of accepting both the 'good' and the 'bad' things as equals. Only if we accept what is real can we also live in peace and happiness. It is in our essential nature to embrace them both and to know everything placed before us is now and ultimately for our highest good. Along with the love-based assistance by other human beings, the Earth, and all the beings of light, we have co-created each one of these elements of learning for a specific value and purpose, leaving nothing to chance. In addition, because our life situation is the result of our own intentional and purposeful creation, there is really no need for judgment or separation.

We don't have to learn anything or even try to be free of judgment. It comes by itself. Each moment comes equipped with everything we need in order to proceed on the path of self-evolvement. One of the greatest discoveries we are about to make is just this: 'It comes by itself'. So far, all we have done is try to change things because we thought they were wrong or not good enough. What we are learning *now* is to give in to the moment and see the treasures it brings to us. By allowing ourselves to experience duality shifts from right to wrong, yes to no, good to bad, etc. often enough and intensively enough, we find that the confusion this generates within, is suddenly lifted and replaced with clarity.

This is how you can free yourself from the binding influences of emotional upsets:

Immediately, or soon after, an emotion comes up in you, simply express how you feel about a certain situation or someone else (if there is no one to listen to, speak it into a tape recorder or write it down), without (the emphasis is on 'without') trying to explain or reason why you feel this way. This quickly removes the discomfort and lifts the weight off your heart. Looking at the symbol displayed on the cover of this book helps you to connect with your Higher Self and stay centered within your heart space.

Friedrich Nietzsche aptly pointed out: "The will to overcome an emotion is ultimately only the will of another emotion or of several

102

others." Trying to control emotions only leads to an endless chain of new ones. If someone has expectations of you that you do not wish to meet, such as going to a movie, then instead of finding excuses, just say that you don't feel like going. It is simply that, no reasons, no excuses. Using arguments moves a situation into your head, whereas this is a matter of emotion or feeling, a matter of the heart. It helps to resolve any emotional conflicts easily and without causing scars by keeping it there.

The more often you apply this simple method of honest introspection, the sooner you begin to realize that is absolutely OK for you to have any kinds of feeling, and, what is most remarkable, nobody can really get offended by this. People get offended only when you try to *justify* your feelings. You justify or explain your feelings out of fear of criticism or not being loved anymore. However, fear draws people toward you who point out your low self-worth and thus seem to put you down. When a fearful situation confronts you, simply feel and express this fear! Instead of battling fear (this gives it power), give in to it or sit with the anxiety. It is bound to dissipate. Know that you have created these situations yourself so that you can clear the fear completely, simply by experiencing it.

Fears always represent something that does not exist. They are lies that tell you they are real. When you let them be, they disappear. You may want to acknowledge to yourself or to someone else how you feel: "Alright, I am scared" or "I am afraid to admit that I made a mistake" or whatever it is. You don't need to do anything when you are gripped by fear, except to be with it. Its only reason for being there is to release and to move you into your power. **Stepping *into* the fear rather than trying to *avoid* it is the first step in crossing the bridge of judgment and entering the world of freedom.**

It is time now to accept our humanness. By accepting our humanness, we naturally rise to our Higher Self nature. The era of casting judgments on others for their presumed wrongdoings was a useful method of survival and karmic interaction, but it is ending. We are sometimes painfully becoming aware that nobody else is our responsibility. Our only responsibility in life is to align ourselves with our Source Love. The rest are details taken care of on their own. Without Source Love, we are thrown into turmoil and chaos, like fallen leaves in the wind, with no direction or purpose. Like blind people led by the blind, not knowing our real roots, we live by what the masses say and want. Being slaves to judgment, we cannot feel free in ourselves, and this lack of freedom becomes a desperate cry for justice. Yet justice remains an evasive dream.

You are light, I am light; we are all light waves upon this plane. We see each other's effervescent skin, the thrill of the dawning age shimmer upon our eyes. Like looking upon the surface of a lake, one sees the reflection and yet also feels the sparkle of the light and imagery as it plays back upon our own seeing mechanism. We are but mirrors for each other. Snap them on and take them off. We serve this role beautifully and faithfully for we are in the dressing room of tomorrow, trying on an assortment of lifetimes and possibilities for one another.

George Washington Carver
in reminiscing on his life's past at a
carriage house in Alabama in the 1860s
Channeled on January 5, 2001

Chapter Seven

Injustice - The Greatest Illusion of All

*This is a time of peace and
equanimity. Be as brothers to one
another; serve yourself and your
country. Be at arms only with
rebellious thoughts, for in haste
we often make an imprecise
decision that may wrong us in our
fortitude and take the breath
away from our livelihood and
spirit. Take the time and have the
will to persevere, for in fact this is
a great and noble gift endowed
upon each of us.*

Thurgood Marshall
(United States Supreme Court)
Ended legal segregation in American Life
Channeled on 5 January 2001.

The Law of Non-Interference

The universal Law of Non-Interference can perhaps best explain the
meaning of justice. Without it, we will forever wonder why some things
are considered right or why some things are considered wrong. This
universal law applies to every area of life, including human relations and

the field of justice in particular. As beings of Spirit in human form, this law binds us all. It is to our advantage, though. The universal Law of Non-Interference is our only password to eternal freedom, for without it we would forever be entangled in the web of karma. What's more, interference is actually a complete impossibility in the universe. Unless we invite interference (and then we cannot call it interference any more), we are only left with what we create for ourselves or co-create along with others. In fact, since nothing and nobody can exist in true isolation, co-creation is all there is. Furthermore, every person involved in co-creation has given their consent to what is happening to them and to everyone else.

The perception of injustice, in whatever area or form, is based on the concept of interference. It implies that there are people out there, situations, laws, organizations, societies, or even entire nations that have the power to prevent me from fulfilling my needs and desires or affect me in a negative way. We have been taught from an early age that there always has been, and continues to be, great injustice in this world. By opening any history book, we face event after event that tells of relentless bloodshed and tremendous suffering in almost every society that has lived on this planet. Millions of apparently innocent people have lost their lives because of wars fought out of greed for more land and worldly influence, or through acts of crime and terrorism.

We have come to believe that many people out there have only one thing in their mind, that is, to steal from others to enrich themselves. Furthermore, a large number of them do not even hesitate to take the life of another in order to have access to more possessions or greater degrees of power. Some merely want to take revenge for the injustice they believe has been committed against them or their loved ones. The more recent 9-11-2001 landmark assault on thousands of civilians by terrorists using commercial jet planes as weapons of mass destruction seemed to have been one of the most senseless acts of hatred seen in history, completely beyond human comprehension. There are scandals popping up in every sector of society revealing how a few people with ill intentions can manipulate and cheat the rest of us. Drug cartels have infiltrated both the poor and rich sections of society, even using children as cheap distributors of life-altering drugs. Millions of innocent children are victims of slave labor or used as prostitutes. The stories of injustice in this world seem endless. From the simple act of stealing chewing gum in a grocery store to the large-scale exploitation of the world's poorest countries, injustice appears to have infiltrated everywhere.

Born in Germany nine years after World War II, I became a witness to the painful aftermath of the war and the forceful division of my family and my country into two parts, and so I learned to believe in injustice as everyone else did. In addition, I felt so ashamed about what the Nazi-Germans had done to the rest of the world that I couldn't wait to leave Germany after high school. For years, I tried to hide my German identity and rid myself of anything that had to do with my country. If anyone had told me then that there was no injustice in this world, I would have said they were out of their mind; they would have to be someone who lived in a fantasy world of peace and harmony. Today, I cannot but think differently. I am aware that this is one of the most challenging concepts to understand and to accept, but it is also one of the most liberating ones, and it may perhaps be the only one that makes any real sense.

Injustice is an illusion that is currently in the process of demystification. Already, the old systems of serving justice are crumbling. Although law and order are still being maintained, laws cannot guarantee justice. Many nations have had a high level of law and order, but at the same time, there was great injustice to their people; for example, in East Germany, in the Soviet Union, in Tibet and in China. We are about to witness the birth of a new justice system that is not based on human laws but on Divine Law.

Manmade laws are needed greatly at a time when polarity thinking dominates the collective consciousness of the population. As long as we inject the idea that there is a 'right' versus a 'wrong' into the atmosphere of collective thinking through our own thoughts and actions, we essentially create 'injustice' in this world. If this most basic form of judgment - seeing one thing as right and another as wrong - ceased to dominate our awareness, there would be much less injustice around us. This is actually happening already. Manmade law is being replaced gradually with natural law, and a daily-increasing number of people look toward nature, the natural environment, and the spirit within to know how to live their lives. Much of the current strife and struggle is a result of this transformation. The search for natural alternative energy sources, the cleaning up of our rivers, lakes and air, the attempts to save and preserve species that are dying out, the emergence of alternative forms of medicine, etc. are all definitive indications that natural law is already awakening in the mass population. This, however, creates conflict, the struggle of having to let go of the old before we can accept the new.

A person experiences injustice in life because of a need to bring to the surface of awareness any form of injustice harbored in his or her own heart. Whether this injustice is rooted in the present life or previous lifetimes is irrelevant. Because they have not come to terms with an internal discrepancy, these people literally, though unconsciously, seek a situation that permits them to get in touch with their unforgiving feelings and judgments. Humans do not err, lie, cheat, steal, etc.; they only *pretend* to. They unknowingly play these roles for the sake of learning from each other about themselves.

Since the Law of Non-Interference cannot be broken, no matter what the circumstances, there can never be a true victim. And if there is no victim, there can be no victimizer. A presumed victim and their corresponding victimizer co-create a situation together which outwardly looks like a conflict but in truth is a spiritual dance. It is a process of gradual awakening that involves the clearing of dualistic perception and opening to the Love Source that they are. This mighty task has taken many of us innumerable lifetimes to tackle. Now, when the perception of duality is losing its frequency basis, we are collectively moving through the illusion of injustice. The purpose of creating the illusion of injustice for everyone on this planet has been a grand one. It has given us the opportunity to learn all about our three-dimensional world, and work through all the nooks and crannies that make it up, until we find our essential self (The One Eternal Spirit) reflected in it. The recognition of Spirit in matter *is* our process of ascension. This will bring both fulfillment to the natural justice system of the world (replacing the illusions of injustice) and also restore peace and harmony on Earth.

Mass consciousness is currently undergoing a tremendous transformation that requires the experience of injustice. Anyone who still has roots and beliefs of separation feels agonizing pain and suffering when exposed to personal and collective calamities. When terrorists attacked and destroyed the World Trade Center in New York and the Pentagon in Washington D.C., the senseless loss of human life was incomprehensible to almost entire world population. It shook the very foundation of safety and security, and the belief in goodness as such.

On the other hand, it demonstrated to all of us that human life on Earth is the most precious commodity there is and that we can only survive and live through catastrophes like this when we pull together and become one united force. We realized that the petty things and differences that have so occupied our lives in the areas of politics, economics and human relationships are not that important anymore. The grave 'injustice' of the Attack on America carried a blessing of unconditional love, brotherhood and sisterhood into the masses that would otherwise never have been experienced by humanity. Many brave and honorable souls volunteered (on the level of their Higher Self) to initiate this urgently needed transition in the world by giving up their physical lives in the inferno of the 9-11 events - perhaps the world's most important distress call ever made.

The distress call was and continues to be a wake-up call for us all. It urges us to find answers to the following questions: Do we continue supporting and encouraging injustice by condemning it or do we begin to forgive and respect those that incur it? Are those who commit such crimes not also people who are driven by incredible amounts of fear, anger, disappointment, abuse or other grievances that none of us has really given any attention to? Do we truly believe that the attacks were indiscriminately placed and that we have nothing to do with them except being innocent victims? Weren't these young men, who blew themselves up to destroy others, once also beautiful, innocent children who wanted to be loved and held but were not? Who made them this bitter and why? Haven't we all directly and indirectly contributed to the economic imbalances that have led to the extreme poverty and anguish experienced in the world today? How much do we really care about those living in horrid conditions of poverty and exploitation?

When I lived in India and other poor nations, I saw hundreds of thousands of people who literally owned nothing but their bare skin and only survived (or died) by eating scraps decomposing in massive heaps of garbage that contained, among other things, leftover foods. Children, dogs, cows, and millions of flies partook of the same 'free meals'. The situation is even worse in Afghanistan. Have we not been breeding the very terrorists (through our insatiable desire for wealth and power) that now enter our space like angry sharks coming to our beaches in order to kill? Is retaliation the only answer to this problem? When Mahatma Gandhi stated: "An eye for an eye makes the whole world blind", he knew that seeing and retaliating against the injustice done by others in truth fosters it even more and initiates new cycles of karma, pain and suffering. We have become so blind we really believe that when adversity comes to us someone or something else is responsible for it, not us. We will only be free of anger, terror and fear when our so-called enemies are free of anger, fear and terror. And this can only happen when we see others and other countries in the Oneness that underlies them all.

As long as we *see* injustice in the world, we *create* injustice in the world. And we create more and more of it until we discover the deceptive nature of this perception and move beyond the need for judgment. Justice and injustice are opposites that appear to be so real in

109

life that we have a hard time not taking sides. Yet behind their appearance, they form a common bond. Both serve our Higher Spirit Self to become the only reference for how to live our life.

Justice is but a Heartbeat Away

During my involvement in the Transcendental Meditation (TM) Movement (1970-1992), I was fascinated by the fact that hard-core convicts could be rehabilitated to gentle and kindhearted people, simply by teaching them to meditate for 20 minutes twice a day. I vividly remember about hearing the story of one inmate who was serving three life sentences (if that is humanly possible) at a maximum-security prison in California. I will refer to him as Nick here. This man, who had killed three people out of rage and revengeful feelings, and injured several others, never felt any remorse for his actions and continued being a 'hardened criminal' throughout his imprisonment. One day, Nick and a number of other prisoners attended a lecture at the prison auditorium, given by a local TM instructor.

As Nick listened to the TM instructor speaking about the beneficial effects of meditation, he felt so touched by the gentle, loving kindness of this teacher that tears came into his eyes. He had never seen someone in his entire life who was genuinely interested in him and who didn't care about the bad things he had done in his life. Here was somebody who valued him for who he was, without casting a judgment. Why would someone want to come into the dangerous and dark world of a maximum-security prison, and without getting anything in return, give him something that would help him find peace and joy? At the end of the lecture, Nick went up to the teacher and asked him if he could learn from him how to meditate. It wasn't so much what the TM teacher said during the discourse that had inspired Nick to approach this man. When asked about this years later, Nick said that it was the man's radiance of inner peace, joy and the non-judgment that intrigued him the most, so much so that he wondered whether there was any chance he could become somewhat like him.

Nick signed up for instruction and literally, within the first few seconds of his first meditation, he immersed into a sea of love and peacefulness that would change his life forever. During my 20 years of teaching TM around the world, I had seen dramatic internal shifts happen in some people, but I never thought it was possible for a murderer to turn into a saint within moments. What unfolded was a story that could only

110

warm hearts. It shows that evil isn't real, love is, and it is there in everyone. For Nick, justice was but heartbeat away.

Beauty in The Beast

Having never had any respect for himself, Nick had no way of valuing anything or anyone else in his life either. Since he felt there was nothing worth living for, he believed that life as such, anybody's life, had no value at all. And because life wasn't worth much to him anyway, he felt no remorse for killing someone else. Having had nothing within him that he liked or appreciated, he naturally attracted only people and circumstances in his life that reflected back to him what he saw in himself. Consequently, there had never been anybody in his life who liked or appreciated him. Everyone he met treated him like a piece of dirt or avoided him so as not to get into trouble. This only confirmed and furthered his idea that life was a sheer waste, with no joy or purpose. He was a beast in the wilderness of life where the law 'Survival of the fittest' was the only rule he knew to obey.

Now, for the first time in his life, after having reached the limits of low self-respect and taken three people's lives, the pendulum began swinging back and opening a completely new and exciting chapter in the book of his life. One tiny spark of love that tingled in his heart-space during this first dive into himself set off an avalanche of events nobody could have anticipated. The moments of peace he experienced during his first meditation were moments of non-judgment, self-appreciation and self-love. Nick, from this moment onward, had this uncanny, tremendously powerful desire to share what he had experienced with his fellow inmates. Those he considered as his strongest adversaries just moments before now suddenly felt like being his closest friends. He no longer wanted to control or hurt them; instead, he wanted them to feel what he felt.

To cut a long story short, it took Nick several years of continuous writings to the Governor of California, to members of the media, to the leaders of the TM organization and other rehabilitation centers to rally support for the official inclusion of TM courses in the rehabilitation programs of his prison. Several years later, after many disappointments and rejections, his unwavering persistence led to the first American study on the psycho-physiological changes occurring in prison inmates who practice meditation. His prison became his home and his fellow prisoners his family. He, in fact, became the most loved and respected inmate of

111

his prison at that time. According to him, this was already more than he could have wished for, but it got even better.

One fine morning, a woman TM instructor, who heard of Nick's success story, came to visit him. They fell in love and were given permission to marry, within the prison walls. Soon after that, Nick was released from prison, something unheard of given the three life-sentences he was to serve. But instead of staying away from the prison and enjoying his freedom outside, he decided to train as a TM instructor himself and go back there and teach his inmate friends how to find the same love and peace within them that made him a person worth living for. This time, though, he went into prison as a free man.

This, incredibly, is a true story. I believe it happened so that others can see that life is not clear-cut, that our future is not set in stone, even if it seems hopeless and bleak. Judgment doesn't allow us to perceive the goodness that is concealed by evilness. There is a Beauty in every Beast. We all have all parts in us. We carry hidden within us unconscious memories of experiences from this life or other lifetimes related to low self-worth, where we felt put down, rejected or humiliated. Each one of us, in one form or another, has suffered abuse, was attacked, tortured, or killed by someone else. Then someone comes along whose behavior becomes the trigger for us to release the trapped feelings and bring them to the surface of our awareness. Then suddenly, without being in control of the situation, we act out these feelings to the point of criticizing, attacking, or even killing someone, as it happened with Nick. However, no person is worse than another, whatever they have done. We all have abused our power, hurt others, fought battles and killed. It is irrelevant whether we did this yesterday or ten thousand lifetimes ago.

We Only Judge Memories

Just because most people on Earth perceive time in a linear fashion, it doesn't mean that time behaves this way. Anything that has occurred in our past can be brought right into the present moment. That is why Nick, while acting in the field of duality, was simply reactivating his past experiences, hurting others in the same way as others had hurt him before. Past and future are only concepts we have created on Earth so that we can perceive separation or duality. Whereas our Divine mind can only perceive the eternity of the present moment, our human mind subdivides timelessness into past, present and future. Our human mind tends to allow memories and past experiences to create the present reality. By contrast, our Divine mind chooses to let the future create the

112

present. And *the future is what we make of it*, at every moment. It is our challenge here on Earth to free ourselves from the shackles of memory by realizing that time is an invention of our consciousness, which we can change whenever we choose to.

As soon as Nick transcended the field of duality and surrendered to the field of oneness during his first meditation, he no longer felt like a guilty man. He had stepped out of time, even if it was just for a moment, and he knew who he really was. He still remembered that he had killed people before, but that memory was no longer real to him. He no longer saw himself as a mean man who was out to hurt others. The memories of his past had no more hold on him, because who he was then was no longer there. Having been a murderer before doesn't make him a murderer today. He now identifies with his true self, not with the memories of evil actions that are just as unreal now as my memory of having killed a mosquito in India fifteen years ago. Memories are fictions of the mind, they aren't the real thing. Nick was able to change his past by no longer letting it influence his thoughts, feelings, and actions in the present.

When we judge others for what they have done in the past we can only really judge *what we remember* about their behavior, thoughts or roles they played. We can never judge the person, because in reality they are not any of these appearances. So our judgment of others is really only related to memories, our memories of them. And these memories are tainted by subjectivity, the subconscious impressions we have of ourselves. The net result is a very distorted understanding of reality.

Anyone can think negative and evil thoughts but that is all they are, negative, evil thoughts. Many people have such thoughts but this doesn't make them evil, even if they turn the thoughts into evil actions. The thoughts are merely the result of not knowing one's true identity, which is the root cause of all fear in life. One glimpse of oneself can dispel that fear and along with it all the false identities, for example, being the victim of abuse, a thief or a murderer. Once that reconnection to one's true essence is reinstalled to whatever little extent, life automatically takes a new direction.

The Upanishads claim: "He who sees all beings in his own self and his own self in all beings does not suffer from any repulsion..." Nick suddenly felt love in his heart, love for himself. The moment he opened his eyes after his first meditation he became aware of the love he felt for everyone else. This was the end of repulsion by, and for, others and the world. He had *built his own prison* by denying himself and prompting others to do to him what he was doing to himself. Then he *created his*

113

own freedom by accepting himself. Like Nick, we are the creators of our own problems and our own solutions.

Mirror, Mirror on the Wall…

Seeing faults in others, that is, casting judgments on them is expressive of a person's compulsion for self-judgment. Unkindness occurs when you judge yourself, and then take action towards others because of it. Jesus made this point when a group of 'honorable' folk gathered around a prostitute, intending to stone her to death. People desire to hurt others and punish them for no other reason than to justify their own actions from the past. Jesus challenged everyone's conscience then and now when he asked those who had never sinned before to throw the first stone at this woman. All that Jesus did was 'place a mirror' in front of everyone and let them see that their judgment against the woman, and the desire to kill her, stemmed from within themselves as a consequence of being unconscious of their own past sins and deviations from the path of love. He helped them see that no one is better or worse than another and that we all are caught up in the web of duality and make 'mistakes'. There is no one, not even God, who has the right to judge another, for this would violate the universal Law of Non-Interference. To make certain that this law is inviolable, there is the overseeing law of karma: "He who judges another is judged in return."

Manmade laws, on the other hand, do not recognize the natural justice system of natural law. They single out those who harm others or go against the specific rules and regulations that maintain law and order in a particular society or country, and they punish them for these violations. Casting judgment on someone in a court of law or otherwise is based on the deeply ingrained belief that there are individuals or groups of people who intentionally do harm to others in order to enrich or empower themselves in some way. This, however, is only true on the duality level of perception. But in true reality, the Law of Non-Interference does not allow such one-sided occurrences.

People who are robbed find it very difficult to accept that they brought it on themselves, but the universe simply could not function if interference was a possibility. As hard as it may sound, victims cause their own crime; the victimizer merely facilitates it. If you tell this to people walking in the street you may push many buttons in them, in fact it can bring up pure rage. Why? Because deep inside they know that this is true. Otherwise, it wouldn't bother them. Seeing one's shadow self in the mirror can be an overwhelming experience.

114

When assaulted, it is almost impossible for someone to see that they are the co-creator of the crime. Why do so many battered wives leave their abusive husbands, only to return to them and be beaten again? Who or what is making them do such a self-destructive thing? Why do so many people feel guilty when they are sexually abused? Why are so many of us trying to defend ourselves when criticized, and why do we feel so uncomfortable or embarrassed when someone discloses our faults or weaknesses to others? Strange as it may sound, these questions contain their own answers.

Nick *believed* he was a victim from a very early age. This belief or thought attracted non-resonant and destructive people and situations into his life, which reinforced his belief. Since he didn't like anything about himself, he made others (without their conscious consent) support and execute this self-destructive verdict of his. But once he began to perceive the spark of love and peace within, the same power that had manifested 'trouble' in his life instantly transformed into an incessant drive for manifesting *love* in his life. "That which is done out of love always takes place beyond good and evil," said Nietzsche. Nick's love transformed his cold and hostile prison environment into a place of hope and peace, where everyone could find a deeper inner meaning to life, *if they wished to*. Not everyone responded to Nick's call, for they needed to work through their victim issues, as he did. Every person finds their own mirror image reflected by the behavior of those with whom they meet and interact. This happens for reasons of higher learning and growth, and the unfolding of unconditional love.

Some people get very upset when they hear about all this. They argue that there is no way that an innocent child who is being abused and murdered can have unresolved victim issues and attract their own killer. This is where not knowing our 'past-life history' gets in the way. Because there is no gap between past and present, or present and future, except the one imagined in our mind, the events of a past (or future) life are happening right now in a parallel form of reality. But since most of us are not consciously aware of this parallel reality, which we conveniently refer to as 'past lives', we face great doubt and confusion whenever we witness a seemingly unjust situation like the murder of an innocent child. These past life issues, however, are intrinsically connected with a person's present experiences and life lessons, even if they involve death at an early age.

The confusion, however, that arises from not being able to consciously remember our own and other people's 'past life' situations is necessary in order for us to fully act out the emotions we need to experience as part of our soul agreements with one another. If we had known the larger picture behind it all, the truth that there is no interference and therefore no victim, we would be deprived of developing negative emotions and thus not learn about separation and how to bridge it through the power of love and compassion. It is our collective mission on Earth that we fully understand the dualistic world of separation in every way possible, and through this experience infuse our Divine essence into the density of the Third Dimension.

Not knowing the larger picture of life can leave you hopeless and disillusioned about world destiny. Hundreds of millions of children have their existence in prostitution, slavery and labor, and millions of people are starving to death each year. Many of us feel appalled by such gross transgressions of justice. Those who have lost faith in their religion often lament: "God cannot be a God of justice, love, and compassion if he allows such things to happen." But then, they need to experience separation from the fictitious God they have created in their minds *in order to find the true God within*. They may even need to judge God for being unjust and merciless before they can see and accept that it is His/Her/Its ever-present love that brings 'enemies' together so that they can learn from each other about the ways of duality and oneness.

The most important thing to understand about justice is that you can *never* interfere in another person's life affairs unless asked to and invited by their Higher Self. The farthest you can go, without an invitation to help or assist another soul, is serving as a catalyst or mirror. You don't do this, though, for purely selfless reasons. Your reward in playing the catalyst or mirror for someone else is seeing yourself, thus allowing you to learn about and unfold your own vast inner potential. Seen from a higher perspective, the idea of someone harming another is pure fiction - as is the notion of injustice.

Where is the Justice in Holocaust and Ethnic Cleansings?

Many people nowadays accept that the role of karma (often stated as: "As you sow, so shall you reap and not otherwise" or "What goes around comes around"), plays an undeniable role in the area of human interaction. For them the idea of victims co-creating their own victimization is not only plausible but the only reasonable explanation there can be. Yet the understanding of such a universal system of restoring justice is challenged when a few individuals with tremendous worldly powers negatively affect large portions of a population. Recorded history is filled with instances of mass killings, such as the

116

genocide of millions of Armenians, the Holocaust of World War II, the eradication of Kurds, the slaughtering of thousands of Algerians and Tibetans, or the Kosovo and Bosnian conflicts, to name a few. In most of these situations, one or several people are blamed for causing such atrocities.

All these instances may raise serious doubt about the role of karma as a reliable system of natural justice. Take the Holocaust, for example; how could anything in the world justify the killing of millions of innocent people who had only one thing in common, being of Jewish descent? Yet the question arises whether the hate of just one fanatic man from Austria was sufficiently strong to make hundreds of thousands of Germans believe that Jews were pests that needed to be exterminated. How could millions of people be wiped out by a few, and have nothing to do with their own demise? Is natural justice so unfair as to let anyone get away with mass murder? These questions are not answerable in a satisfying way, just as a physical problem cannot be resolved by understanding its symptom. The *causes* for both remain hidden and are seemingly unrelated to their *effects*. Yet behind the scenes of what occurred in the concentration camps and on the battlefields of World War II lurked a deeper meaning; one that weaved the complex threads of individual and collective karmas together to lay the ground for an unprecedented spiritual awakening that would perhaps not otherwise have occurred.

The immense suffering that the German Jews experienced and finally succumbed to was part of a drama of unprecedented proportion played out by the Germans and the Jews, as well as many of the world's nations. As horrible as it was, the holocaust was experienced with the permission of all the souls involved. The mass trauma was, in fact, a tremendous release of the destructive, non-allowing and judgmental ideas, dogmas and behavior of the people living on Earth at that time.

The war wasn't just one person's fault, although we like to see it that way to avoid taking responsibility. Even those that resisted, hated, and judged the Nazi Germans, were feeding them with negative energy. The Holocaust received its energy to make itself manifest because there was so much destructive energy floating around the Earth. Hitler and those who aided him were fed by that energy; it was up to them how and where to focus the destruction. Given the intensity of the collective stress and fear at the time prior to the war, the destruction would have been of a similar impact even if there hadn't been a Hitler.

Almost all the people in the world suffered in one way or another because of the war, whether this was due to economic hardship, the loss

117

of loved ones, or the destruction of their homes and towns. Their suffering occurred in direct response to the conflicts and wars within their own minds. They went through these incredible hardships not because they deserved to suffer, but because their souls asked to be released from that burden of collective tension to which they had contributed, each in their own way. Those who lost their lives didn't lose anything, they simply chose to move on to the next level of their spiritual quest, and at the same time clear much of the collective and individual energies that were preventing mankind as a whole from raising its vibrational level.

Until the eruption of the greatest war this Earth has ever witnessed, the world's population wasn't ready for a spiritual revolution. The karmic knots were too hard to undo in a more gentle way. They needed to be cut, and although this was painful to all, it brought mankind closer than ever to the extreme side of the pendulum, representing the darkest night of the soul or the most extreme state of duality. Almost everyone at the time was involved in the dreadful labor pains that accompanied the birthing of a new era, and the destruction of the old one that was no longer appropriate for the growth of humanity. Within the relatively short period of the war, much of the karmic burden that had accumulated on the Earth during thousands of years of abuse was undone. It was a massive undertaking to get hundreds of millions of souls to incarnate on Earth in order to play out the drama of World War II and pave the way to freedom from duality.

Death - The Greatest Teacher of All

What we consider life and death is merely part of the illusion of duality that we are learning to dismantle. The idea that life begins when we are born and ends when we die eventually needs to be abandoned altogether if we are to be in our true essence while here on Earth. We all had to die in physical form many times throughout our human experience on this planet. As long as we are afraid of dying, or of other people dying, we need to continue experiencing the cycles of life and death. Without accepting death, we will not understand what life is. Although death is not a punishment, it is generally seen this way.

Most people deny that death exists, or 'postpone' it until they meet it face to face. We try so hard to avoid death that we actually stop living while still being in a physical body. In other words, if we try to hold life, we are already dead. Much of our time and effort throughout life is spent in safeguarding ourselves against the unavoidable. We work hard to put

118

aside money so that we don't have to die of starvation when we are old. We insure ourselves against illness so that we don't die for lack of proper medical treatment, should the need arise. Doctors do everything possible to prolong a patient's life, even if the patient would rather choose to die. Our relationship with death is so fear-based, that even the economy carries the stigma: 'If you don't have enough money you cannot make it in this world.'

People are not actually afraid of dying as such; rather, they fear living because it constantly reminds them of death. They are afraid of losing what they own: family, houses, and possessions. The uncertainty of life itself can cause the fear of death in many. At every moment, we are faced with the uncertainty of life. A deadly earthquake could strike anywhere at any time, and there are numerous other unpredictable ways that can end life. Millions of people around the world leave the Earth plane in this way each day. It is necessary for us to experience and treat both life and death as equal partners, for they represent the extreme ends of duality. By going through enough cycles of life and death, we increasingly learn to accept them willingly and without fear. We will finally discover that there is no beginning and end to life. We never die; we simply *are*, forever evolving. To break through the illusion of the life/death cycle more quickly and more easily, our Higher Selves agreed to let our human selves (egos) die in large numbers and more frequently. This required major collective dramas of famines and wars. World Wars I and II were two of the most important ones.

The death experienced by huge numbers of people in the Nazi concentration camps and by those who died during the bombing raids on German and European cities, as well as on the battlefields, removed, on the one hand, an enormous amount of fear of living from the collective consciousness of the dying masses. On the other hand, it generated a tremendous wave of fear of death in those who were left behind. The wave still hasn't stopped, today. Never before had the world population become so in touch with the core emotions of separation as during those years of war. This was very important for the emergence of a new world order that would help future generations to eventually transcend the boundaries and limitations imposed by the duality stigma of life and death and ascend to the immortal structures of their true selves.

Being in the Bubble of Maya

The whole issue of justice is painfully difficult to understand because we are having such a hard time living in a 3-D world. While living in duality, we are so completely misled by the appearance of concrete space-time events that it takes many lifetimes of experience in the physical arena to eventually conclude that the truth of things is exactly the opposite of what it appears to be. Almost every person in the world has seen the sun rise in the East and set in the West. When you tell young children who have seen the daily movement of the sun from East to West that this is not true at all they may be perplexed at first. They are confronted with a challenge that is hard to resolve. Do I believe what I see? Alternatively, do I believe what is completely contrary to what I see? If the sun was really stationary and we were moving around it, it would make sense that there could not be a sunrise or a sunset ever, yet my sense of sight and daily experience tell me we have sunsets and sunrises every day.

Seeing the sun move around the Earth is an illusion created by the sense of sight; knowing that the sun doesn't move around the Earth is a fact. Eventually both the understanding of this phenomenon and what we apparently see must be reconciled. Although they completely contradict each other, once understood, we can comfortably live with the illusion and the fact. For practical purposes though, we follow the cycles of day and night caused by the seeming appearance of the sun in the East and the setting of the sun in the West. Even our hormone-producing glands are tricked to believe that there is a movement of the sun; we call it Circadian Rhythm. The cyclic secretions of hormones are precisely linked with the sun's 'movements'. This provides the physiological basis for following a phenomenon that isn't really occurring.

The same principle applies to everything in our physical universe. The world as it appears to us with all its diverse phenomena is a giant bubble of illusion, which the ancients called *Maya*. As long we are in this bubble we have to play its game; sometimes we seem to lose and sometimes we seem to win. Yet if we were to step outside the bubble, we would know why we played it and there would be only winning and no more losing.

Playing the game of duality long enough and often enough helps to further our understanding of the nature of the bubble. We have been granted the experience of disillusionment so that we might be released from our illusions and increase our ability to discern the truth. Without first becoming enveloped by false impressions, we might otherwise never discover what it is like to be free of illusions. Once we know how Maya works we then find ourselves outside the bubble, observing it as if from a distance. Simply observing our world around us with calm and discernment helps to us to see the purpose of the bubble of Maya. On first impression, the sight of someone hitting an innocent bystander makes us believe that this is an obvious act of violence that justifies the prosecution and punishment of the perpetrator. The victim, on the other hand, should receive protection and help. We can only respond in a reactive manner if we are looking at the scene from within the bubble of Maya. In contrast, if we observe the situation from the sacred space of our hearts, we can only feel love and compassion for both the victim *and* the aggressor. We will begin to realize that those who unconsciously display negative energy in their thoughts and actions are like a vaccine, causing the rest of us to become immune to the lure of drama.

A judgmental response reveals nothing about the real nature of the event that took place. Without seeing through the eyes of the heart we have no way of knowing the underlying truth of the event, its real causes. This makes us automatic participants. Hurling our anger towards the perpetrator has more to do with our own unresolved anger issues than we realize. In truth, we are actually adding momentum and intensity to the situation if we become emotionally involved in it.

Quantum physics tells us that in the real world the observer of a particular event such as the movement of an electron exerts a *direct measurable influence* on whatever they observe. The law describing this phenomenon is known as 'Observer-observed relationship.' Reality changes with the viewpoint of the observer. Studies on water solutions, animal behavior and computer models have shown that the outcome of scientific experiments is largely determined by the subjective expectations and preconceived notions of the conducting scientists. Since everything in what we call the 'real' world is a form of energy, nothing is truly predictable; every situation or thing is subject to change. And according to the latest research, even the effects that past events have on future events can be altered. Nick, for example, drastically changed his predictable future of having to serve three life sentences into one of joy and freedom by infusing his past, vicious self with love, forgiveness and compassion. Our attitudes, insights, feelings and emotions count more than we realize and they can be held accountable for everything that happens around us.

No Victims, No Perpetrators

Among a group of people who become witnesses to a crime scene, very few can be considered innocent bystanders; everyone else is a participant. Generally, we participate by adding our own fuel of anger to the anger that already exists in the criminal, before they even commit the crime. Anger is a vibration, a field of influence we carry around with us, and it links up with those who have a similar vibration. This is especially true for densely populated cities where many people live very close to each other. Crimes occur much more frequently and with greater intensity in areas where the anger field is more concentrated. The combined anger reaches a saturation point and then bursts out into a wave of violence and thus becomes released from the energy field of that area. This makes crime more a collective phenomenon rather than an isolated one that involves just a few individuals.

In most cases of violence, the person who causes hurt to another is not in conscious control and later regrets having done it. In disbelief of their own actions, they cannot understand what overcame them. Little do they know that they weren't the only one involved in the crime; they were simply the most suitable candidate around to carry out this deed due to their karmic connection with the victim.

Being in the bubble of duality, we don't have much choice about our bipartisan reaction to the witnessed crime because this comes from our emotional body. Emotions can be suppressed for a little while but they cannot be controlled. If we try to control them, they only become more intensified. What *is* up to choice is how we deal with them once they have arisen. This is where knowledge and understanding become helpful.

When seeing someone hurting someone else, we may get in touch with two types of emotions. As our heart opens up and we feel an overwhelming compassion for the victim of the crime, we are actually sympathizing with the role of the victim that we ourselves have played so many times, whether in this or other lives. The next moment, while directing our anger towards the perpetrator, our heart closes again, following the duality nature of change. It closes because we are now facing the unconscious knowingness that we have been the perpetrators ourselves in either this life and/or other lifetimes. We can only resonate with these roles because we have played them so often in the past (which is just a parallel reality).

Becoming a witness to a crime is a non-coincidental opportunity our Higher Selves have co-created, along with other souls, to accept and embrace both the compassion and the anger in our own lives. Nothing in this universe is useless or without specific meaning and purpose. So it is with our endless stream of thoughts and the emotional responses we have to any situation in the areas of personal relationships, health, God and religion, abundance, economics, politics, or justice. The urge to see the perpetrator of a crime receive proper punishment is our own personal issue, and remains there as long as we are still angry with ourselves. We express our desire for punishment of another because we still feel guilty for having played a similar role so many times before, to whatever degree. And since we cannot run away from our emotional body, which is a collection of all the emotions we have ever created during all our lifetimes, we must eventually confront and balance them.

If we dare throw the first stone at the whore who has 'ruined' so many families with her seductiveness, all we do is express, or bring to the forefront, the 'sin' of having done something similar ourselves. *We are the crime we judge.* If we see injustice in the crime, we are unjust ourselves, for there is no other crime than the one we see. When we have no more ill-feelings left in our heart that need to be subdued or cut out, we can also no longer have any desire to see others punished for whatever 'wrong' they might have done. In the story of Jesus and the prostitute, Jesus passed no judgment against her. He simply accepted her for who she was. And he also saw the reason behind the revengeful feelings the crowd harbored against this woman and pointed it out to them. When they saw they were no different from her because they all had sinned before, the same people who were about to murder the woman became suddenly aware of what they were doing and walked away ashamed but more aware of themselves. Within a moment, Jesus had showed them that the prostitute represented a mirror reflection of their own behaviors from the past. They tried to find error in someone else because they didn't dare to expose their own faults. The past counts because it is present always. We all had to be perpetrators at some stage so that we could learn how to stop assaulting aggressors; mentally with our judgmental thoughts, emotionally with our feelings of revulsion and in any way physically.

Jesus once said: "Forgive them, for they know not what they do." Where there is forgiveness, judgment becomes obsolete. By forgiving the prostitute, the crowd was preparing the road for self-forgiveness, which is just another word for self-acceptance. Forgiving another is the same as accepting another. Accepting another is no different from accepting oneself. We only have difficulties with others if we cannot cope with some aspect of us. This circle runs through every successful relationship. Every relationship we could possibly have in life is a perfect reflection of the relationship we have with ourselves.

In this story, not only the crowd learned their lesson. The prostitute, who was put into the victim role, lost her fear of victimhood. Not being judged by the Son of God must have meant to her that she was worthy of his love and forgiveness/acceptance. Her self-worth increased and she saw value and purpose in her life. Having gained a sense of self-appreciation she was able to change her ways and stop abusing her body and herself. She became healed and rehabilitated almost instantly. Nick's situation wasn't much different either. The TM instructor that so impressed him wasn't the Son of God (or maybe he was), but he certainly was God *sent*. He came at the right time to the right place, just as Nick had reached the worst period in his miserable life. What Nick saw in this man was that he himself was worthy of peace and of being loved, something no punishment could ever have accomplished.

Punishment - A Cause of Crime and Injustice?

On the surface level of consideration crime appears to be such a persistent 'weed' of society because we don't punish enough. Crime statistics show that since the introduction of tougher prosecution measures and computer technology, some types of crime have dropped to their lowest levels in years, whereas others have remained the same or have even increased. It is actually very difficult to determine what increases or decreases crime. People commit criminal acts because of emotions of fear, dissatisfaction, unhappiness, greed, low self-worth, anger, aggression, or hate. No matter how strong the deterrent may be, when people no longer are able to retain their emotions, they will seek a way to release them. Robbing a bank, for example, can bring about a feeling of success in people who were never successful in anything. Using a gun may give them a sense of power they never had; by being a 'nobody' before, a criminal act makes them feel like a 'somebody'. The bottom line is that lack of worthiness - the root cause of every crime - cannot be resolved by any form of deterrent or punishment The real issues remain. And if the frustration cannot be expressed outwardly it will become internalized. Such a person may suffer severe depression, take drugs, become an alcoholic, contract a serious illness or commit suicide. Whether frustration is externalized through crime or internalized through self-destruction, it persists as long as punishment exists.

In the case of the prostitute, she was only able to change her ways because she wasn't judged and punished for her past actions. Had she been punished, her body would have been stoned to death. Yet her spirit would have continued, and in a future life she would have had to play the role of the victim again, or become one who would throw stones at others, depending on her reaction at the time of her physical death.

While living in duality, punishing someone for committing a crime is equal to committing a crime which itself will be, in turn, punished. Those who pass judgment on others will receive judgment themselves; the process is automatic and foolproof. Therefore, today's judges are in a challenging position because they have created a situation which forces them to pass judgment on others. Even though they are addressed as "Your Honor", they are actually the victims of their own judgments - unless they begin to consciously recognize and develop a sense of 'honor' and respect for those they judge. Seeing them as Children of God, as equals, regardless of what they have done, would bring fulfillment to the judge and inspire those who receive sentence to get in touch with their innate integrity. Even further, those who judge themselves, judge others in the same way. We must remember here that punishment and judgment only *appear* to be negative, and although they feel negative to those involved, they are merely tools for learning and growing. True crime prevention begins in the mending of the heart and that can be achieved in a moment.

Have you ever wondered why rehabilitation programs in prisons have such high recidivism rates (the number of released inmates who commit new crimes and return to prison)? One of the main reasons for this is that there is no program made available to the inmates that opens their hearts. There are over six million people imprisoned throughout the world, many of them for life. In the United States alone, there are over one million prisoners. The inmates are virtually forced to defend themselves against other inmates. Violent aggression and attack become a means of survival. The average prisoner has multiple scars from stabbings by inmates from self-made spears and knives and other objects that can cause injury. Also, drug abuse is rampant throughout prisons. Over 20,000 gangs control the lives of the prisoners. Not belonging to one of these organized crime groups, which operate both inside and outside the prisons, is life threatening. The prison system offers no real protection to the inmates at all. 'Survival of the fittest' and being extremely vigilant about everyone's movements are the key rules controlling prison life. Even the toughest guard systems in maximum-security prisons cannot change the fact that there is *more violent crime within the prison walls than on the streets*.

Many people think that these criminals deserve to be incarcerated and should be kept there like chickens in small cages for many years, even their entire lives. This thought pattern is exactly how those who feel this way, being part of the collective consciousness of society, become active participants of the drama of crime. The exception being that they don't end up in prison for their thoughts, at least not physically. Prisons throughout the world will remain the most stressful and the most tension-generating places on the planet so long as the rest of us have an attitude of punishment within us. Because we still carry so much guilt in our hearts for all the things we have done wrong in this and other lifetimes, which is self-judgment, we feel better somehow if we project it outwardly and condemn others for not being as perfect as we would like to be. You can feel guilty for almost everything you do or don't do. Maybe you feel bad for not having done enough to help a friend in need, for having criticized others, for having manipulated or misled a customer, for having broken off a relationship, for having hurt those you love most, etc.

The suffering world serves as a reminder to us that we still harbor these judgments in our hearts. *Judgments keep the heart closed* until we are ready to open it for the entire world to see and share, even with those who we believe deserve punishment. This belief is a *self-imposed limitation* of the heart, an imprisonment in fact; if we want to break free, the limitation must give way to love for *all* life. If we see evilness when one person tries to hurt another, we are only able to see it as such because we have not yet embraced and accepted our own 'evilness' from sometime in the past. All of our lifetimes are filled with events of greater or lesser injustice, and now we face them again as others create them for us to see and deal with.

Through almost-instant means of international communication, the media now enables us to know what is happening in any part of the world, as it happens. War footage, news about disasters, disease outbreaks, terrorist attacks, etc. comes right into our homes at the push of a button. Many people say the media is manipulating us by giving us their censored opinion, and the true picture of things is never really given.

Yet this manipulation is exactly what we need *at this time*. Collectively, we are still in need of constant mirroring back to us what we are doing to ourselves. What we get upset about is not what happens out there, but what we still have stored inside us. The current situation out there serves as a trigger for us to forgive and accept ourselves for having done what we at one time felt to be wrong, and around which we created guilt. It doesn't matter in the least what we have done in the past; what matters is how we deal with it *now*. Even if we were a liar, a thief, a prostitute or a murderer, regardless of whether this was yesterday or 200 lifetimes ago, this is only what we did; it is not who we are. Once Nick felt the place within him that was holy, in a moment of peace and love he was a changed man. All he had to do was accept that part of himself that he never knew he had i.e. the capacity to feel love and respect *for himself*.

126

Once Nick had made peace within himself, he wanted to share his newfound love with his enemies. The desire to be friends with enemies who were only out to harm and subdue him came not because of punishment, attending a rehab program or by studying the word of God. It occurred naturally after he had reached the fullest possible saturation of negativity, aggression, and hate against himself and the world. The pendulum had to swing back. At that very moment, fate, which is just another word for Divine calculation, decided that someone had to come into his life who could trigger a feeling of hope in him. This person had to be free of judgment and fear to enter into the living hell of a maximum-security prison. All that this person saw in Nick and the other inmates was the potential for love and peace.

After large groups of inmates had been instructed in meditation, the most astonishing thing the prison wardens reported was the peaceful and tension-free expressions on the faces of the inmates, and the total lack of fear of being stabbed in the back. Never before had they seen rows of inmates sitting peacefully with their eyes closed for even a minute, much less twice-daily for 20 minutes. And never would they have imagined working in a prison that had so little violence and tension as that prison during the time of the experiment. Unfortunately, since most prisons have been privatized, in is not in the interests of those who own and run the prisons to rehabilitate inmates. Prisons have become one of the most profitable businesses, much more 'successful' than most luxury-hotel chains taken together. It pays to keep a prison a dangerous place, for this ensures that inmates are most likely to return to jail eventually. But even this is part of the larger picture.

Punishment is a two-way process. For one, it involves those who have the inner urge to pass judgments for personal reasons, that is, to bring to the surface what they do not like in themselves. Second, it compels those who feel judged to deal with being in the role of the victim, which is, having a sense of low self-worth that naturally attracts attack or criticism. Every stick has two ends, each one pointing in opposite directions. A victim consciousness requires a victimizer to learn about itself and a victimizer consciousness needs to find a victim to know what playing this role feels like. A murderer may for a while feel the power that comes with being a perpetrator, but once caught, they feel the vulnerability of a victim. The prosecutor of this criminal now becomes a perpetrator, that is, one who seeks to punish or victimize another, for whatever 'justifiable' reasons. One follows the other. We have all played both these roles many times over. And both roles are needed as long as we live in our own creation of duality. In fact, punishment of perpetrators serves them well until they finally come to the point of accepting themselves for whatever they are, regardless of their past deeds. Retribution by another, gives them the chance to release some of their bottled up feelings of guilt. Battered women often feel relief when their husbands beat them up. Yet once they see room for getting an upper hand, they will assume the role of victimizers, often with their own children.

Therefore, even prisons have served their purpose in society until now. Prison inmates have remained 'stuck' in the ever-alternating roles of victim and victimizer. Every victimizer has been a victim before and every victim has been a victimizer before. We all have both roles within us in potential form and we all have expressed them in one way or other throughout our lives. The mass media reflects this drama in daily news coverage, and through movies, best-selling novels, soap operas, etc. Fortunately, the pendulum of time is turning now. Soon we will be able to give up the necessity for punishment as a way to gain justice.

Although true justice prevails at all times because the Law of Non-Interference can never be violated by anyone, the *illusion* of injustice will soon dissolve for everyone to see. Crime will simply stop serving as a means of learning and self-reflection. Instead, humans will recognize each other for who they really are, Divine Beings in human form. Just by discovering and claiming our own divinity, the oneness with our Source, we will automatically see it in others too, regardless of whether they are in the form of a criminal or a priest. The more people who experience this, the less punishment will be used as a measure of correcting behavior. Without using punitive action, our power of seeing the true nature in others will increase. This in turn will create the precondition for any criminal to rehabilitate within a very short time, if they choose. Crime will become minimal. At the same time, the news media will be much less inclined to report negative news, because the population will have very little need for negative mirror reflection. In the new world order, casting judgment on others to become aware of one's own guilt and dissatisfaction will subside, because self-love and self-acceptance will dominate almost everyone's behavior. We are right in the middle of a colossal transition from a life of judgment and seeming injustice to a life without judgment; to life with true justice and peace. However, we are not quite there yet, and it is our challenge to discover the way that leads us to transcend the duality of appearance.

Gaining the Power of Acceptance

You can only see, perceive, feel, hear, and understand what is in your highest good, no more and no less. Each moment is a Divine moment. *Accepting what is* versus controlling, manipulating or rejecting it is perhaps one of the most powerful things you can do to solve any kind of problem in life. This is not to say that resisting or judging is wrong, given the fact that it helps you understand the purpose of duality. But by *accepting what is*, you actually transcend duality. Acceptance is the key to developing that serenity within which allows you to let go of the past with all its mistakes and regrets and become free of all expectations that bind you to future events that have not even happened. It takes you onto the road of the eternal present. Projecting your thoughts and desires into the future is the old way of creating reality. The new way of creating reality is based on being in the moment and emanating energy out, not to the future per se, but into all moments of time.

One of the primary laws of life is the Law of Free Will. According to this law, each soul is free to accept, reject, or ignore all the souls around it or even to disregard the Creation itself. But ignoring or rejecting the responsibility for our own needs and those of others can greatly affect our well-being. For example, failure to surrender to the loss of control over life may result in numbness of hands and arms, or even paralysis. The desire to control is the opposite of accepting what is. It arises from the fear of not being in the moment, the only safe place there can ever be. The spiritual or mental drama of not taking responsibility for oneself is enacted in the physical body, for learning from the experience. The desire to avoid carrying one's mental or spiritual load i.e. not accepting it for what it is, is the primary reason for physical and mental illness.

Accepting whatever presents itself in life is the key to healing any type of illness, even cancer; attempting to control the things that happen to us is a sure way to create illness. Those souls, who, from the depth of their being, seek love and oneness in their human lives, empower their progress with a tremendous multiplying effect. All they do is accept responsibility for the potential for spiritual learning in each moment of their lives. They give spiritual meaning to everything, even to anger, hate, and suffering. Seeking love at every moment can never be fruitless because each moment contains love, no matter what disguise it might assume.

The Magic of 'Yes'

By accepting into your life whatever occurs in each moment without immediately compartmentalizing it or deciding whether it is something good or bad, you are able to open up your heart. Acceptance doesn't imply that you will always be perfect. What it means is that the heart never needs to withdraw or close down because it knows that *everything* that comes along is acceptable. This permanent 'Yes mode' of the heart allows you to see as much value in imperfection as in perfection.

By loving and fully embracing all your experiences, all your reflections, and all of your body, you rise to a completely new level of heart, the heart of oneness. You cannot free yourself from fears and limitations until you say "yes" to all of your dilemmas, heartaches and pains. Embracing and loving your body with all its faults and difficulties brings you giant steps closer to inner and outer freedom. Since every cell and even every tiny wrinkle is a creation of your God Self, it has Divine purpose, even if you have no idea what this purpose is. So by accepting and loving every inch of your body, you align yourself with your Divinity.

It is easy to love the beautiful things in life. In fact, it is difficult not to love the flowers, trees, dolphins and butterflies, or the sunsets and rainbows. But it is a true challenge to love that which reflects you at each moment. Saying "Yes" to all the choices and decisions you have made in your life allows you to see their Divine purpose. Having done this, you have no more need to judge, criticize, analyze or rebuke them. This instantly takes away the reasons you may have had to judge someone else or worry whether your spouse, child or friend is doing the right thing. You will know that each person has to have their own learning experiences, so that they too can embrace and accept their Divine nature.

Let us assume you have a mother or mother-in-law who blames you for everything that goes wrong in her and your life. One possible reaction to her nagging criticism is to defend yourself, to say that she is wrong and you are innocent. By defending yourself, however, you simply throw back at her what she is throwing at you, while not resolving the conflict. Instead, getting all her own stuff back from you causes her to be even more relentless in her pursuit of finding fault with you at every occasion. So what can you do to end this vicious circle of events?

The next time your mother or mother-in-law lashes out at you, instead of rejecting her negative energies, say "Yes" to them. Invite them into your space in the knowing that they are only there for you to go beyond judgment and to expand your heart. By telling her "Yes, I am guilty of everything you have ever told me", regardless of whether this is so or not, something magical begins to happen. The first experience you will have is that you no longer feel guilty of any wrongdoing, which also means you no longer feel the need to defend yourself. The second experience will be that your mother or mother-in-law is also going to be relieved of her guilt, and the responsibility for herself and her actions, because you stopped returning her accusations. By accepting the criticism, you are giving her the chance to experience for the first time how it feels to be without the urge to put you down. This teaches her a lot about herself. You become a role model for her because you accept responsibility for something you didn't even do. Instead of getting defensive or feeling sorry for yourself, you stand there with an open heart and simply say "Yes."

The magical "Yes" is so effective because in reality, that is to say from a spiritual perspective, everything that comes your way belongs to you. For your Higher Self it is no coincidence that you are being criticized. You choose the people who play the role of button pushers in your life in order to free yourself from all guilt and low worthiness. Saying "Yes" to everything you resist is your road to freedom and infinite possibilities. And by accepting those whose energies seem to be attacking you (which, from a higher perspective is only an illusion) you become invincible to attack in any form.

Acceptance is the heart's best defense. There is no more need for self-protection; each moment is welcome and doesn't need to be judged. This does not mean you give up your discerning ability. On the contrary, once you are able to accept everything that happens to you, you can then fearlessly select from it whatever you wish or require for your happiness and fulfillment. You begin to realize that everything that occurs in your life is tailored to perfection. You will know intuitively that the people, spiritual guides, angels, entities, or animals you encounter all help to further your growth and evolvement toward full awareness of your essential nature. We all are masters of co-creation and nothing ever happens to us that, in view of the final outcome, isn't in our best interest. This is one of the best-kept secrets of human living and it applies to every person and every life form.

Each moment of your life is sanctified and blessed with Divine intent, even though it might feel like you are going through hell. Nick's circumstances, having murdered three people and caused bodily harm to many more, were dire to begin with. He had no self-respect and therefore no respect for others, which is perhaps the 'worst' place of isolation one could be in. Yet experiencing living hell in this present lifetime

131

eventually allowed him to taste heaven, and it brought him the tremendous gift of giving hope and purpose to others going through life with a closed heart. With every trial we pass through there comes a gift. Nick's gift was that he received the opportunity to step into the place within himself where heaven and hell could meet and not be in conflict. Accepting both, he was able to bring love into his fear-stricken world and transform his life. The more emptiness or vacuum we have created in our lives, the greater will be the empowerment and fulfillment. When the shift occurs, we call it a miracle.

You Are What You Feel

One of the most revealing insights of life is that we, that is to say our consciousness, become what we perceive. You are the person you love and you are also the person you fear. You adopt the qualities of beauty, courage, honesty that you so admire in a friend but at the same time you manifest the qualities of guilt, hate, or aggressiveness that you dislike in an adversary. Your consciousness can assume any role in life, which is in accordance with its highest good. If you meet a person who is angry, either with you or with someone else, it is because *you* have a need to face your inner anger. Anger, however, is nothing but an expression of fear, the fear of separation. It is the disconnection from your own Life Source that makes you look for substitutes to fill the emptiness of not knowing who you are; yet if you cannot get what you desire, e.g. money, power, romance, you become frustrated and angry.

If you have gone beyond the illusionary appearance of anger, there is practically no way of recognizing it in another person; you simply have no more reference for anger in your consciousness. To reach this place of peace and harmony, however, you first need to become exposed to this emotion through others. Recognizing anger in another is our personal experience, and we become what we experience. We become it because we resonate with it. In addition, we resonate with it not because we like feeling resentful or angry, but because it triggers in us what has laid dormant in the substructures of our consciousness. Seeing anger in others is a way to bring our own anger to the surface of awareness and see it for what it truly is - love in disguise. As always, we can choose to give either a negative meaning to anger, or a positive one. If we choose to honor others for delivering to us messages of anger, we cannot not help but be in love with the world.

There are no right or wrong ways to live our lives, regardless of how we behave with other people, how we dress ourselves, or what we eat.

The 'good' and 'bad' we attach to everything and everyone stems from the mostly unconscious projection of what we have learned is good and bad. There are plenty of reminders, which try to keep us in line, to make us conform to the norm. Some norms, like laws or medical drugs become outdated and discarded and are replaced with new ones. Others are disputed or subject to personal opinion.

We are All in this Together

Take for example the sport of hunting animals. Some people feel revolted by the act of killing animals for no other reason than personal enjoyment. Proponents of hunting claim that it is a wonderful sport, which makes you feel good about yourself. This is true; killing does make you feel good - if you have a need to overcome a weakness of personality or suppress a sense of victimhood. A gun is not just a physical tool that can destroy life but it is also a symbol of power, stronger and more powerful than a bear or even an elephant. Using the gun causes the hunter to feel in charge, in control, invincible and protected, whereas in normal life they may feel just the opposite. Hunters have the need to experience these qualities so they can feel good about themselves and at the same time suppress their feelings of low self-worth and inadequacy. Since the euphoria of having placed a victorious shot, i.e. having proven their power, is only short-lived and real life is still waiting around the corner, they do not get the lasting fulfillment they seek. This results in anger and frustration, which drives them back to do more killing. The pent-up emotions release at the point of shooting the animal (as if the animal was an enemy). But releasing anger in this way only dissipates it temporarily, it does not get rid of it. They have yet to face the animals inside themselves that they are really out to kill, so they are drawn into the game over and over again. Hunting does to a hunter what drugs do to a drug addict.

This principle can also be extended to the killing or harming of human beings. There is only a value difference between killing an insect, an animal or a person. The basic reason for killing remains the same. Killers may be more drawn to killing an innocent victim, someone who has not done harm to anyone, than another villain, probably due to having been in the role of the innocent victim either during this or a past life. For example, if abused by their father while still a child, they will be desperate to free themselves from that inner feeling of victimization. By killing an innocent child, they believe they have finally seen justice done. They may even be proud of this for a while but since the satisfaction

133

doesn't last for very long, they are often drawn to look for another victim.

However, all this doesn't make them criminals who deserve punishment. They are not vicious people who have no capacity for love in them. Their ultimate difficulty is to face, embrace and accept the fear of becoming victimized again. Being powerful and tough seems like their only way out of the situation. When it no longer works, they are eventually forced to deal with it in other ways. Imprisonment can sometimes cause self-reflection, though it rarely does. Accepting this type of person for whom they really are, rather than for what they have done, has a much better chance of opening their heart to love than punishment does. But merely desisting from punishing them or locking them away without giving them the opportunity to free their heart-space from hatred poses a grave risk to others. But as long as society is afraid of them or angry about what they have done, they are likely to continue their violent behavior.

Intentionally causing the death of another person can, in itself, be enough to shock the killer and awaken them from the illusion of having previously been the victim - a notion unconsciously used to justify their actions. With the shock of realizing what they have done, many murderers have suddenly turned to God, their own inner goodness, and asked for forgiveness. They are just as good as the rest of us who have been in similar situations during other lifetimes. Every person, no matter what they have done in the past, has the potential to transcend their self-imposed limitations and judgments and know that they are just as worthy and loveable as everyone else. With this recognition begins a new phase of life.

Unfortunately, all of this is particularly hard to accept for those who still believe that there *really are* victims in life. When, for example, an 'innocent' child becomes the victim of a horrendous crime, a lot of people get very upset because such an incident triggers all the cellular memories of victimization they have neatly packed away in their unconscious. Any past life issue related to having been treated unfairly erupts as anger, which in turn forces them to deal with these hidden issues. So when such a crime is committed, if anger is your reaction, take the opportunity to see more clearly what the drama is really all about.

For Your Eyes Only

We see that taking sides throws us into our polarity mode. First, we identify with a past victim in us, one that was similarly mistreated. This

134

generates fear. The next moment we assume the role of a perpetrator, wanting to see the person punished or even killed. This puts us in touch with our deep-seated anger. Once again, desiring someone else killed or punished, for whatever reason, stems from a profound sense of low self-worth or a judged personality within. We don't really attack the attacker, we merely attack that which we don't want to see or recognize in ourselves. When we want to assist or help a victim, we do that not only because of feelings of compassion and love but also because of memories of having been in a similar situation. And we condemn the victimizer because we have not yet either forgiven our victimizers or accepted ourselves for having played a similar role some time in our life stream's past. In this sense, the situation of 'injustice' is for our eyes only. Injustice is a purely subjective experience and has nothing to do with objective reasons. That many people might agree with your viewpoint (of injustice) only means that they, too, have similar victim issues of their own to resolve.

Being there for others in need, without having any personal judgment of the event or people involved, is an act of unconditional love. However, if you feel love and compassion exclusively for the victim and foster anger and hostility towards the victimizer, there isn't much true love involved. Such biased behavior is rooted in one's desire to be a better person than one is (self-judgment) and at the same time, seeks to reduce the feelings of guilt of not being good enough for others or oneself. True love does not discriminate between the two parties. For the person who sees through the eyes of love and compassion, both the victim and the victimizer are equally valuable and advanced souls who are simply acting out their respective roles. They are in fact helping each other become aware of the whole range of duality - the creative and destructive parts - attraction and repulsion, suppression and release. They learn about giving, taking and being receptive and unreceptive. Eventually both role types are bound to wake up to their heritage of unconditional love, just as Nick did.

Conflicts End With the End of Victim Consciousness

Conflicts of any sort will only last as long as there are people with victim consciousness. It is the victim who requires a victimizer just as a patient requires a doctor or a student needs a teacher. At their soul level, victims literally *ask* for the transgression against them because they condemn or judge those same aggressive aspects of themselves and need someone else to play that role as a mirror for them. Everyone with low

135

self-worth, guilt, or the belief of being a sinner who does not deserve the love of God or other people, has the potential to manifest an adversary in their life.

Although it happens unconsciously, we actually are *always* in control of everything that happens to us. We make it happen. We may be robbed because we ourselves have robbed, or we have condemned robbers for what they have done to us, fulfilling the law 'You become that what you judge'.

I personally had to be robbed three times in order to arrive at the point of relinquishing the illusion of victimhood. The first time this happened to me, I was shocked to the core of my being. Just 15 minutes before I boarded a plane at Frankfurt Airport to fly to India, a thief snatched from me a small bag which contained $2,000 in cash (all the money I owned at that time), one of my two passports, and my one and only address book. When I contacted the airport police, they shrugged their shoulders and said there was nothing they could do. Left with nothing but a passport and a return ticket, I decided to go anyway. It all worked out fine in the end, but at the time I felt very upset and angry with the thief.

The second time, during a four-month stay in New Zealand, I was robbed of my credit card and a few hundred dollars, but the damage was minimal compared to the first time. This time I really got in touch with my own naivety and sense of victimhood, that 'poor me' feeling.

The third and last time I was robbed was in 1992 at the railway station in Rome when two extremely 'skilled' gypsy kids (about seven and ten years old) relieved me of ten cash checks worth $1,500, my passport, and my airline ticket back to Cyprus where I lived. Although it is practically impossible, and in fact illegal, for anyone to travel by air to another country (especially Cyprus) without being in possession of a passport, not only did the Italian police let me board the plane but, most astoundingly, the Cyprus immigration officials allowed me into the country without my passport. Apart from the expenses of a new airline ticket, I had no further damage done. The organized crime gang in Rome, which the gypsy kids worked for, managed to cash my checks straightaway. Fortunately, I was insured and received my money back.

During that third time that I was robbed, I released a lot of fear about losing what I considered essential or important in life. At the same time, I gained the insight that life always goes on and that I am always taken care of, no matter how difficult a situation may seem. I also saw clearly that, in various lifetimes, I had been all the players in each of these episodes.

In one past life, I was a young monk in a monastery in North India; I was the gatekeeper. Although my superiors told me that this was a very important job, I didn't quite share their perspective. I was to make certain that only 'good people' entered the monastery. In India at that time it was (and still is to some extent) the custom to offer travelers food and shelter. One day, in my naive and unsuspecting nature, I opened the gate of the monastery to a group of thugs who pretended to be tired travelers seeking shelter. Once they were inside the monastery, they robbed us of all our valuables and treasures. I felt very guilty about this because I was responsible for the safety of my brothers and the monastery. A few years later, still in charge of gate keeping, I once again let in a group of robbers but this time they killed all the monks and threw me over a cliff.

During this present lifetime, I have had the same naïve nature I had back then, which led me into similar, although less severe, situations with robbers. The situations were striking enough, though, to let me feel what it is like to be a victim of crime. Upon my return home to Cyprus from India, after the first robbery, I was still so angry that I even asked a good friend of mine, the famous clairvoyant, psychic surgeon and healer Daskalos, also known as 'The Magus of Strovolos', to tune into the thief and find out where he was. (During my previous lifetime in India, Daskalos was like an uncle and caretaker to me. My mother had left me at the age of two at the monastery because she felt she was too young to raise a child on her own.) Instead of helping me find the thief, Daskalos pointed out that the robbery happened so that I could master one of my greatest lessons in this life. He said, "It isn't in your best interest to seek justice for something that is right and just already." When the gypsy kids in Rome robbed me, I had almost no angry feelings towards them, nor did I feel guilt for being fooled again. Instead, I felt euphoric and almost invincible when I entered Cyprus without a valid form of identification. I am convinced that I have not been robbed again to this day, despite having traveled through many 'insecure' countries, because I no longer feel a victim when something 'happens to me'. I sense no more guilt in my heart for having done something wrong in my life.

During a healing session with a past life regression therapist, the monks who were killed in the monastery as a result of what I had assumed to be 'my fault' suddenly appeared in a circle, smiling at me and showing me that everything was in right order and that no one could ever be a victim in life. They were not killed because of me, in the same way that I wasn't really killed by the robbers. They also showed me that they weren't dead at all, that no one who seems to die, really dies. Yet we feel guilty for causing the death of another when, in truth, death is a

137

figment of human imagination. Guilt is also an illusion that creeps into our awareness when we get involved in the duality mode and cannot see the larger picture. We see death because we believe it exists. We are so attached to our physical form that when it ceases to be, we believe life is over. Yet nothing happens to life, it continues as always and forever. For the monks, it was just another opportunity to get closer to uncovering the truth of eternal living; for me it was about finding out that victims don't exist.

We perceive both the victim and the victimizer as being the two main roles that our body awareness or ego plays for us in order to become integrated and complete ends of the experience of crime and conflict in life. Simply seeing, whenever one role seems to dominate, that we actually play both roles, jailer and jailed, automatically cancels both out and sets us free. So long as we act out either polar aspect, we are bound to undergo the ego shifts from being a victim to becoming a victimizer, and vice versa. Accepting that all this is very useful removes the stigma of crime and the need for punishment. The time for punishment as a way of restoring justice is ending because victims and victimizers are running out of fuel for conflict. The fuel for conflict is karma, and karma is ending.

We are in fact experiencing the final remnants of all conflicts that ever have occurred on this planet. The new energies that are moving planet Earth and us into the higher frequencies of the next dimensions cannot sustain duality and karma. These energies bring to the surface everything that stands in the way, so they can finally be understood and released. Those who are not ready to let go of their guilt and karmic accumulations are likely to 'self-destruct', for these new energies only support oneness. Their decision not to let go of duality is a soul choice, made on levels not consciously known to them. However, they too, only do what is best for them. Those of us who consciously want to move on and ascend to our own higher forms while being in physical expression are in the process of tremendous clearing and healing. We are finally relieving ourselves of the heavy loads we have carried on our shoulders throughout our existences on Earth. When we are ready for freedom, it will be there waiting for us.

True Ownership Lies Within

Fighting for freedom is not a means of attaining freedom; it is only an attachment to something we are yearning to have. We form attachments to things or people so that we can learn what it is like to be without them.

Right now, we are perhaps going through one of the most painful times in human history because we are prompted to let go of every attachment that we ever have created. Parting from what we believed was rightfully ours brings up fear, rage, and even violence. The conflict between Israelis and Palestinians over the role of Jerusalem is not really about historic rights over territory or religious sites. It is rather a reflection of the deep division that exists within the hearts of those who claim they cannot live with one another peacefully. Since they do not feel one with their own Higher Selves they are desperate to identify themselves with a home outside themselves. This inner separation is expressed in their beliefs. They insist that they have rights over land that their ancestors had owned before them, calling it homeland. If they cannot own this land, or at least have free access to it, they feel they have the right to take it by force. For lack of owning themselves, they attach themselves to something outside of them that they can call their own. The attachment to material things such as a house or a piece of land can become so intensified that, when there is a danger of losing it, panic sets in. This shakes up the attachment.

The truth of the matter is there is no solution that could ever satisfy everyone, except the one that unites everyone. This oneness, however, cannot be dictated or given; it comes naturally once the grip of attachment is loosened. Both parties will only get what they want when they are able to let go of their limited focus and make peace with *themselves* first. Then it will not matter who lives in which part of the city and it will be no threat to the other if the one calls it a capital city. When oneness dominates, in our awareness, all opposition ceases and everyone finds their right place.

The violence in the Middle East is a necessary part of the process of releasing the separation consciousness that has hovered over this region for thousands of years. The conflicts there look very real but they are not. The real issue is the painful letting go of the great attachments that mankind has been enveloped in for eons. When separation consciousness leaves, it can bring up resentments and struggle for survival. If unity is to dawn and peace be created, separation must vanish. This is what is happening right now. It is not in the highest good for either of the two sides to claim ownership for the land or sacred sites that exist there. It is impossible to own anything but oneself, whether it is property, land, or even one's body.

True ownership lies within. By being yourself, you are also one with others - the land, mother Earth, and the universe. Once all of these are owned in your heart, it is no longer important to own it in any other way.

139

It ends conflict of any kind. But not everyone is ready to move into oneness. Those who have decided to remain in duality consciousness, in alignment with their self-assigned roles of promoting division and suffering, are most likely going to 'self-destruct' with regard to their physical existences here on Earth, for the new energies will no longer support separation consciousness. This act of self-destruction is what is being displayed every day on television for the world to see. The same applies to all the armed conflicts, such as guerrilla warfare, suicide bombings, and natural disasters that cause loss of life.

It matters not in what role they are leaving the planet, whether as victims or victimizers. Those who hijacked jetliners and used them as weapons of mass destruction in the 'Attack on America' had lost their true sense of self and were overcome by the illusion of separation. When they died along with their victims and their souls departed from their bodies, they looked at the destruction they had caused with great sadness and confusion because they realized that none of this saved them a place in Heaven after all. They saw that life and its lessons do not end when they destroy the physical body. Many of the victims of the attack made their transition with ease and joy in their hearts, for they (their Higher Selves) had chosen this route as a possible way of reuniting humankind. Both these groups learned from this event that true ownership lies within.

Those who stayed behind received the opportunity to strengthen their ability for forgiveness, love and compassion. Each one of us was asked to make the decision whether to keep up the wall of separation and be trapped within the world of blame and continued external threat or to create a new reality based on showering those who seem to cause us harm with love, forgiveness and acceptance. So when you say "God bless America" for example, or any other arbitrary grouping of humanity, also give blessings to Afghanistan, Iraq, Iran, and in fact to the whole planet. To ask God to bless us in our pursuit of retaliating against our enemies is futile and nonsensical. According to the words of Jesus, executing and dispatching a negative spirit into the ether causes it to return to the Earth plane; but it does not come alone, it brings along seven others. Killing terrorists *breeds* terrorism. Many of those 'enemies' that fell at the hands of Americans during the war against the Native Americans, or during the Great Civil War, World War II, Vietnam and the Gulf War are now back to set the record straight. The outcome of the conflict is being determined by our individual and collective thoughts, speech and actions. It is for us to decide whether we want to stop the cycle of karma or perpetuate it.

Many people repeatedly pray to God to follow in the footsteps of Jesus Christ, to become like him. But if their wish is fulfilled, they are likely to face highly challenging situations that really put their faith to the test. It is not a real accomplishment to feel love for those who are kind to you. In the wake of a terror attack like the one we witnessed in New York in September 2001, how many people are truly able to act like Jesus, who at the time of his physical death asked God to "forgive them for they know not what they do"? Major calamities occur from time to time to test the degree of true love and inner freedom we have achieved and to apply these in a practical way.

A large portion of the world's population passed the 9-11 tests, others didn't and they are still following the old ways of dealing with such external threats to their lives. They still believe that the physical person of an Osama Bin Laden or Saddam Hussein is an evil force, and that by destroying that person, the evil will be gone too. But it is not the human brain or the body that devises acts of hate and terror. It is the consciousness, the intelligence or the mind behind the scene that uses a brain or body to execute its intentions. This light being (soul) is indestructible by physical means. The desire and will to eradicate all evil and evildoers from the planet is an old concept that has been attempted by Caesar, Hitler, Stalin and Mao Tse Tung. Each one of them wanted to cleanse the world from what they considered 'filth'. But trying to eradicate terrorism by killing those who have radically different views of justice than we have only sets up the stage for yet more violence and suffering.

Those with the greatest attachments and narrowest belief systems are the least likely to endure the sweeping power of the new energies that have begun to infuse human life and the Earth. Within less than 20 years, separation consciousness and the power of manipulation, exploitation, abuse and conflict are likely to vanish from the surface of the Earth, along with those who seek to keep dualism alive. This is going to affect every area of life in the most glorious way. We will discover that the outer appearances of our physical nature, accumulated wealth, and intellectual abilities simply do not compare to our true strength within. Everyone, no matter what the circumstances, is a God in embryo, waiting to be born.

The strength of another man is
measured by the strength within.

141

You can count every hair, every fiber of his being and this will not add up to the wellspring of capabilities he carries within him. For what is shown to the world, what is externalized can never be an adequate reflection of that which lies within. It is simply a displacement, a reverberating image of that which is stored and encased within the human body. But the true inner strength and tenacity is immeasurable.

Achilles
Channeled on December 26, 2000

Chapter Eight

Our Hidden Agendas

*The war of the mind is a fierce
battlefield to work within. The
skirmishes are many, the battles
are few and fiercely won but we
are steady and solid soldiers and
warriors in our own right. We can
stem the tide or accelerate the
fury at will. The force of our
intentions is mighty, the power
lies within each of us and we will
win this war within and come out
victorious. Of that I am sure.*

Winston Churchill
Channeled on December 21, 2000

Returning To Oneness

One morning I noticed that my partner had put on a black tee-shirt
and black pants, a color that I had strongly disliked for many years.
About two years before, I had shown her through a simple test that
wearing black cloth had a weakening effect on her mind and body and
that she would be better off avoiding it. She agreed and changed her
wardrobe except for a few pieces.

While I was questioning in my mind why my partner would want to
wear a black outfit, I instantly received the answer that the color she had

143

chosen to wear that day was the exact color that she and those she was going to meet needed to see, either for self-reflection, to become vulnerable in some way, or to release withheld emotions. And it wasn't for me to even know why. In that moment I was allowed to take a peek behind the obvious and see that nothing we do, think or desire, can ever be wrong or in conflict with our highest good.

To return to oneness is the one and only software program that all human beings have built within their souls, and there is nothing that can permanently erase this program or prevent them from achieving this goal. All life situations, regardless of their nature, are geared towards reaching the oneness we left, in order to find it. No matter how difficult life may seem on the surface, underneath it is simple and straightforward. The difficulties we meet on the way back to oneness can serve as some of the greatest stepping stones towards a meaningful life. It is not necessarily an indication of high evolvement or enlightenment to have a struggle-free life. Many of us were born in a hostile, unloving environment in order to mature into a person of great love and strength. You do not become strong by seeking those situations that make you feel secure and protected; you become strong by navigating through all kinds of storms, finding your direction and purpose from within.

Some of the greatest men and women who have lived on Earth often struggled more than the average. Think of Mahatma Gandhi, Mozart, Van Gogh, Lady Diana, and Jesus Christ. Their struggles formed their personalities and led to achievements, which united millions of people in the spirit of love, compassion, and forgiveness. Mother Teresa in particular exemplified love like few others that have lived on Earth. The main theme that ran through her every thought and action was 'return to oneness'. She truly 'walked her talk' when she gave this advice to us:

"People are often unreasonable, illogical and self-centered; forgive them anyway.
If you are kind, people may accuse you of selfish, ulterior motives; be kind anyway.
If you are successful, you will win some false friends and some true enemies; succeed anyway.
If you are honest and frank, people may cheat you; be honest and frank anyway.
What you spend years building, someone could destroy overnight; build anyway.
If you find serenity and happiness, they may be jealous; be happy anyway.

144

The good you do today, people will often forget tomorrow; do good anyway.
Give the world the best you have, and it may never be enough; give the world the best you've got anyway.
You see, in the final analysis, it is between you and God; it was never between you and them anyway."

We were all one in Spirit before we allowed the perception of separation to dominate our lives in human form. Of course, before incarnating on Earth we did not know what it would be like to lose that intimate connection and that love bond that held us together as one unit of life, similar to the cells of the body being held together as one living organism. Our minds functioned in harmony with each other, not against each other, and our hearts were melting pots of bliss where everyone felt welcome. We came into physical form in order to evolve to full consciousness but the path was thorny. A tree can only bear fruits if the blossoms that precede them die off first. To create a new world it was necessary for us to become a non-resonant and destructive human race first, one capable of destroying the old world. Moving the entire human race and its 3-D planet into the high frequencies of the fourth and fifth dimensions takes an enormous shift of energies. There has been much pain inflicted on Earth, upon her species, and upon humanity by humanity. All those memories need to be erased and let go of in order for the new Earth to become a place of love and purity. We are collectively and individually erasing that memory right now.

Ending All Division on Earth

The memories of injustice and disharmony are becoming more vivid to us now than they ever were before. Some people cannot help but publicly point out the wrong done by others. They believe that addressing the problems that still trouble mankind through uprisings, demonstrations or anti-this and anti-that groups may force those who are 'responsible' into finding solutions. However, we all are responsible for everything that happens on this planet. The human race, though segregated on the surface, is nevertheless one united human race underneath it all. Mass demonstrations in the former German Democratic Republic succeeded in bringing down the Berlin Wall, but it hasn't been able to create the sense of unity between the two parts that everyone had expected from 'reunification'. The division needs bridging in the hearts

145

of the people. It is no longer good enough to break down walls; we must undo the memories of division within us.

Each human being is responsible for one's self only and not for others. One nation telling another nation that it is violating human rights and should therefore be placed under an international embargo and be isolated like Iraq or Cuba is doing exactly that, violating human rights. It is a sign of great weakness and incompetence on behalf of those who try to 'help others' by creating division among nations or people. Using tactics of unity are far more powerful, but they can only come from a place of unity. And unity begins within every individual. It is no use trying to change others. Problems that seem under control through manipulation tend to reappear somewhere else, but with greater severity than they were before.

The time has come to resolve all thought forms and beliefs of separation and division from everyone's past and from the present. If we don't do this, the quickening energies that are coming into our and the Earth's energy centers will exacerbate these mental and emotional blockages to the point that more and more physical diseases will manifest. Most people who are falling ill at this time are those who have harbored persistent thought-forms and beliefs that support division, confrontation, competitiveness, and/or attachment to wealth, land, or past achievements.[3] The faster and higher the Earth is raising her vibration towards lesser and lesser density, the more rapidly will those who still resist the oneness of all life become diseased or face other survival issues. If they are still unable or unwilling to take responsibility for their lives and physical bodies, they are likely to die from diseases, accidents, or other 'unnatural' causes. This is what is happening all over the world, especially in the Middle East, Asia, Africa, and South America.

The new world can only be born after the old world is released. The old world exists as memories from the past. If we cannot forgive those who have caused a holocaust, a nuclear explosion, or a Gulf War, we cannot move on to the 'promised land'. We will have to play out our separation issues elsewhere, for this Earth will be one of unity only. Our choice now is between duality and unity. If we choose unity, we must know everything about the nature of duality. This has been our story on planet Earth. Although this story is ending now, it may help to learn why it really happened so that we can accept and release it with joy and understanding.

---

[3] To better understand the connection between mind, body and spirit, you may refer to the book *It's Time to Come Alive!* by the author.

How It All Began

Our first experiences on the Earth plane were ones of great harmony and happiness. The dualities of life had very little impact on us and we enjoyed our paradise out of respect for all life forms. The first race that inhabited the Earth had such an intimate connection with the kingdoms of nature, the animals, plants, water, mountains, the air, and planets, etc. that there was practically no fear and therefore no conflict among them. There were no rebellious cells or cancers in this giant organism of humanity. There was no one who attacked, so no one needed to defend himself or hide. But the longer we dwelled on the Earth plane, our sense of oneness became gradually overshadowed by the opposites that give rise to the physical appearance and diverse nature of the world.

Constantly being in a very dense physical environment, we began to 'discover' greater and greater differences between our feminine and masculine nature, between us and the stars, the animals, the land, and our God Source. These differences, which at first weren't challenging our sense of Oneness with the All, eventually became so dominating in our awareness that we began to feel an emotion that arose from the perception of separateness - the emotion of fear. We learned to distance ourselves from the world and even to fear everything and everyone we believed was too different from us. So out of fear we created our own enemies, beasts that started attacking us, natural disasters that destroyed our crops, people who robbed us of our livelihood, and the entire world drama up to this very day. Out of fear, we sought power, but instead we became subjected to the dominance of others who were more powerful. We looked for ways to enrich ourselves, motivated by greed, but felt poor despite the riches we had amassed. We criticized and subjugated others and then found we could not trust them anymore. Out of guilt for having 'sinned', we even created a 'God of Punishment', one who judged us from Heaven, who expelled us from paradise and threw us into the emotional turmoil of polarity existence.

The journey through the opposing values of life, though, was a necessary step towards the integration of our human selves with our Divine Source selves. This binding back to the Source (*religere*, Latin) became part of life and formed what we know today as religious beliefs. These religions became our crutches, without which we had no way of knowing which way to go. Other than during times of crisis, religions now attract fewer followers than ever before. This is not because we are becoming less spiritual but because we are finding our God-Source from within. We are discovering that the kingdom of God lies within, something that Jesus taught over 2,000 years ago. We are beginning to realize that we can have a direct link with Spirit and need no textbooks, churches or doctrines to tell us how to live. When Jesus taught that everyone would be better off to *first* seek the kingdom of God, he emphasized that all we need is to *be*, to be like the children. There is no need to beg or pray for anything else, for it will come to us without effort. *Being* is our most natural state, it is who we are, and we are one with God. Praying to God has kept us away from being one with Him/Her/It.

Tap Your Eternal Memory Bank

During our journey through the previously uncharted territory of life duality, we began to think and act based on being separate from Spirit, from the members of our soul family, and from our surroundings. We learned to love things and reject them, to accumulate wealth and to lose it, to appreciate life and to destroy it, to use wisdom to allow and to use force to control. Every experience we have ever had throughout our many lifetimes, both past and future ones, is a living record that is fully available to us at every moment. The collection of these records is the book of life, also known as the 'Akashic Records'. These records are the infinite parallel realities, or time lines, that reoccur at every moment in time. These 'eternal' events exist outside physical 3D reality and are therefore not bound by the illusion of time and space.

David Cousins, a good friend of mine and well known healer and clairvoyant from Wales, not only sees the present day reality of a person, a house, or a place; he can literally see at least dozens of parallel realities that are related to each one. One day while we walked past an old unoccupied building, David was able to describe to me the people who used to live in that house about 50 years ago and what they did there. For him, this isn't just an experience of the past but something that occurs right now. At the same time, without causing a conflict to him, David was able to see the house as it was 100 years ago and the place before they built the house. He saw battles that were fought, crops that were raised, and whatever else happened there, right down through the corridor of the ages. For David, time has lost its surrealistic appearance. To him, time is all time, not otherwise. He is not trapped by the illusion that something starts at some time and ends some time later. For him time has no beginning and no end, it is simply eternal. All events are seamlessly interwoven. At any moment, while in the present he can be at

148

any time in the future or any time in the past, depending on what he chooses to see or be.

On another occasion, we went to a beautiful waterfall in Cyprus. While standing at the edge of one of the pools he saw the different things that had occurred at that place, one of which was the death of a woman who felt so drawn by the energies of the pool that she jumped from the cliff into the water and died. When I later inquired about this, it proved to be true. The same day when we came home, he commented about the many 'unfinished' activities that were happening underneath our neighbor's house. He said that there was an old cemetery there with many trapped souls who begged him to help them move on. When I asked the neighbors about the cemetery, it was again, confirmed to be accurate.

My friend has unlimited access to the Akashic records of anyone or any place. It is as if he can see an entire movie at once, not just one frame at a time but the entire sequence of pictures, whereas most of us can only see one picture at a time. In 'normal' life, we take one picture after another, and give each one a place in time. We call this our past: "I was born in...when I was 20 years old I trained as ... then at age 25 I moved to... I got married when I was 32, and now I live in..."

In traditional record keeping, we completely miss out on what we did before we were born, and we usually don't remember our previous lifetimes either. If we had access to the entire record of time, we would eventually go back to the memory of the Big Bang of the universe. Then we would want to know what was before the Big Bang. At this point, we would simply lose our concept of linear time. We would be where we always were but didn't know consciously - in the eternal moment of no time, where the memories of all the possible pasts and all the possible futures are experienced as one time. There would be no more limits imposed by time or space, and the conscious mind would have access to infinite possibilities.

The reason why each soul keeps a memory bank of every moment in life is quite simple. The Akashic Records serve as a giant supercomputer, which organizes life in such a way that none of the words we utter, none of the people we meet, none of the numerous events in our lives, none of the 'accidents' that happen to us, are misaligned with our ultimate purpose. Nothing happens by accident since nothing can escape the law of cause and effect. If some effect happens to me, either 'good' or 'bad', it is because I have created a cause for it, some time or lifetime ago. Everything is available to us at all times and each little step, regardless of whether it is a happy or painful one, is geared towards taking us where we belong - to be masters of time and space instead of their slaves.

149

Collectively we are now moving into the no time zone. More and more people experience time as 'flying' or 'running out'. In fact, there is less time in a day than there used to be even two years ago. Instead of having 24 hours in a day, there are now less than 20 hours at our disposal. What used to be one hour long now feels more like 45-50 minutes. This gives us the nagging sensation of having less and less time. The speeding up of time is a precursor of the imminent dimensional shift the Earth and her inhabitants are about to go through. In order for the shift to occur, time is collapsing to create a new dimensional space. Likewise, space, as we know it, is collapsing to create a new dimensional time. Until recently, time and space on Earth have formed a relationship that allowed us to perceive duality and to experience past, present and future as apparently separate things. The collapse of time and space means that the dimensions can finally interface. This in turn will allow us to live more and more in the present moment. The *now* will be our permanent playground, for it will trigger the DNA to sustain physical life for as long as we desire. But the genetic shift can only occur if we have fully experienced duality (as created by the illusion or appearance of time and space).

Thank God for Duality

Duality is a peculiar concept. Although it is at the root of all the suffering that has ever occurred in the world, duality's illusionary essence permits us to create and explore our own free will. Without free will, we would not be able to choose a greater oneness than we had ever known before. The same free will that propelled us to choose such pairs of opposites as joy and sadness, fear and love, right and wrong, is the same free will that gives us the opportunity to step into the oneness of our essential self. This time, however, the oneness is an enriched oneness. The wholeness is more than the collection of its parts. To achieve such wholeness we had to know each of the parts first, we had to learn everything about separation. We learned that being a king, a president, or leader of a country or community didn't really make us powerful because we had to give it all up again, even if we only came to this realization at the time of physical death. We also learned that being a beggar in the street didn't *really* mean we were less worthy than being a rich merchant or a king, yet for some time we needed to experience it this way. The law of karma is also the law of 'history repeating itself'. It taught us that if we forcefully take from others what isn't ours, we are given the choice to undo this act in a future, similar situation, by giving something instead of taking it.

The Akashic records make certain that no lesson, once learned, need be repeated. Opportunities keep presenting themselves again and again until we have finally balanced them. Then we can step into another situation and pull that into the oneness that we are. Gradually we overcome our slavery to the world of duality and enter the joyful knowledge that we are powerful creators, not passive recipients who have no other choice but to take whatever comes our way. Once all our hidden, unresolved agendas have surfaced and we have recognized them as our personal guideposts to help us achieve integration and wholeness, we then truly represent what the universe does so eloquently - that is, being in unity with all of diversity. The verse of uni-ty tells the song of dual-ity, the all-ity of two.

To feel and know *what* we are one with, is entirely different than just *being* one, the condition we were in before we started our journey into separation. There is a difference between coming back home after having traveled the world and being home without ever having gone out and experienced the world. A pregnant woman and the fetus she is carrying share the same heartbeat and live from the same blood. They are practically one with each other, sharing the same body and the same breath. During the birth process, however, this oneness splits and the process of separating the one life into two lives also becomes a process of creating a new kind of oneness. The oneness that a mother and her baby share during the pregnancy is certainly rewarding, but it is not enough for either of the two. The new oneness that arises from their painful separation during and after the birthing process can be many times more blissful and enriching for both of them. The experience of growing together in love and joy creates a more powerful wholeness than it was before. When reading the word *love* backward it becomes *evol*, which stands for evolution. Love, which is the uniting force of creation, grows when we evolve. We evolve when we delve into the division, the separation that makes up duality and then discover the bridge that connects all opposites and harmonizes all differences. That bridge is love. Once that bridge is created, evolution takes place. Love and evolution occur simultaneously.

Evolution also encompasses the destruction of something old so that something new can emerge. In the example of the mother giving birth to her baby, she needs to discard her placenta, which at one moment is so absolutely vital for the baby's life and the next moment isn't. In time, the atoms that make up the placenta disassociate from one another and reassemble into another form, such as soil, food, air, or perhaps even another human being. New life, which is one of the purposes of evolution, is only possible because of the destruction of the old. Both are needed. We have all the possible opposites within us that we could ever experience outside us. One sets the tone of the creative force, the other the tone of the destructive force. While living in duality consciousness we tend to exhibit one mode over the other, and we move into a state of imbalance where we consider one thing, situation or person to be 'better' than another. Being divided in consciousness it is impossible to see opposing values as equally important and valuable. One thing must be worse or better than another. This inner need to make choices of preference is what lies at the root of judgment.

Judgment - A Flaw in Perception

The best way to describe our obsession for preferences in life is perhaps through a simple but enlightening story from the ancient teachings of the Vedas. This is how it goes.

Once upon a time, there was a water bearer who lived in a small village in India. He had two large pots; they hung on each end of a pole, which he carried across his neck. Everyday he went along a lengthy path from his master's house to a small stream and filled up the pots with water. One of the pots, though, had a crack in it, while the other pot was perfect. Upon his return to the house the perfect pot delivered a full portion of water but the cracked pot arrived only half full.

This went on for two years. Each day the water bearer delivered only one and a half pots of water to his master's house. Of course, the perfect pot was mightily proud of itself for all the good work it had done, fulfilling the purpose for which it was made. However, the poor cracked pot was ashamed of its own imperfection, and miserable that it was only able to accomplish half of what it had been made to do.

After two years of what it perceived to be a bitter failure, the cracked pot finally found the courage to speak to the water bearer one day by the stream. "I am very ashamed of myself, and I wish to apologize to you."

"Why?" asked the bearer. "What reason do you have to be ashamed?"

In a dismal tone the pot said, "For these past two years, I have only been able to deliver half my load because this crack in my side causes water to leak out all the way back to your master's house. You are working so hard carrying this load but because of my flaw you are not getting full value from your efforts." The water bearer, who knew much about life, felt sorry for the old cracked pot, and in his compassion he

152

said, "As we return to the master's house, I want you to notice the beautiful flowers along the path."

Indeed, as they went up the hill, the old cracked pot took notice of the beautiful flowers on the side of the path, and this relieved some of its anguish. But at the end of the trail, it felt guilty and bad because it had leaked out half its load, and so again it apologized to the bearer for being a pot not good enough for the job. The bearer said to the pot, "Did you notice that there were flowers only on your side of the path, but not on the other pot's side? That is because I have always known about your flaw, and I took advantage of it. I planted flower seeds on your side of the path, and every day while we walked back from the stream, you have watered them. For two years now, I have been able to pick these beautiful flowers to decorate my master's table. Without you being just the way you are, he would not have this beauty to grace his house."

While living in this world we are all 'cracked pots'. We may have qualities that others, and we, could perceive as flaws but this is only a flaw in perception. What I may think is an imperfection in me may just turn out to be a wonderful gift that enriches other people's lives. A flower needs the sun, water, soil, and air to grow. It doesn't feel incomplete because it cannot provide all these by itself. It thrives in the knowledge that it is one with all the elements and that they are there to support and nourish it. We only feel flawed and incomplete because we create a wall of separation between our surroundings and ourselves. We deprive ourselves of the nourishment, the abundance, and the happiness that is always there for us to enjoy. We have the capacity to love and appreciate all the different people who live on this Earth, yet we deny ourselves this because, like the cracked pot, we believe we don't have it. Yet even cracks can be a blessing.

Seeing the Perfection in Every Relationship

Since it is often very difficult to detect our own cracks or hidden agendas, our Higher Selves arrange for us to meet others who hold up mirrors so that we have a better chance of experiencing and understanding what isn't complete within us yet. Our friends and foes are all willing to play their respective roles for our benefit. We learn that we are all the things that we don't like in others, but we also discover that we are all the things we like in others. Both are challenging because they require acceptance on our part. How many times do we feel we are not worthy to receive, not beautiful enough to please, not intelligent enough to be of use, or not skilled or competent enough to make a difference?

153

When we meet people who personify all those qualities that we deny we have, we may feel very attracted to them. We may love those qualities so much in the other person that we want to experience them all the time. We feel at a loss if they are not there, as if part of us was missing.

Many new relationships are formed on this basis. You may have had at least one such experience. Whatever you feel you do not have in yourself, you desire to get from another. However, as soon as your friend or partner stops holding up the mirror that reflects this expectation or need, the love bond seems to dwindle and the relationship begins to fade. If it is a romantic relationship, you may feel that the other person has changed so much you no longer feel the same excitement and joy you did before. You may decide that you can no longer stay with him/her.

On the other hand, a fading romance might reveal a true, lasting love that remained hidden until then but now has the chance to blossom and grow. Once expectations of how the other person is 'supposed' to be, begin dwindling away, our hidden agendas that had been hidden re transmute into pearls of wisdom. They reveal our true identity. We begin to love the oneness we are and the oneness we see in the other; we begin to know from within that my oneness is also your oneness, and whatever you or I do or say does not disturb, stop or destroy this bond of pure love. There are no strings attached to this love, and no expectations that need fulfilling because we recognize that whatever the other represents to us is also in us. In fact, you are only able to resonate with these special qualities because you have them in yourself. By not fulfilling your expectations, your partner or friend helps you to become more complete. You no longer have this desperate need for someone else to 'make' you feel this way.

This kind of independence or self-sufficiency forms the basis of a relationship bonded by unconditional love. (Unconditional love is actually a redundant phrase. There is no conditional love because a condition arises out of fear, not love.) This is not to say that romantic relationships or faded relationships are not based on unconditional love; in reality they are, but this is not apparent. Some relationships are only formed to clear some of the heavier, hidden agendas in our life and they may not last very long. Nevertheless, they occur because of a prior agreement the Higher Selves have made with each other to move forward in greater learning and integration. This agreement is made out of unconditional love for each other. One offers to be a mirror for the other, and vice versa. The mirror reflects all the 'good' and the 'bad' personality features one is able to project to that person. Each exchange, verbal, physical or otherwise is yet another opportunity for both sides to become a little more aware of withholding these good and bad things from ourselves. You dislike in your partner only what you do not like in yourself. This may be hard to grasp, but with a little self-honesty, we conclude that there is no other reason to be *anti anything* other than our own inability for accepting our undisclosed weaknesses.

Conversely, your partner may be fascinated or turned on by certain personality features of yours, because they represent something that they haven't yet been able to find within. You may think nothing of these qualities that they so much adore in you. The infatuation that occurs on both sides at the beginning of a romantic relationship must subside at some stage, if unconditional love is to take over.

You Only Own What You Love

Seeing the high divorce rates all over the world at this time in human history, shows that we are heavily involved in clearing our hidden agendas from this life and past lives with one another. We seem to be in a great hurry to do that and having only one major relationship in life may not satisfy this need. Each new relationship allows us to tap into more of our unresolved separation issues. After a period of being in love with all those beautiful qualities that a new friend or partner represents, we may start feeling uncomfortable with them. Why? Because we compare ourselves with them and conclude that we are not like them, although we would love to be this way. Or, we are afraid of losing the relationship and try to hold on to it, to such an extent that we make all sorts of concessions or sacrifices to ensure being loved. Admiration for another may turn into envy, resentment or jealously and, in extreme cases, feelings of hate.

Comparing ourselves with those we love can also manifest as severe self-judgment and depression. Although this seems to be negative and undesirable, it directs our attention inward and prepares the way for filling the underlying unworthiness with the very same qualities we first admired and then rejected in the other.

In time, we learn that we own everything that we love. It is not important whether I know how to play a concert piano or paint beautiful pictures. The very act of appreciating something is being it. By contrast, comparison causes a division that separates me from other people and the environment. Once there is enough self-acceptance, we begin to expand our individual boundaries and include others and the world as our extended self and find the same joy they feel when they are expressing their uniqueness to us. Thus, 'uniqueness' becomes a means of uniting

155

rather than separating people. The role reversal is significant. Someone else's joy is your joy if you have joy in your heart. Someone's love can become your love if love is already there in you. Likewise, someone else's pain can be your pain if you perceive pain in your heart. Accepting the contrasting attributes of life as being part of our perception of duality makes us whole. Rejecting joy, love or pain makes us feel isolated, incomplete, and separate from the world.

Our hidden agendas are our true gifts in life, although they seem so far from being rewarding. Having 'come' from the omnipresent source of oneness and getting 'lost' in the extremely dense and bewildering diversity of 3D reality has not been easy for us, to say the least. And for most of us, the current phase in our journey of discovering the oneness of diversity is the most challenging one of all. In order to create this new world of oneness of diversity (5D reality), which will have no limits to our creativity, we are compelled to face every hidden agenda that is still stored as 'unbalanced' in our Akashic Records. Everything that binds us to the illusion of duality must go. It is as if we are going back in time, although in truth we are simply switching our attention to our parallel realities (lives), searching for any unattended and thus unbalanced experiences that have caused us fear and still do so now.

Ending All Fear

We are at the threshold of a new era where being influenced by duality is no longer useful or necessary. Our next stage in the evolution of human consciousness will take us beyond all limitations of time and space. The many boundaries and difficulties that mankind is currently experiencing have mostly to do with accepting and clearing the remnants of the 'old' duality that have brought us to this point of global transformation. Moreover, it is coming to us now all at once. We are dealing with all kinds of fears, restlessness, doubt, guilt, anger, hostility, and self-destructive tendencies. As they come up, triggered by perfectly timed circumstances and situations, we are receiving the opportunity to bring forward all their opposite counterparts. Simply by becoming aware, and accepting what *is,* the unbalanced issues become balanced. By allowing what *is* and not doubting that it is good, we begin to feel safe inside and develop the aspects of lovingness, intuition, calmness, affection, and self-appreciation.

The opposing parts of duality alternate or oscillate back and forth with such speed now that we may feel confused over what is happening to us. Because the changes occur so quickly, there is not even time to

156

analyze what is going on. Parts of left-side brains dealing with intellectual analysis are currently being demobilized, which compels us to deal with all that on the level of emotions. Our right brain, which processes our emotional experiences, is more active than ever. Indeed, there is no other way to consciously enter the world of the soul than through the window of emotions. The mother of what we call 'negative' emotions is fear. It is the emotion of separation. Before we can transcend separation and reunite with our Source, we may need to experience, and master, fear.

Feeling the anguish of fear and going through it from the beginning to the end, which is what acceptance means, is one of the quickest ways to free ourselves from its clutches. Since the illusion *fear* is merely caused by 'not trusting' and 'not knowing', it disappears when we allow those things that we don't trust or know to come into our conscious experience. This gives us the vantage point of being both involved and uninvolved. We feel the emotion but it no longer grips us. Although life may not have changed on the surface, our perception of it is different. Now negative things make as much sense as positive things.

The giant jigsaw puzzle of life, with all its innumerable, small and great, right and wrong, good and bad events gathered during all lifetimes, is about to be completed. Once the last piece is placed into the picture, we will have no more fear, because every part of the puzzle, regardless of the emotion it embodies, will have proven its value and purpose of existence. Each one has been essential for creating the picture of timeless living. To be free of judgments we had to experience every major facet of judging and being judged. Going through the dualities of life helps us to transcend them altogether. We stand at the edge of infinite freedom where we will not even be able to conceive of being limited in our creative powers. This is the promise of our time.

The Mirage of 'Finding' Happiness

Every person will eventually conclude that happiness is not something that can be found. Whatever one finds cannot be permanent and therefore isn't real or lasting. It cannot be possessed either. If happiness has a beginning, it is destined to end again. Unless you *are* happiness, looking for it remains fruitless. All you are doing is chasing a ghost of memory; you wish to bring back to life those moments from your past that you so cherished and which made you feel so good inside. These times of happiness may be defined and even exaggerated through times of upset and sorrow. In other words, we are more likely to seek

157

happiness if we experience sadness or feel unhappy. This kind of happiness, however, is sustainable by separation consciousness.

Such expressed feelings as "You make me so happy" or "I am so happy in this place" imply that without 'you' or without 'this place' I cannot have the same happiness. And because you and this place may not always be there for me, my happiness stands on shaky ground. The very words "I am happy" show the relationship of the 'I' to a quality that is heavily influenced by its counterpart: sadness, or even depression. Identifying with anything different than my 'I AM' puts me automatically under the spell of duality. It is therefore not possible to find true and lasting happiness in life through anything or anyone else other than through the relationship with yourself. One popular song suggests "The greatest love of all is the one I have found in me." Once we stop chasing it outside us, we find that we *are* love. It is our nature. And nothing that we *are* can ever be taken away from us. *Being love* means also being independent, non-discriminating (i.e. blind to duality), without strings attached, eternal and unshakable.

Whatever we feel we cannot get from within ourselves, we seek to obtain from outside. We are doing this so that we experience temporary happiness coupled with sadness and thereby understand the illusion of separation and duality. The hunger for outer happiness is ego-based, controlled by the awareness of our body, which seeks gratification of its senses. There can be no permanent satisfaction from this because the receiver of love and happiness, which in this case is the human ego, is a highly changeable entity itself. Eternal love and happiness, however, cannot be found; they are intrinsic to the essential nature of one's never-changing Self. Every thought we have and everything we do in life is the result of our incessant drive for happiness. We create desire after desire to take us through the whole range of duality until we reach the end of the road and stop searching for happiness. When we stop looking for happiness, the ego becomes married with the Higher Self and the world of separation turns into a world of unity.

Love versus Happiness

The force of love for oneself is the greatest force we have and it always succeeds. When something goes 'wrong' in life, we only consider it wrong because we do not see the larger picture of things. When something goes 'wrong', we actually get a little closer to stepping outside the cycles of duality. We are gradually breaking through the mistaken belief there is anything out there we need. Being eternally one with the same Source that constantly creates and recreates this universe, we have everything that we could possibly need inside us. All that we so adore in others, we are it, too, although we have chosen not to express it outwardly because this may not be necessary or be to our advantage. It would be a boring world if everyone were a Mozart, a Michelangelo, an Einstein or a Mother Teresa.

When we search for happiness outside, we practically deny that we have it inside. Looking for happiness because we are not happy is a major source of conflict. We become addicted to the things and people that can fill this void. If they do, we feel happiness for a while, until it is eventually replaced by a bigger void. We call filling the void, love. Yet true love never wants anything, it just is and shares itself. By 'being' love, we no longer desire happiness. Love unites opposites; desiring happiness creates separation. Both, though, have their value. Relationships that exist only because two people feel that they need each other to be happy are bound to end in separation. They feel terrible if apart and great if together. Being addicted or attached to one another is only a small part of what we are here to learn. When the addiction ends, we no longer look to borrow happiness from others.

We base new relationships on the love and respect that we have for ourselves. The more fulfilled we are within, the more beautiful and rewarding our relationships will be. Two happy people bring much more joy to a relationship than if only one is happy. The cup of love each one carries in their heart keeps overflowing when together, yet always remains full when apart. The beauty of all this lies in the fact that each one of us is perfectly capable of creating a life in constant love. A mechanism in us determines whether what we desire comes true or not. I call it the 'art of desiring'.

She speaks, but hears not the words of others. She judges, yet has no concept of the word, or the deed. She sees with eyes wide open, yet the winds of change continually obscure her vision.

She is timeless, ephemeral, loving. She is you.

Lady (Princess) Diana
Channeled on April 14, 2001

Chapter Nine

Resolving the Abundance Issue

We are will of the wisps fluttering here and there, abundant in our effervescent love, swaying to and fro with palm fronds and the fig leaves of delight. We are attuned with merrymaking of the universe, for this is our natural instinct, the intuitive veins which run deeply, like riverbeds in our heart spring. We evermore ask for your hand in marriage of the minds. May we reap the joys and plentiful good nature that come with this united blessing.

We are man and woman, father, mother and child, all blessedly entwined in the same ball of love knots. We are and can survive this mighty time of insecurity and doubt for there is plenty to keep us in abundant high spirits and to cater to our heart's desires when it appears that the setting sun will stream no more of its goodness upon our eyelids. May the dew in the glistening morning's light retell its tale of yonder nature, for each tear drop upon the petals of mother nature has cascaded down this waterfall of life before, never ending, just beginning its journey through time.

It is unsettling to consider that time has neither a beginning nor an ending but this is as it should be, an enigma for the mind's eye to toy with. May you never doubt the genius that went into this creation, for it was born out of love, as were we.

The revived soul of Elizabeth Barrett Browning
Channeled on January 7, 2001

When Desires Just Remain Dreams

Have you ever wondered why most of our desires don't become fulfilled? The answer can be found by looking at the way we desire things, the *intention* that drives the desires. Whenever you wish for something that you do not possess, the desire to have it derives from dissatisfaction with the current situation. Desires are linked to what you need or want or haven't got and are therefore future oriented. They take your attention away from the present moment, which naturally brings up fear and insecurity. Unwilling to accept what each moment presents to you, the mind pursues change in order to overcome the fear. So the motivation to have something better than what you have now, such as a new car, a faster computer or a pay raise, is really based on not being happy with the old car, the slower computer or the current salary.

The desire to be or have something more in life stands on very shaky ground, the ground of perceiving *lack*. In addition, lack attracts more lack, according to the law 'Like Attracts Like'. "I don't like this house anymore, so I want a better one" is a typical example of how a dislike becomes the motivating force behind desire. As a result, we are confronted with exactly the lack we are trying to avoid or run away from. The desire may even become fulfilled but the frustration of not being happy with the old house simply is transferred to the new house. The

162

lack is still there, but it isn't outside; it exists within. Soon the new house isn't good enough either, and the cycle repeats itself over and over again. If the desire doesn't come true, we may become frustrated and angry. We may even blame God, other people or circumstances for not letting us have what we want.

In reality, though, there is no outer force that has the power to stand in our way and block the fulfillment of our desires. The only force there is, is our own. Each one of us is a master of creation, whether we know it or not. We relentlessly propel each thought into the world and it cannot be stopped by anything, not even by God. A thought of lack will create lack and a thought of abundance will create abundance. This, you might say, would make it very easy then to have everything we want in life. All we would be required to do is change our thoughts and practice some positive thinking. Not quite so!

Thoughts are much more complex than words written on a piece of paper. No thought can be devoid of feeling, intention and emotion. Before a thought can develop and assume its meaning, we must *intend* it. Moreover, before we can intend something we must have *a subtle feeling* about what it is we want to express or desire. At the same time, the body creates a specific response to this subtle impulse of feeling, which is what we term 'emotion'. All these aspects of a thought are intertwined with every thought we have and those we had a minute ago, or yesterday, last year and all previous lifetimes. For example, if I decided today to climb Mount Everest, I first have to have a subtle feeling that I can do this, based on the knowledge that I have climbed big mountains before, during this or other lives. Then I must intend it, which will eventually get me to join a team, go there, and start climbing. The emotions that this thought-impulse must generate in the body, through the mind body connection,[4] must be ones of excitement, joy, and enthusiasm; otherwise, the body won't cooperate in the desired endeavor.

The bottom line is that all these various aspects of a thought, decision or desire must be supportive of and in alignment with one another; otherwise nothing will come of them. A feeling of doubt that may arise when I think about climbing the mountain can be sufficiently powerful to sabotage my desire. The mere thought of climbing Mount Everest may prompt my adrenal glands to pump powerful doses of the stress hormones cortisol and adrenaline into my bloodstream, causing

---

[4] The mind body connection is explained in detail in the author's book *It's Time to Come Alive!*

sensations of panic and anxiety. Such emotions are hard to ignore when you plan to go on an adventure that entails a life-endangering risk.

None of the above aspects of a thought can be changed through conscious efforts, with the exception of the content or meaning of the thought. Even if you change the *meaning* of the thought "I hate snakes" to "I love snakes", the *emotion* of fear of, or apathy to, snakes remains the same unless the underlying feeling that causes you to hate them vanishes, too. Perhaps a snake bit you in this or a past life, which may leave you with the fearful anticipation of suffering a snake bite in the future.

Each time the word 'snake' comes up in your mind, it reactivates this cellular memory, along with the corresponding feelings and emotions. There is a reason why this emotion pops up repeatedly during conversations or trips to tropical places, or in symbolic form during dreams. The fear of snakes, which is a block that for the time being prevents you from being in your full power, seeks the opportunity to be balanced by a love for snakes. Unless we are able to love and respect everything that exists, there will always be something that seems to attack or dislike us. In addition, there will be this deep inner longing for something else in life, something that we can never quite reach. Once in unity consciousness, the need for desiring stops altogether because everything is provided automatically. This state of awareness already *is* everything; hence, there is no lack and therefore no desire to fill it with something else. Roadblocks on the path of fulfilling desires exist only in duality consciousness. These roadblocks are our own creation. Most of them are rooted in a misaligned ability of graceful acceptance. In other words, how you perceive yourself determines how much abundance comes into your life.

Unlearning the Old Ways of Desiring

Since having desires belongs to the realm of duality, they are subject to the laws of duality. It is impossible to receive full satisfaction and enjoyment from trying to fulfill one's desires if they are based on lack. Robert H. Schuller once wisely said, "The only place where your dream becomes impossible is in your own thinking." In most cases, nothing ever happens with our dreams and desires because the awareness or thought of lack only creates more lack. Letting go of them or suppressing them is equally frustrating, for this would mean emotional suicide. Without desire, we simply would stop growing in life. Judging your desires means you are judging yourself. Being afraid of your own desires means you fear yourself. You may even feel guilty to have everything you want and need because deep within you feel you do not deserve it. In this mode of self-rejection, you are unable to receive and your desires remain unfulfilled.

There is a much more satisfying way to deal with your desires. It is the willing acceptance of whatever comes your way in life, which keeps the flow of fulfillment going. So if you are looking for more abundance in life, start by accepting your present situation, this moment of not having enough abundance, and bless it. Lack of abundance is an essential, although temporary, part of your toolbox to construct a marvelous life of total abundance for yourself and others.

There is only a minor difference between total lack and complete fullness. The two are so closely bonded that when one is present, the other isn't far away. By accepting lack in the same way you would welcome abundance into your life, you will come to appreciate its real role and value for you. This not only takes away the stigma of negativity, fear and pain but also delivers its counterpart - abundance - right to your doorstep. It is certainly not your destiny to live with constant fear of lack, emptiness or deprivation in your life. So to help you transmute this fear, your Higher Self is surely guiding you to have exactly those 'negative' experiences (of missing out on abundance). Fear is the darkroom where negatives are developed. They help you understand the role they play for you and why you draw them toward you. Remember: you are the creator of all your life's situations and you do this for good reasons only.

Wanting to have abundance in your life simply because you feel you have nothing or you wish to rid yourself of poverty *only manifests more lack*. Your belief in lack actually determines your experience of abundance. No matter how hard you try to satisfy your hunger for abundance, it will not bear the fruit of satisfaction and happiness; instead, it will take you to a point of resignation and hopelessness. This inner void may be exactly the turning point you need in order to stand back and allow life's events to unfold. When you resign yourself to "Oh, it doesn't matter anymore", you are actually beginning to accept your current situation. At that moment, as your attention curves back from wanting greater abundance in the future or from the agony of not having had enough of it in the past, you become locked into the present. This is the magical moment of 'no-time' where all miracles take place. It is the moment where you are at your most powerful, where you *are* abundance. Everything you could ever want is available in the present moment. By contrast, all the things that you don't want in your life such as bad luck, illness, fatigue, pessimism, etc. result from not being in the present moment.

During the letting go of all expectations, you are left with nothing, i.e. with nothing but your Self. You can only fill a cup, which is empty and sometimes you need to empty a cup first before you can taste a new, fresh beverage. Then both the emptying and the filling of the cup serve the same purpose - preparing you for a new experience of taste. Thoughts or desires that have no strings attached to them (that are neither projected into the future nor are limited by past memories), naturally revert to the present moment. They just are. Those thoughts and desires are beyond the influence of duality; they are one with the Self and thus cannot remain unfulfilled.

How to Choose Abundance

Life organizes itself in such a way that it brings us to crossroads of major change. The old road we used to drive may have served us well in the past, but when we decide to head for a new destination, we may need to take a new road. Of course, there are options. Once we have decided we want abundance in every area, the universe takes care of the details. However, the manifestation of abundance can only occur if we *are* what we want. This makes abundance dependent on the area of self-worth. Feeling blessed by *whatever* we have and are *is* that consciousness of abundance, which opens up the gates of infinite possibilities. Feeling unloved, unworthy, or lonely, on the other hand sets us up for being a victim of poverty and lack.

Every situation in life prompts us to choose between abundance and lack of abundance. The real choice, though, occurs within. How do I see myself at each new moment? Do I consider myself blessed, even if I do not possess anything, or do I doubt my worthiness despite having everything I could possibly want? In other words, the abundance issue would not come up if I knew my essential Self. There are no limitations to energies, regarding wealth or health, other than self-worth issues. There is no force, no government, no economic system, no gods, no devils, etc. that impose limitations on us in any form; we create these ourselves. It is our task, therefore, to undo and release the self-imposed myth of limitations and allow abundance to flow freely and without restriction.

True abundance is far too complex for our human mind to figure out. To open ourselves to the abundance of the universe we must employ the God force itself. God's mind, which is the ever-present consciousness of

166

our Highest Self, cannot fit into the limited frame of the ego mind. Our ego mind chooses the field duality to form the impulses of a desire, whereas our God mind relies on the 'Oneness of the All' to bring that desire to fruition. Therefore, to organize all the necessary details that are involved in the fulfillment of a desire, sprung from the lips of the ego, we have to rely on our Higher Selves. These often very complex arrangements normally escape the conscious awareness of the limited ego mind. While we are still entangled in the jungle of duality we have a very hard time understanding that becoming empty before we can become full is part of the Divine plan of awakening us to our essential nature - which is abundance in every conceivable way.

Each one of us *is* infinite abundance by nature, but our ego mind doesn't have a conscious knowing of this, so we devise all sorts of methods to try to find it. These methods are bound to fail eventually because none of them reveals 'Who We Are'; they merely show what we identify with. However, and this is equally important, they do show us what we are not. The immense power of the President of the United States is insignificant to the tiny power of a deadly virus, should it strike against him. What is the wealth of a Bill Gates worth if it cannot prevent a massive earthquake from taking away his family? Having the influence of a pope is meaningless if he cannot love himself. None of the worldly powers compare with what we truly are.

Each one of us is *everything* that exists. To revert to our true power, wealth and influence we must learn to bring our ego-mind into alignment with our cosmic mind. For this to happen, a president may need to resign, a Bill Gates may have to give away his wealth, and a pope may need to concede that he isn't so 'holy' after all. This emptying of the cup of our ego-mind surrenders it to the *real* power, wealth and influence that we are. This makes it easier to understand why 'bad' things happen to us.

Why 'Bad' Things Happen To You

Your wallet or car may be stolen *because* you asked for true abundance in life. Your home might burn down *because* you are terrified at the thought of being homeless. A lifelong partner whom you have given all our trust and love for so many years may suddenly decide to leave you *because* you feel life would become so empty and useless without them. What follows the *'because'* in each of these situations highlights a particular type of fear that remains hidden until you lose what you have, a fear that forms the basis of separating yourself from the stream of life. Having a full wallet, an expensive car, a comfortable

167

home, and a reliable, trustworthy partner are all wonderful and well-deserved things as long as we can exist without these just as well. If we believe we cannot, then it isn't in our best interest to have them anyway.

We have been living in this dream world that (successfully) tried to convince us we were worth something only if we owned something else, such as a good name, a successful career, a house, a car, and/or a family. We have come to a point in human history where we measure or value people by how much money, power and influence they have. The media and entertainment industry display and promote the image that those people who do not have these or similar things in their possession are failures, poverty-stricken, and even outcasts of society. Yet however far the truth has been twisted, even the rich and famous, the powerful and admired members of society face the same challenges in life; they only truly own what they are able to let go of. So life's lessons include the acquisition of all these things and, if need be, also their loss.

Some of the most admired and successful movie stars and singers are facing their demons within; they take recourse to drugs and alcohol, they have life-threatening accidents or suffer from such diseases as Alzheimer's or Parkinson's. It forces all of them to deal with the same old question humans have been asking since the beginning of our time: "Who am I?" And the world may say this: "What a shame, what a waste of talent!" When these events happen, everyone loses something; yet their loss is in fact a gain, not only for those involved but also for the world to see. It is for everyone to learn that a great loss is the beginning of a great gain, and we are given the chance to accept it for what it is.

Loss is not meant as a punishment but as a blessing. Because what we gain by freeing ourselves from the blinding effects of ego-gratification and attachment to the illusion of owning possessions is priceless. The difference lies in being in command of all streams of abundance versus being at the receiving end of a small trickle of abundance. It is our destiny on this Earth plane to end our enslavement to fleeting riches that have no lasting bearing on the quality and evolution of the soul, and to assume mastership of everything we need and want. We are meant to enjoy as much abundance as the universe has to offer but as long as we are attached to it or try to own it, which is poverty consciousness, abundance cannot offer any lasting enjoyment and therefore leaves you empty-handed and empty-hearted. The laws of the universe ensure that only abundance consciousness can manifest abundance. Trying to have abundance because you feel you do not have it in your life just manifests more lack and more emptiness so the most important element of abundance is to realize that there is just as much abundance out there as there is within you. How much abundance you deserve depends on how you value yourself. By being grateful for who you are and what you have, you honor your inner abundance and begin to open the gateways to outer abundance. So dare to love yourself and give yourself the permission to improve the quality of your life!

The Power of Gratitude

Accepting what is at this moment creates a natural feeling of gratitude and recognition that every moment is a precious gift of all possibilities. Although 'accepting what is' sounds so simple and easy, we may have spent numerous lifetimes to experience such a moment of grace just once. Now the world is being prepared to make this moment permanent. We are asked to leave our minds behind because acceptance is a matter of the heart, the entry point to the soul within the body and the seat of our Higher Self.

Life is uncomplicated and simple for the heart but complex and complicated for the mind. The heart honors all our desires, even if they blind us, conceal our spirit self, or cause violence. From the heart's perspective, everything that happens to us and to the world has a favorable reason that is supported by a larger picture. The larger picture, being a puzzle to the mind, is like an open book to the heart. It honors and cherishes all desires, even those that appear evil. Evil desires, should the need for them arise, make us aware of our fears and struggle and may in fact be indispensable for our growth.

Sometimes, to jump forward you may first have to take a few steps back, which may appear to be negative. The heart knows that detours have meaning because it trusts in the perfection of the moment; the mind, however, is the one that raises doubts. The doubting mind has its value too; it helps you clear a path through the jungle of duality until you see the light of Self. *Being grateful for both* is the key to spiritual and material abundance. Thus, being grateful for each desire you have ever had and will ever have, safely leads you through life until you desire a life of oneness. Your desires are your guideposts on the way, each one telling you where you are in your spiritual journey.

At each moment in life we have the choice to accept everything that happens to us, not passively or as a victim would, but with loving anticipation of what we have created for our world and ourselves. Allowing and embracing the moment is assuming the power of co-creation. Jesus once taught those who questioned their own powers: "Is it not written in your law, I said, 'Ye are Gods'?" *John 10:34.* Moreover,

169

on another occasion Jesus said: "Ye are Gods, and all of you are children of the Most High." *Psalms 82:6*. It is time to become aware of our creator roles and enjoy what we create with everyone to share.

With the New Age Movement came a renewed desire for creating abundance in life. The idea spread that to receive abundance one must deserve it, implying that those who don't have abundance don't deserve it. This is however only true on the superficial level. Everyone is deserving of abundance and has always been. Lack of abundance can be just as good a sign of deserving to grow as having it. The difference lies in the kinds of learning that an individual soul has accomplished. Some learn earlier than others that if your attention is on what you don't have you remain stuck there unless you shift your attention on to what you do have. If you look deep enough you will find that there is a lot you can be grateful for. The longer you look, the more treasures begin to reveal themselves to you. Once you are thankful for everything then abundance will flow by itself. And abundance can come in many ways.

Being thankful that you don't have everything that you desire allows you to look forward to something new. If you are grateful that you don't know certain things, you derive great pleasure from learning more about them. Your gratitude for the difficult times in your life gives you the opportunity to grow stronger and wiser. Being thankful for your mistakes helps you to learn valuable lessons. Therefore, if you can find a way to be grateful for your troubles, they inevitably become your blessings.

In truth, human beings do not make mistakes. The saying "to err is human" stems from an incomplete perception of reality. The so-called mistakes are an integral part of the drama of life. Each time you make a supposed mistake, a chain of events is formed which leads you a little closer to the goal you and your Higher Self have set for yourself. It is like a new movie where the audience doesn't know how it ends but the director, the film crew and the scriptwriter do. Your Higher Self is the director and producer of your personal drama in life. Every little detail counts and every mistake made is important in the overall scheme of your life. The movie of life must contain mistakes, controversies and conflicts in order to bring the drama of duality to a closure. When the drama ends, it is going to be a happy ending.

Don't therefore judge yourself for making 'mistakes', instead, be grateful for having made them. Become aware that mistakes are always disguised as opportunities. Also, acknowledge that, like you, other people do not make mistakes either. This removes a great deal of fear from your interactions with others. Everyone on Earth is a Creator God, acting out a specific role that serves the whole. Some are here to create light and love; others are here to create darkness and deception. In the course of evolution, destructive powers are equally important as constructive powers. While gripped by the illusion of duality, one is seen as 'bad' and the other as 'good'. When the veil of illusion is lifted from awareness, former enemies treat one another as the best of friends. We see setbacks as wakeup calls, as timely opportunities for change and growth.

It is very easy to be grateful for the good things in life. But real abundance comes only to those who can also be thankful for the setbacks. Conversely, giving energy to what is not there, such as lack of money or love, or focusing on what doesn't work in your life, is like multiplying '0' with any number. However large that number may be, the result always remains zero. In other words, there is abundance in everything and especially in 'negative' things. 'Getting' that, really comprehending it, fills you with gratitude. Suddenly you realize you have so much for which to be grateful.

By accepting and blessing everything that you do have, you automatically begin to accept what you do not have. This places you instantaneously in the stream of abundance and affluence of every kind. And remember to bless others in their health, their work, and their relationships. Bless them in their abundance, their wealth and possessions, bless them in every conceivable way, on the street, in the stores, or at work. Also bless them in their mistakes and judgments, their aggressions, illnesses and unkindness. This brings a sudden ray of sunlight through the clouds of their sky. This is a direct way to dissolve the consciousness of division and bring to your own life all the wonderful things you wish others to have. Whatever you need to live comfortably and joyfully will land at your doorstep, somehow, someway, some day. When, how, and through whom this comes about doesn't need to be your concern. A president of a country doesn't need to know all the details of how to obtain this or that, they just need to know that what they ask for is in their power to achieve. Once the preconditions for the fulfillment of the desires are met - acceptance and the removal of self-doubt - you will begin to live your dreams.

With this comes the realization that there are no adverse circumstances, ill fate, or even bad luck in life. Being grateful for everything that comes your way also implies that you cannot suffer any disappointments in life. On the other hand, expecting gratitude from others for what you do for them is really 'being ungrateful' and is bound to cause disappointments for you. Therefore, if you do have expectations of others, it is in your best interest to become disappointed by them,

171

otherwise you will keep trying to 'buy' love and attention from others instead of giving these to yourself. Just as the withering of a plant is the result of not watering its roots, not having 'enough' is the consequence of not nurturing oneself. Gratitude is the best form of self-nurturing, of blessing yourself. It is impossible to bless and to judge at the same time.

Such commonly used expressions as "I will always be poor" or "I can never make ends meet" are self-fulfilling prophecies, ever perpetuating themselves until we change the prophecies. We are the creators of our own lives and destinies. What we command must occur. There is no place for independent forces, which randomly pick out the less fortunate and deprive them of the right of equal opportunities. If we decide to experience poverty for a while or even a lifetime then this is our choice. Understand that being born into a family that has no material possessions or enough food for every member is no more coincidental than driving your car from your home to your office. Both are subject to need and want. In reality, none of the choices are harmful.

Abundance doesn't need to be generated; it is always at your fingertips, no matter what the circumstances may be. Yet it needs to flow, like a stream. The flow is only interrupted if you stand in its way. You block the flow by insisting, albeit unconsciously, that you are not worthy of it. The beliefs that uphold the idea of unworthiness are often rooted in the guilt of having deprived others of abundance before, in this life or other lives. You may have even abused your wealth, power, and influence to obtain what you wanted. To balance these karmic distortions you may have chosen an equally extreme situation, one that lies on the other end of the spectrum of duality, offering poverty and deprivation as an opportunity to nourish the qualities of humility and gratitude.

Keep the River Flowing

During my frequent travels to some of the most underdeveloped regions of the world, I noticed repeatedly that some of the poorest of people had the most genuine love for their children, their parents and for each other. Their faces glowed with joy and peacefulness, despite their hard lives of constant struggle and strife. What perhaps astonished me more than anything was that they had a lot of time just to be, as if time didn't exist. By contrast, the rush of modern life in order to get everything a modern person thinks they need to own, has left many without time to even think, reflect, or be quiet. In modern cities, we see far more stressed faces than we do relaxed ones. So I came to the conclusion that true abundance cannot be measured by how many

172

possessions you have, or even how much wealth and power you have accumulated, but *by how good you feel about yourself*, about others, and about the world.

There is no real pressure or stress from the condition of being poor; the pressure only arises when being poor is interpreted as a sign of not being good enough. That is when the river of true abundance stops flowing. Like a river, obstructed in its flow by the wall of a dam, our perception of lack even more assuredly stops the ever-present potential stream of personal abundance from flowing. The pressure that builds up in us, as in the case of the dam, is what we experience as stress and not having enough time to do all the things we think we need to do to keep the abundance flowing. Yet in order to really know and master the flow of abundance, we may first need to fully experience the pressure and anxiety that comes from the feeling of never having enough. There is that inner void, that disconnectedness, which we try to compensate for by filling our lives with pleasures that have no lasting effect, except to further increase our feelings of emptiness. This is how it needs to be. Our acceptance of this feeling of lack, void or emptiness (or whatever words we may choose to describe our dissatisfaction with life), and embracing it for all its worth, is an indispensable step toward allowing more abundance into our lives. This total acceptance completely removes the block that holds up the stream of abundance.

Many of those who were born with a 'silver spoon' in their mouth, and those who have made it to the top by their own means, may need to lose all their possessions and wealth in order to feel what it is like to have nothing at all, and be at the mercy of the government to receive their daily bread. This was one of the main reasons, why the masses co-created the Great Depression in the 20th century, affecting lives everywhere. The Great Depression then laid the basis for a giant wave of affluence that spread all over the globe. The experience of mass poverty at that time was a portal to a new era that brought freedom and greater possibilities for so many and prepared the way for the spiritual revolution now taking place.

The Poor Wealthy and the Wealthy Poor

Strange as it sounds, wealthy people often feel incomplete and empty because they have no real reference of knowing what it is like to have nothing. In the same way as shadow defines light, poverty defines wealth. For a Nepalese man who lives out in the country, an income of eight dollars a month may be the normal average. If he comes to town and sees others earning as much as $100 a month, he considers them to be rich. By contrast, however, Americans would regard themselves as below the poverty line if they made $1,000 dollars a month. In turn, they would see someone with a monthly income of $5,000 being well off. Yet many of those who make that amount and more feel they have nothing to spare when they see a homeless person in the street who may collect even less than the Nepalese man in the countryside.

So those born into very wealthy families, with free access to everything they could ever want, may not be able to appreciate their wealth at all. It may in fact become so meaningless to them that they spend it on things they really don't need or even enjoy, except perhaps for a fleeting moment. Yet they are often very reluctant when it comes to giving part of it away to help those in need, except occasionally as donations that are tax deductible. They find no real purpose for what they own.

By contrast, many people born into very poor families learn to appreciate small things as great gifts, and have a better grip on using their wealth wisely when they step into the flow of incredible abundance. They are more likely to remain humble and receptive and put their wealth to good use, both for their personal benefit and that of society. They know that poverty at an early age helps them to appreciate their life, their family, and their world.

For others, the reaction to having a poor start in life could be different; they might feel so inferior that, in desperation, they choose to try to get out of their poverty dilemma by acquiring wealth no matter what. This extreme anxiety shows that they weren't able to accept, and therefore *live with,* poverty. Instead, they will fight against it and will do almost anything to avoid it, even if it means the use of unlawful methods, such as theft or trickery. Their fear of lack is so strong that they can never find enjoyment in whatever they have, even if it is more than they need. Driven by the incessant urge to accumulate and hoard wealth, they gain no satisfaction from it. Inevitably, at some point, their Higher Self nature will put them face to face with poverty again, until they free themselves of the fear of not being good enough - which is the cause of all poverty. *The fear of poverty manifests poverty.* In most cases they will, for example, gamble their possessions away on the stock market or in the casino, go to jail if they acquired them illegally, or become depressed and resort to drugs or alcohol in order to lose them all again. And even if they manage to hang on to their assets, they will still feel poor at heart, because 'feeling poor' is what they hate and fear so much. Poverty for them represents 'unworthiness' which puts them outside the stream of *true* abundance and locked in their fear of lack. Stockpiling wealth for wealth's sake is just a reflection of their insecurity, fear, distrust, and low self-worth. These persistent, nagging, inner feelings of insecurity compel them to devote their lives to accumulating 'things' (money, property, possessions, power and influence) to try to alleviate their fears. (You may sometimes have experienced these tendencies yourself to some degree.) Even though this incessant drive to have more sentences them to relentlessly living in fear, the thought of being without the comfort of the motivation to be running faster and faster on the treadmill like a rat in a cage terrifies them to death - literally.

In the realm of duality, every state of extreme excess must be balanced by a corresponding state of extreme lack. So wealthy people aren't necessarily living in abundance. They may indeed be poorer than those who own very little but are filled with the richness of love, kindness and a trusting knowingness that somehow their lives are always taken care of. In this, as with most situations in life, the true meanings remain hidden and unrecognized by the vast majority of people. The fact is that the only truly abundant people are those who have accepted nothingness in their lives, they have no more fear of lack or poverty in them. But fully accepting nothingness does not mean that they cannot have or enjoy all the finest material things in life. Quite the reverse. What happens is that they are automatically provided with whatever they need *and much more* because their desires are rooted in the fullness of knowing that they are worthy of receiving the support of the entire, ever-abundant universe.

Give and You Shall Receive

There are no expectations in the awareness of abundance due to the presence of fullness, yet there is expectancy, which is another form of trust that all is well and cared for. We naturally expect changes to occur when we are in abundance consciousness, but we know that all these changes will be in our favor and occur with perfect timing. Only an inner feeling of emptiness, of not having enough and not being enough can produce expectations, which are often mistaken for desires. Expectations are rarely met, at least not to a point of satisfaction, and when they aren't met it results in frustration, stress and anxiety. The body's emotional responses show that having our expectations fulfilled may not be in our highest good because they only further our dependency on physical means, like money or power, in order to fill the inner lack of spiritual emptiness.

175

We fare much better if we accept lack of abundance for what it is: a precious opportunity to accept and embrace our bare human self and learn that we are just as worthy as everyone else of receiving abundance in life. We are worthy of receiving because we are capable of giving. The simple statement 'give and receive' represents the balance of duality. We are as worthy of receiving as we are capable of giving. The fear of not having enough causes us to forget how to give, because we are so concerned with receiving but the truth is that the very moment we give, we also receive. It is in the giving that our heart expands and recognizes its beautiful essence, its inner abundance. We realize how much we *are* able to give simply by being there, by being ourselves. Giving of yourself greatly enhances your self-worth. This helps you to see yourself as more precious and, in turn, you become more receptive.

Effortless Living

Lack of outer abundance in life can push you to the brink of desperation, which is just another way to disclose to you that you are the most precious thing you could possibly own. By being you, you can become anything you want, even if circumstances look as dire as being in a maximum-security prison. Nick proved this to himself, and everyone around him benefited from it. Expecting others to make changes to please you, love or support you, only creates more dependency and less abundance. That is what we do when we look for external means to 'make it' in life. How many people in this world keep trying repeatedly to force abundance into their lives through struggle and effort but never get anywhere? We are talking about masses of them. Is it indicative of our failing political/economic systems, or a result of a few exploiting the majority, that most of the wealth in the world remains in the hands of a few hundred billionaires? Or could it actually be that *the unequal distribution of wealth is a much-needed lesson for the rest of us* to assume our creator roles?

When we are feeling the extreme agony of not having enough abundance, we become emotionally and physically tired and eventually give up trying altogether. This is a turning point in life. This usually coincides with a situation that gives us the opportunity to do something for somebody else, freely, from the heart, and without any expectations of a reward. This opening of the heart space removes the dam that has prevented the river of abundance from flowing through our lives. The pendulum swings back and suddenly all that is needed to bring abundance toward you will be in place, magically and by itself.

Because abundance is naturally present everywhere, it becomes available when you stop trying to obtain it. It may be hard to catch a butterfly but if you sit still, it may come and softly settle on your shoulder. There is no effort displayed in nature. Even though trees, animals and human beings grow against the force of gravity, there is no strain, stress or noise involved in the process of growth and evolution. The Earth moves effortlessly around the sun. The galaxies of stars require no jet engines to move around, and they move with unimaginable speed. So there are no natural laws that support effort, strife and struggle.

Trying to escape poverty is an effort based on the fear of not getting enough, which is equal to a feeling of not being good enough in life. The fear takes you out of the present moment, the only 'place' where everything happens. The resentment of what was in the past and the worry about what is going to be in the future leaves you empty-handed. Nevertheless, as soon as you give up trying, you enter the present moment and the laws of nature begin to step in and support you in your intentions and desires, effortlessly, without struggle or noise. In fact, living in the present moment is so effortless that you don't even require to intend or desire to get what you want and need. You will find that being truly in the now requires that you actually let go of intent altogether. Intent still separates you from reality, for it implies that you are not there yet. Being in the present moment means that you are YOU, the 'I AM', and your free will has risen to be Divine Will - the will of your higher nature. And your Higher Self always knows what is needed at every moment in time.

The present moment is a Divine moment, our only connection to true abundance. True abundance is the kind that is independent of outer riches. Accepting any lack or need of whatever kind, and feeling it through to the end, removes the fear of not having enough. This places you right into the Divine moment of eternal abundance. It is like a stream that knows it can never be without water because new water keeps flowing in. When you have mastered abundance in this way, you are not concerned with what the economy of a nation or the world can offer you. You are your own source of abundance, independent of all forms of outer means of security or methods of wealth building. You have no more fearful attachments to either having wealth or not having wealth, and your life will always sustain itself effortlessly by the incessant stream of *true* abundance of every kind.

We take the tide of life and dredge forward and back within it. Tarry not within the muck and mire of stolid existence. Guide your steed and ride forth in the night, fast begetting your own future. Bountiful it exists. Clear your vision, for the beauty of the hour makes the time, not the minute hand. Taste the livelihood of the moment, and simply transform your image of the now into wonderment.

Julius Caesar
Channeled on April 14, 2001

Chapter Ten

The Spiritual Economy

Be beside the lamplight of my desire; express your whimsy, your toil, your outcry and Mother Nature. Be not complacent about your birthright, or the wanton pleasures of the night speak forth. Be guided by your purpose, not the earthly pleasures of your daily life. For in these are the stirrings of the Great Masters and Mistresses of time lost and there is so much yet to accomplish. Beget the night, give rise to the day and let your full beauty blossom in the lamplight's glow of your divinity.

Oliver Wendell Holmes
Channeled on December 26, 2000

The End of Competitiveness

All natural systems in the universe undergo evolutionary processes that enhance the purpose and potential of life within them. The world's economies have so far served the purpose of allowing both, the rich and the poor, to experience the entire range of material and emotional reality. Although the free market economy has been instrumental in dividing humanity into classes of high, middle, low, and even no incomes, it cannot be considered faulty as such. It has played an important role in manifesting division, competitiveness, segregation, conflict and isolation of the people. Collectively it was important for humanity as a whole to go through this stage (of division and imbalance) in order to manifest what I call the 'spiritual economy'. Since division, as such, is coming to a rapid an end on this planet, the prevailing money-oriented economies must be metamorphosed into unity-promoting generators.

When the World Trade Towers of New York City crumbled to the ground in September 2001, it symbolically represented the demise of an era where economic power ruled the world. The towers had housed myriad corporations, investment firms, financial institutions, insurance companies, businesses and traders from around the globe. The two towers stood for the duality of material existence on Earth. When they fell, mankind became infused with the spirit of oneness. This marked the beginning of the end of the old corporate structure and the consciousness of greed and reckless selfishness. It also strongly undermined the abuse of power that has resulted in the distortion of the medical system, the pollution of the Earth, crime, corruption, famine, poverty and war.

The world hasn't been the same since the September 2001 attack on America. Economics mingled with human values. And who is responsible for all that? Our own Higher Selves are directing all the numerous simple and complex events that shape the world. In fact, there is nothing left to coincidence, including the struggles and setbacks experienced by so many today. All these events are helpful nudges designed to shift the focus of our human thoughts and actions from division toward oneness.

Those who continue to rely on the old methods of keeping a commercial edge over their competitors will increasingly find themselves struggling as if they were swimming against the current of a mighty stream. Companies, which merge, however, are likely to be many times more successful than they were before the merger took place. Although they may not be the true pillars of the new economy, mergers of large corporations are setting the trend for our future. They not only symbolize but also point to the power that lies in unity. At one moment, they are strong competitors, and in the next moment they are pulling on the same rope. Eventually, all businesses will form into one unified whole where no one needs or even wants to compete with anyone else. As this begins to happen, the growth of any economy still based on duality thinking (the

180

manipulation of supply and demand and the competitiveness that results), will become heavily undermined by unity thinking and will eventually fail to work altogether. It is obvious that this will generate a great deal of aggravation among those who hold on to the old concepts of economy.

We are seeing already that predicting a company's success rate for the next few years or months is pretty much anyone's guess. In so many cases, it is even impossible to forecast business trends a mere few weeks in advance. This increases the uncertainty among those who have made investments, for money that was here today might be gone tomorrow. Forecasts of stock market trends are becoming more unreliable than long-term weather forecasts. Why is that? Because the economy is not just about distribution and circulation of wealth, it has a higher purpose. And unless it fulfills its purpose, it will remain a major cause of imbalance, stress and fear for those who are under its influence (and that is practically everyone in the modern world today).

Money - Our New God

Although economics is being taught in schools and universities under the umbrella of science, it is more influenced by subjective, emotional trends than by objective, rational ones. A sense of uncertainty about the outcome of an election, a major social event or national tragedy, a gut feeling about a company's future performance, the production of a faulty product, the untimely announcement of merger plans of two major corporations - all these and more - are powerful triggers for emotional responses. These emotions then translate into strategies for money management. Some of them will make logical sense; others will not.

Any unexpected financial market upheaval can take a large proportion of the population into the unpredictable whirlpool of emotions. If the unforeseen turnabout triggers in the mass consciousness the fear of losing the majority of their assets and wealth, it shakes the very foundation upon which all of modern life is built. For most of those whose lives are anchored in the world of business, God is no longer the foundation of life; money is. Therefore, when money undergoes major fluctuations, it puts the fear of God into them. It seems that God becomes more important in people's lives when something goes wrong or when there is drama that cannot be resolved through rational means.

As long as life remains 'normal', the need for a God is less pronounced. Instead, we rely on the most sought after thing in the world - money. Today it is *money, not God,* which rules the world. Money can buy you everything you want, everything that is 'real'. I once actually

181

heard someone say" "Without having money, not even God can help you." A 'practical' person believes that they are better off relying on money than on God. They know that just praying for their daily bread doesn't fill their stomachs. Asking God to send them a new car or TV set may have been their way of getting their desires fulfilled when they were a child (In fact, at Holiday times, God seemed to be more readily available for answering their prayer wishes than at other times). But since adolescence, for them God has vanished, at least from the arena of daily living. They argue that God has no place in the practical world, or that it is only relevant for 'spiritual' people. And they act on this philosophy until, of course, something happens that cannot be fixed or obtained with money: a terminal illness, the loss of a child or spouse in a disaster, or something so simple yet so hard to obtain as peace of mind. In truth, the point of awakening doesn't need to be dramatic, but it often is. For everyone, there comes a time in life when neither our concept of God nor money can provide what we are truly looking for. This is such a time.

Looking up toward a kind and generous God who could give us what we want or need in life, or relying on money to do the same, are both attempts to avoid taking self-responsibility for everything we are and want to be. Having a lot of money by itself is no guarantee of a fulfilling life. Being rich can be a wonderful asset for someone who respects all life. But in the hands of a person who suffers from low self-worth, money may become a means of manipulation and self-indulgence and subsequent self-destruction. For so many people the 'good' food of modern life and the 'amazing' conveniences of an automated lifestyle have become traps or vicious circles, from which it is so difficult to escape. The sedentary way of life has led to more than half the American population being overweight and obese and to numerous health-related problems that require even more automated systems of transportation, remote control operations, etc.

Both Money and God Are Powerless Unless...

Just having more money doesn't make you a better person in life. Likewise, dedicating more of your time to God is not going to do the trick, either. I spent almost fourteen years trying to follow 'God's words' and be a 'good' Christian, yet this was one of the worst periods in my life. But because of it, I discovered that *it is up to me* how much I respect and accept myself; neither God nor anyone else can do that for me. How much I love myself determines how much I love others, my world, even

182

my chosen God. Praying to God may make me a better person is another way of telling myself that I am basically a bad or undeserving person. It also means that I am at the mercy of a powerful entity that controls me and everything else in this world. Someone who is truly great, however, never sees himself as being 'above' or 'greater', but rather as 'one with'. Putting God into the role of a *superior* being is just a mental concept that arises from the experience of the human dilemma but has no real substance to it.

Praying to God in the hope of having your desires fulfilled is just as unreliable as leaving a bottled message out in the sea and expecting someone to pick it up and send you a response. It implies a division between God and you. Yet God, or the universal field of love, has no interest in keeping itself separated from anything, in fact nothing can exist outside this field. The division between the universal Source of all and myself is merely an artificial one; it creates the *illusion* that there is someone or something greater, more important or more powerful than I AM.

Some people use God as a means of getting the things they want out of life just like others use money to do the same, yet neither way can be a permanent source of happiness and satisfaction. As long as you see God or money as separate from you, you cannot honor and respect either of them. God is your own Divine light permanently shining within the core of your being; money is just another form of energy, just as you are. If you look for God or money outside yourself, *you deny your own power*. This renders God, the universe and money powerless for you. It is the acceptance of yourself as child of the universe, which brings God and money to your life. You create both of them, for without you neither of them exists. *You always create your own reality.* How you perceive God, life, money, love, relationships or anything else is completely up to you, and nobody can change that unless you want to.

The Love-Based Economy

Truly affluent people live fulfilling lives in abundance, with or without money or possessions. Truly spiritual people i.e. people who identify with spirit as their true self, don't ask God to do for them what they cannot do themselves. They are of spirit, not outside spirit. They are one with God, not separate from God. Spiritual people, who perceive themselves in the oneness of spirit, do not pray *to* God; instead, they may pray *with* God. Duality awareness will end when the people on Earth stop praying to God, money, or anything else, in order to improve their

183

lives. This will be the dawn of a love-based or spiritual economy. Abundance manifests automatically if we allow ourselves the experience of passion and joy. There won't be unstable fluctuations in the spiritual economy. When God and money (money is a form of energy for us humans) are no longer treated as separate from us, the economy will be a constant source of success, affluence and fulfillment for *everyone*.

Many people are already aware of the signs of this transformation. It is as if something clicks inside them, like a sudden awakening from a dream, which tells them that the way they have lived so far isn't how they want to live any more. Spirit-based economy will infuse love into the business world. In fact, an economy without the uniting power of love will surely break into fragments, each not knowing how to relate to the whole.

The economy as we still see it today is primarily the result of many different enterprises and individuals who have a vested interest in a 'healthy' growth of the economy, one that procures higher profits. The majority of them do what they do because they want to enrich themselves. If they advertise their products or services in a clever enough way, they succeed. If they told the masses the truth about their real intention, they probably would not. For example, pharmaceutical companies more often than not finance and publicize research according to their requirements to support their claims. If they told the public that most of their studies are flawed and manipulated, then many people would stop buying their products. In this old economy the practice of dishonest honesty has 'worked well', it has divided humankind into the camps of the powerful and the enslaved, the manipulators and the manipulated, the exploiters and the exploited. This has been necessary to lead to the eventual and inevitable empowerment of the individual.

The Birth of the New Consumer

In today's economy, money makes you powerful, *or so it seems*. In tomorrow's economy, being powerful will be synonymous with the full-hearted intention to make *everyone* as prosperous and comfortable as possible. Those who continue operating on purely selfish interests will suddenly find themselves like fish out of water. Since unity thinking is increasingly permeating collective consciousness, we are starting to withdraw the influence of duality from every sphere of life. Those attitudes that create division among people or groups, for example, "I am wealthier than you are" or "My product is better than your product" are rapidly losing public support. It may still take a little while longer before

184

the large and small corporations that comprise modern economy begin to realize that unless they bridge these divisions and are willing to cooperate with each other, they will become highly unattractive to the consumer.

Consumers are in the process of awakening, which means they will increasingly follow their instincts when it comes to choosing a product or a service. They are moving out of victim consciousness and out of their slavery to materialism. Their naïve and trusting nature has for so long allowed, and even demanded, such extreme nerve and blood poisons as, for example, the artificial sweetener Aspartame to enter the food chain and escalate some of the worst illnesses we have today. Now there is a public outcry as one food scandal after another comes to our attention. The population is beginning to realize that it has suffered great abuse by the food, drug and medical industries (or rather, it has allowed this abuse). Those in control of the food and medical sectors of society knew long ago that by introducing processed foods containing harmful ingredients, preservatives, coloring, sweeteners, pesticides, etc., people would gradually become ill. These illnesses would then require medications and other medical treatments. Both cause side effects that then require even further treatment and drug dispensing. The insurance companies are also 'doing their very best' to be of service to the people. Spiraling health care costs benefit everyone *except* those who are sick.

This self-destroying trend, however, is a necessary element in the development of self-responsibility and this trend is bound to reverse with the rising consciousness of the people. As duality thinking is receding into the background and unity consciousness is dawning, the new consumer is growing in their desire to respect and honor life, all life, especially their own. For example, they will want to know why The Food and Drug Administration (FDA) continually allows cancer-producing growth hormones in milk and dairy food. And when they read about research published in the major medical journals that 85% - 90% of all medical procedures and treatments used today lack any scientific basis, they will question their basic safety when seeing a doctor or entering a hospital. The new consumer will want to be treated like a human being. They will seek loving acceptance as a human being requiring more than mere physical repair work. Health practitioners whose own love of self and self-acceptance extends out to the world will become their choice of healer.

The new consumers will prefer to obtain whatever they need in their life from those who give with joy and gratitude, rather than from those whose intents are driven by greed. They will know that a product, food

185

or service given with love is many times more valuable than one sold just to make money. This is a time when the true intentions behind any business are relentlessly brought to the forefront for everyone to see. Hence, there is much confusion and instability in the current economy.

Bridging Material Wealth and Spiritual Wealth

Confidence and insecurity, success and failure, gain and loss are the gripping aspects of duality that are being acted out now in order to bring to an end the paradigms that have controlled life on Earth almost since the beginning of humanity. We have measured our degree of well-being in terms of how much money we possess, what jobs we have, how much skill and expertise we possess, and how much influence we are able to exert over others. None of these are exempt from major changes. Although being money and power oriented has been appropriate until now, it is becoming increasingly uncomfortable for us to emotionally fluctuate like the stock market does. We are starting to sense that there must be much more to life than just satisfying material desires. Since we have been taught right from kindergarten that acquiring a career, a house, a family and possessions is what a 'good' life is all about, when the economy begins to shake and tremble, our belief system is rocked at its foundation.

Economic instability, however, is not a bad thing at all; like everything else, we are collectively creating it for a reason. It helps the masses to see that money, a good career, health insurance, riches and possessions, however useful they appear to be, have become crutches without which we can no longer walk. Hundreds of thousands of homeless people in our cities remind us that having no money also means having no shelter and no food. Nobody wants to end up like that. Having a regular income of money has become our assurance of living a worthy and comfortable life. Yet this is only one view of reality, and a very limited, if not highly deceptive, view at that.

Whether someone lives a healthy, successful, and fulfilling life is not determined by the possession of money. The key determinant behind every single move or event in your life is *the way you feel about yourself.* Our self-image has great power. If you see yourself as a failure, you can only end up as a failure. When you view yourself negatively, without love and compassion, you present a dismal face to others - and they reflect it back to you. Mirrors have no choice but to show what we present to them. They cannot be held responsible for reflecting what is put in front of them. Failure, problems and suffering have no power of

186

their own; they are merely projected images of you reflected back by others, and by situations and circumstances. Conversely, if you regard yourself as being gentle, caring and passionate, you present a positive image that inspires others to be the same way with you. Seeing yourself as creative, unique, gifted and kind hearted, and you will naturally display those exact same qualities in your relationships, behavior and business. Seeing yourself as God (not just imagining it) fulfils human destiny that says "You were made in the image of God!"

The Purpose of Economic Strife

For some people, a hidden sense of low self-worth may only last a short time but for others it may take years or even a lifetime to rebuild. People who do not have enough material wealth to support themselves usually have an underlying sense of not deserving what they long for. This prevents the stream of abundance from coming their way. By contrast, those who value themselves and feel they are truly deserving of wealth, draw opportunities and situations toward them that put them into the flow of abundance quite effortlessly. Yet they are not attached to being successful. Their self-worth remains untouched and steady, no matter what happens. A seeming failure only shows them there is more success ahead, which supersedes even the previous level of success. For others, however, failure becomes a threat that 'demands' immediate action, action that is fear-based and reflects their lack of self-confidence. In such a case, the natural cycle of *success following failure* cannot come to its completion and therefore remains a threat to survival. As long as duality influences us, the fluctuations from failure to success and from success to failure are necessary steps of progress and we cannot do without them.

An economy gripped by the fear that at some point the stock market, the property market or whatever may crash is just as vulnerable and unstable as if it is supported by the belief in everlasting growth. They are both opposites, which keep the wheel of the economic illusion spinning. A recession can strike at any time, and so can a huge natural or man-made disaster or an energy crisis of unprecedented proportion (a likely event in the wake of Mother Earth becoming increasingly unsupportive of the use of fossil fuels). Material wealth by itself is highly volatile. Spiritual wealth, on the other hand, is stable and inexhaustible and when owned in your heart takes care of your material needs no matter how adverse circumstances might be. If you own spiritual wealth, you require no health insurance, no protection, nor any other artificial security to

187

survive and live comfortably. The fight for survival belongs only to the consciousness of material existence. If you think you are just your body, you create a reality for yourself that will center on physically sustaining the body and supplying it with all the pleasures it can possibly get. When you fail to satisfy your physical and emotional needs, you call it suffering. If you know you are spirit in human form, your mode of behavior is very different. You play by the rules of Spirit, not those of the flesh. You are in control of the body, not the other way round. Likewise, you also control your economy, rather than being subject to it.

The rise and fall of national economies throughout the world is not coincidental. It serves as a means of bringing the masses in touch with their self-created dependency on material things. Our collective Higher Self is instigating these turbulent times so that we learn to develop new ways of working with the energies of the world. The masses rarely get motivated unless for economic reasons. Without economic hardships, we would not awaken to recognize our immense ability to create what we now consider impossible. They motivate us to make new choices.

New generations would feel completely lost if they had no access to electricity, computers, cars or telephones, things that were rare or even non-existent a mere hundred years ago. The movie 'Castaway' starring Tom Hanks highlights this lack of self-sufficiency, a timely reminder of how superficially many of us still live our lives. We have collectively acquired the belief that material wealth is the most important thing to have in order to survive and live a perfect life. 'Castaway' sheds doubt on this attitude by asking us what remains when we have nothing left but ourselves.

Have we stifled our creativity and suppressed our spiritual human nature by accepting the philosophy of materialism as being the main reason why we are here on this planet? We have indeed done that, in order to learn through materialism that we are spiritual beings after all. We started by becoming enslaved to the dollar bill, forsaking our spiritual nature and happiness, and consequently suffering great hardship and pain. Now we are at last realizing that we are essentially spiritual beings in a physical body. Because of this shift in consciousness, whatever we mistook for being physical and materialistic is becoming infused with spiritual meaning, thereby losing its limiting grip on us. By embracing the spiritual world, we are becoming masters of physical creation, with unrestricted access to the material world. It is a wondrous lesson to learn; that it is in our highest good to enjoy *both* the pleasures of Heaven and the pleasures of Earth.

Self Acceptance—Origin of All Creativity

When the shift towards Spirit consciousness occurs, we know from within that having money is not the crucial factor that determines how well we fare in life; our creativity is. The more we love and accept ourselves exactly the way we are, the more creative we will be. Total self-acceptance will mean total creativity and mastery of life. Spirit and matter become one; God and we merge as co-creators of every facet of life. This merger lasts forever.

The beauty is that we don't need to change ourselves at all to get to this point. All that is required is to accept who we are right this minute, in all our strengths and weaknesses, without self-judgment. We are the pillars of the new economy, which will be driven by the power of love rather than by competition and striving for success. By accepting all parts of ourselves, we are also accepted by the universal Law of Balanced Exchange. Giving and receiving become perfectly balanced, all the time. No one will suffer from not having enough food or not having a roof over their head. Those who have more than enough will want to share their wealth with those who do not, because withholding wealth from others will be seen clearly as the cause of poverty consciousness, sickness and pain. The rich will feel *truly* affluent and the poor will no more feel poor. Everyone on Earth will come to realize that no life form needs to earn the right to live.

The world's economies will merge and become one unified whole, benefiting all nations and all the people around the globe. It will be understood by everyone that if one nation isn't doing as well as the others, the enjoyment of material wealth becomes greatly diminished. So, it will be in the interest of all that no nation suffers any deprivation or shortcomings. Global polarization into groups of poor and rich, powerful and weak, successful and inefficient, etc., will come to an end, for its purpose will have been achieved - one global family growing through the force of unlimited creativity and bonded by the eternal flame of love.

Atop the very mountain that we scale stands the sign and the flag in tribute to those who have come before us. Every achievement, every earnest step taken forward belies the pride and courage welling up inside each adventurous spirit, for there is truly no way to measure a man's energy, determination and drive. A signpost of achievement is but one heirloom in the diary of humanity. Let us not get caught up in the journey of success, of reaching new heights for the sake of climbing beyond one's own ability. Let us be fully at one with ourselves and with our God. Amen.

From A Sherpa lost in the Himalayan Mountain Range, whose spirit sings in the wind.
Channeled on January 11, 2001

Chapter Eleven

The Ego's World

*Have strength and inner guidance
in all you take on, for yourself
and the multitude around you.
Feel the weight of their plight,
their interests and their hopes.
And set upon your own path, with
freedom to ride high and far from
glory, and into the shadow of
your own worldly existence. Have
strength and courage to persevere
in this nether region of selfhood,
for it is here that we learn the
ultimate secrets of hope and
prosperity, and reap from within
the charitable chaste state of
Grace.*

Hercules
Channeled on April 14, 2001

The Importance of Ego

Without ego we would not be able to experience duality and without
the experience of duality we would not search to find out who we are.

The ego permits us to see a world outside ourselves, one that is separate from us. It allows us to explore this world and discover what its surface and depth are made of. This is important for our development, as going out into the world and living through its difficulties helps us to step into the unknown. The ego knows that the unknown is the source of all fear in life. As we fathom the entire range of the world of duality, we grow in wisdom and understanding and we learn where we fit in all of this.

If you meet a stranger, you may first feel the wall of separation that lies between that person and you, simply because you do not know each other. Not knowing them brings up the fear of being too open and, thus you feel, *vulnerable*. As you get to know them better, the fear begins to diminish and the wall of separation crumbles. Eventually you may become good friends, which means you have bridged previously unknown differences by finding out what they are and arriving at a place of unity. Although each one of you is still unique and different, there is a *unity of differences* at the same time. The ego's natural incessant drive of wanting to know what the duality world is made of has dual value; it removes the fear of the unknown and bridges the gap to our Spirit Source. Since the ego is outward oriented, it seeks happiness through external values such as wealth, power and sensory enjoyment. In its relentless pursuit of happiness, the ego *loves* things like cars, money, food, as well as other people, and if it cannot get any pleasure out of these, it develops an aversion towards them instead.

At this stage, the ego's love isn't true love; it is only attachment. It *attaches* itself to anyone or anything that could promise even an ounce of happiness. Thus, the ego is out to grasp, achieve and control but it isn't able to give anything. Eventually, every person who functions exclusively through their ego will be so dissatisfied with empty attachments to external things that they begin to wonder who they are, and whether there can be such a thing as real love in life. When this awakening occurs, the desire is born to give something without expecting anything in return. The ego discovers that freely parting with something doesn't feel like a loss, but enrichment. It learns that the joy of giving is so much greater than the pleasure of taking. This is the beginning of true love. Giving doesn't just mean giving material things but also giving of oneself, which is perhaps the greatest gift of all. When the ego lets go of its original role of grasping and taking, it expands to a less self-centered role, the role of giving and sharing.

In time, loving others and giving freely from the heart isn't enough anymore. The ego's now greatly expanded sense of self, finds there is a deeper love inside that even the greatest love for, or from, another person

192

cannot match. This love is the love for oneself. The world is no longer able to satisfy this thirst for love and the desire arises to be with oneself, to go within, and discover where this love comes from. This begins the search for a higher reality. The ego increasingly surrenders its 'power of causing separation' to spirit's 'power of unification'. Its mission is finally accomplished when there is no more reference to the outer world in order to know itself. Wanting external acknowledgement, social approval or gratitude is no longer required as we meet all needs from within. The rational mind, now guided by intuition, and unending trust and faith, become the unfailing power to accomplish one's desires. Our spirit self becomes as familiar as the material world. Spirit and matter are perceived as one. It is the ego's purpose and role to take us there.

It's OK To Be Selfish

Most of us have learned that it is unethical to be egotistic in life. Humility is highlighted as one of the great virtues that belong to a kind-hearted and caring person, whereas egotism characterizes those who care only about themselves and have little regard for the welfare of others. However, both humility and egotism are very important aspects of our personality. One rarely occurs without the other, regardless to what extent. In most cases, one of them dominates. For example, someone who exhibits 70% humility and 30% egotistic qualities in their behavior with others appears to be a predominantly humble person, yet in truth, they are just as caught up in duality as another person who is 70% egotistic and 30% humble. One side of the spectrum isn't any better than the other. Both represent opportunities to learn and grow until they balance each other out altogether.

Life's purpose is not about suppressing the ego or developing virtues for others to admire. Humility and egotism both serve our development in the direction of oneness. Such frequently heard expressions as: "He is so full of himself" or "He thinks the world of himself" reflect an inflated ego sense that seems unbalanced. However, being full of oneself (self-centered) is just as necessary for our evolution in the physical realm as being empty of oneself (humble). Giving ourselves permission to be egotistic is just as healthy for us as the feeling of being a humble instrument of spirit or God. Neither represents the final truth, but we need both to take us there.

Many times, we don't even realize that we are selfish, unless someone else points it out to us. Yet, whoever sees selfishness in others has the very same streaks of selfishness in them, although it may be neatly tucked away in their subconscious mind. A truly well centered person does not see egocentric behavior as something bad and therefore has no reason to point it out or get upset by it. People who get angry by the egotism of others are the ones who suffer a distorted relationship with their own ego, meaning they are trying to keep it out of the way whenever possible. They ignore their ego desires and cannot accept the fact that they have plenty of (unexpressed) selfishness in them. Because they do not allow themselves to be selfish (out of fear of being judged), they do not let others who are selfish get away with it, either. This prevents them from finding their inner balance because when the point of balanced awareness is attained, the question of being selfish or humble simply does not arise. Avoiding selfishness is a struggle that prevents you from moving to this center of oneness, and it often results in frustration and anger towards those who seem to display their ego character. The resulting conflicts, though, help undo the karmic knots of misunderstanding.

Welcome Your Ego

Because of our own judgment, 'being selfish is bad', we attract those people who readily let us know and feel how selfish we must be. If you think being selfish is bad, it will prove bad for you. The meaningful saying "As a man thinketh in his heart, so is he" clearly shows the immense power of creation that everyone possesses. Feel bad about yourself and you *are* bad! See yourself as egotistic and you *are* egotistic! See others as self-centered and you *are* self-centered! See yourself as humble and you *are* humble! See yourself as one with all and you *are* one with all. There is no time factor involved in this. We instantly manifest whatever we believe in.

The power to create always remains with us. How we use it is up to us. If you feel other people disapprove of you because you show signs of selfishness, you are likely to manifest fear around expressing and fulfilling your desires. After a while, this mental program you have written prevents you from fulfilling your desires and makes you feel guilty when you do. As the cycle continues, you increase the separation between your lower self and your Higher Self. When it becomes unbearable, you look for an escape from the mind prison you have created for yourself.

The only way of going beyond this self-induced judgment that being selfish is bad is to accept your ego nature for what it really is. However, the ego has such a bad reputation that accepting it is difficult at first.

194

Even when we manage to accept any selfish characteristics we may have, there will be others around us who greatly disapprove of our 'selfishness'. This challenge offers great lessons in life; by accepting every aspect of ourselves, we get a glimpse into the hearts of others and understand why they react the way they do.

Rejecting our ego 'cuts' the connection to our Higher Self. Embracing our ego nature 'reties' that connection. When the connection is re-made (although in reality it can never actually be severed), humility naturally begins to emerge and balances selfishness. The two become so entwined that there is no way of seeing them as separate. A strong inner authority has no need to seek acknowledgment. At the same time, there is so much gratitude and joy in the oneness with the All, that there is no need for an individual to display their personal power. The ego or body awareness finds its purpose - to be the loudspeaker of the spirit within. All it needs is to be welcomed.

The Glorified Ego

The reason we feel so uncomfortable when someone points out to us that we are selfish is not because this is a judgment or criticism directed against us, but because we have learned in the past that selfishness is wrong - a weed of personality that has to be rooted out if we want to live a decent life. Thus, putting the self-judging label on ourselves we are unable to locate and embrace our Divine nature. Only through the acceptance of our selfish attitudes as part of our humanness can we find value in them. Once they reveal themselves as our teachers in disguise we are ready to move on to the next level of our journey, the integration of our human self with our spirit self. To know our Divine nature all we must do is accept our human nature. From this point on it is no longer necessary for us to live a self-centered life. The ego begins to blossom in the Light of Spirit, and selfishness and humility lose their boundaries of influence.

Perhaps one of the most eloquent descriptions of this blending of ego with spirit comes from Lao Tsu: "The reason why rivers and seas receive the homage of a hundred mountain streams is that they keep below them. Thus, they are able to reign over all the mountain streams. So the sage, wishing to be above men, puts himself below them. Thus, though his place be above men, they do not feel his weight, though his place be before them, they do not count it an injury." The wise man has no more need to show off his power and influence to others or to prove his

195

abilities to himself for he already owns them. He appears as humility personified and yet, at the same time, radiates the authority of a master.

Internalized Selfishness

False humility arises whenever we deny our selfishness. There are many who appear to be extremely humble and giving all the time. When you ask their opinion about selfishness they will tell you it is sinful and should be avoided under all circumstances. Most of them have learned to be this way as part of their upbringing. The negative relationship with one's ego nature, which is sustained by an anti-selfish attitude, manifests as fear and self-directed anger. Fear arises because of the constant vigilance against showing any signs of selfish behavior to anyone; anger eventually erupts because the fulfillment of one's deepest desires becomes stifled. Both serve as alarm signals. Suppressing the ego creates pressure and tension in life. In addition, whatever is suppressed becomes stronger in time.

The adopted belief that you are only a good person if you live a selfless life doesn't allow the ego to unfold and be expressed externally, so the ego self begins to express itself internally through the emotional vibrations of tension, fear and anger. Because the outer personality is prevented from being selfish, the inner personality begins to be selfish instead. Eventually the cells of the body become 'selfish creatures' that are out of control and grab everything they can get hold of. In their greediness, they begin to devour the nutrients meant for other cells, thus extending their natural life span. Their behavior is aggressive and egotistic in every sense of the word. They are what we call cancer cells.

Cancer appears in those areas of the body where the emotional holding (of anger, fear or guilt) dominates most. For example, the guilt (self-directed anger) resulting from sexual abuse, usually manifests as cancer in the reproductive organs such as ovaries, uterus, breasts, testicles and prostate. Cancer is basically 'internalized selfishness' and thus a desperate signal and final attempt by the body-mind to bring the afflicted ego into alignment with its partner - the Higher Self. Profound healing can occur when we accept both selfishness and humbleness as the two parts of human behavior in duality, which are jointly steering life into the haven of love, peace and harmony.

Unless balanced by selfishness, humility can lead to self-destruction. Fighting egotism by judging or suppressing it through every means available is more than just emotional warfare. It destroys the immune system and paralyses almost every other function in the body. False

196

humility can reach such a degree of intensity that there is no self-worthiness left. Subsequently, the body self-annihilates. The following few examples may perhaps shed some light on the way we treat ourselves, how often we tell ourselves that we are not good enough (negative self-talk), and how little credit we give to our true essential nature:

- I am only an instrument of Divine will *versus* I AM Divine will.
- I am only a doctor doing my job *versus* I AM a good doctor doing a good job.
- I am only a catalyst helping others find their way *versus* I AM a healer in my own right.
- I am just a servant of God *versus* I AM God serving the ALL.
- I am only here to give *versus* I AM here to give and to receive.
- I am only here to learn *versus* I AM here to teach others and myself.

Putting ourselves down for whatever reason has nothing to do with humility but is a sign of low self-worth. In truth, *we are nothing less than the greatest of everything.* We are masters of creation, so powerful that we can create our own hell and self-destruction. This means that there is no other power outside of you, there is no other meaning to life than the one you think there is. If you believe there is no meaning to life, your life will be meaningless. On the other hand, if you give it meaning, then whatever meaning you choose, that is what it will be. You are exactly who you say you are, such is the power of your own creative force.

If you give love, you automatically receive love. If you teach, you automatically learn from what you teach. If you heal someone, you heal yourself. And so on. The field of duality is such that *whatever we project outwardly is simultaneously projected inwardly,* and whatever we suppress inside becomes suppressed outside. Being masters of our own destiny, it is completely our choice at every moment as to what we want to project. Will it be fear or love? Fear allows us to create the illusion of separation and all the conflict and suffering that comes along with it. Love takes us into the realm of oneness and allows us to create a world of unity and harmony. They are both the legs of progress. And (although unconsciously) we all have chosen both of them in order to experience every kind of duality expression. And at the end we will be victorious, for we will have become the masters of both the dark and the light, the above and the below, the near and the far.

It is Divine wisdom to have in one's hands the key to knowledge that resides in the heart. Open your arms wide to this possibility, for within your bosom lies the truth, beauty, glory and immortality of life. For all life stems from the heart of love. This is not only Divine Truth but also Divine Pleasure. We speak as servants and angels Divine, at the side of Allah.

Allah
Channeled on January 11, 2001

Chapter Twelve

Birthing the New Medicine

*Formulae, equations, sentence
structure, laws of theory are all in
perfect order and follow the
universal spirit of energetic
knowingness. We who have duly
departed from this realm bask not
so wholeheartedly in the
teachings and the wisdom of the
theory but in the law, the
universal law of life itself. The in-
breath of life follows its rhythmic
interplay with its rapturous out-
breath, and in this soliloquy of
life, this sine wave of pulsating
life force, we have all the
answers and all the instincts
alive to ponder.*

Ruminations of Albert Einstein
Channeled on January 11, 2001

The Origin of Healing Systems

Our duality (polarity) model also applies to the field of health and
healing. The division of medicine into traditional/conventional and
alternative/complementary did not occur by accident. Mankind as a

whole needed to experience both of them before it was ready for a system of medicine whose purpose would be of a higher nature than is currently available. The new medicine, although it is so unlike the conventional and alternative models, is being birthed by both of them

Other than the Lemurian and Atlantean approaches to healing, it is clear that the 'medicine of nature' has been the most influential in recorded history. Nobody created this form of medicine; it was simply there to be re-cognized or discovered by those who had direct access to the language of nature called *Veda,* which means knowledge or science. The first written records of nature's medicine appeared about 6,000 years ago. They were channeled messages written down by Vedic sages in direct response to the first occurrences of illness on the planet. This system, which kept illness and suffering at bay for hundreds of years, became known as Ayurveda or the 'Science of Life'.

Although Ayurveda only survived the passage of time in India and some in areas of Brazil and China, it remains a universal form of medicine. Today it stands revived to some of its original form. It greatly contrasts with the western approach to modern medicine in that it seeks to address the underlying imbalance responsible for the symptoms of illness rather than trying to alleviate or remove the effects of the imbalance.[5]

Outsmarting the Violation of The Laws of Nature

Before Ayurveda became a textbook science of healing, people knew how to live in harmony with the laws of nature. As a result, sickness, pain and poverty weren't part of life. But as time progressed, we began to replace some of the laws of nature with our own laws, in other words, we violated natural law. To try to address the consequences of this, a system of healing (Ayurveda) was developed to treat the physical and mental effects resulting from the deviations from natural law. A new set of natural laws needed to be employed to undo the damage that was caused by the violation of the original laws of nature. When you dam a stream of water and it flows over its banks, the flooding caused by this action requires a different approach than just letting the stream flow in its own course. We needed to employ new laws and insights to help us deal with the damage once done. The first violations of the laws of nature on

---

[5] For more information on Ayurveda, the causes of illness, and how to restore health, refer to the book *Timeless Secrets of Health and Rejuvenation* by the author.

Earth created the need for a natural system of healing, one that would give us access to those secondary laws that would reduce the damage caused by violation of the primary laws. This system would show us how to release the obstruction that hinders the flow of the stream in its natural direction. Without anyone violating the primary laws of nature, such healing systems would otherwise be unnecessary.

Hippocrates was perhaps the most enlightened father of nature's medicine in the more recent history of our species. He understood that the need for healing (applying secondary laws) resulted from the loss of alignment with one's inner wisdom and intuition. The more humans distanced themselves from their own inner wisdom and the rules of the natural world, the harsher were the corrective measures needed to be taken by the force of nature. So killer diseases such as the plague began to decimate the population, which then generated the urge for a new kind of medicine that would combat disease-causing germs and stop each new one dead before it became an epidemic. This approach is what has become known as the conventional system of modern medicine. Of course, all of this was part of the master plan - to throw much of humanity into the other end of the spectrum of duality for the purposes of greater learning and growth in consciousness.

Breeding Illness

Just like Ayurvedic medicine, modern medicine, too, was unable to prevent the escalation of disease on the planet. Modern medicine was so concerned with the effects or symptoms of disease that it lost sight of the reasons why people fell sick, most of which weren't even physical causes. The discovery of the first antibiotic medicine (penicillin) caused euphoria among the medical circles and general population. Years later, the enthusiasm of developing an effective drug for almost every infectious disease became dampened by the fact that the side effects generated by the poisons contained in the drugs were so severe that they often outweighed their benefits. In fact, they actually contributed to the emergence of an entirely new class of diseases now known as chronic illnesses, such as heart disease, cancer, diabetes, and arthritis. At the beginning of the twentieth century only 10% of all diseases fell into this category. The rest were acute problems, including fractures, infections, burns, etc. By around 1980, *over 90% of all diseases had reached a chronic stage*, meaning they couldn't be cured by modern medicine. They also became known as the killer diseases of the modern era. Since our genes haven't changed a bit over the past hundreds or thousands of

201

years, genetic errors cannot be held responsible for such a sudden and dramatic escalation of diseases, especially when most of them occur only in the modernized world. What's more, having defective genes doesn't mean an affected person is going to get ill. Research on the blood disease *thalassaemia*, for example, has shown that patients who have exactly the same defect in the gene may be extremely sick, mildly ill, or completely healthy. This applies to most other 'genetic' illnesses, too. There may be just as many people with healthy genes who suffer from diabetes or asthma as there are those who have defective genes.

The symptom-oriented approach of modern medicine became synonymous with the revival of the old epidemics that so scared and scarred humanity less than a hundred years ago. The wide use of antibiotics and steroids have forced the targeted microbes, blamed for causing infectious disease, to resist the drugs' action and mutate into what is termed 'antibiotic resistant organisms'. The germs, following their natural survival instincts, are now outsmarting one drug after another, which means that there are now very few effective 'treatments' left for diseases such as tuberculosis and malaria. Millions more people each year are dying from these 'new' infectious diseases than ever before and the current trends suggest it will get worse. Unless medicine takes a complete U-turn in its approach, or healing is practiced in a different fashion, mankind will be greatly decimated once again.

It is highly unlikely, though, that modern medicine is going to save humanity from self-destruction. The side effects of drugs and treatments are breeding so many different diseases and causing so many deaths every minute of the day that it is virtually impossible to even remotely win the battle against disease as long as people believe they depend on any form of medicine, even an alternative one. Since the medical system is primarily controlled by financiers who have a vested interest in keeping it going and even expanding it further, it is not in the investors' interest to find a real cure for the most common illnesses, for this would mean the end of medicine. Modern medicine is not designed to make people healthy; it is designed to make people sick.

Many voices among doctors, patients and alternative practitioners denounce the exploitation of 'innocent' people. However, they have not yet realized that the same medical system that is misleading and enslaving mankind and robbing millions of people of their sense of sovereignty and self-empowerment, is also instrumental in birthing a new medicine, one that will make everyone their own best healer. The government, health care agencies, medical associations, insurance carriers, and drug companies have no idea that they are key players in the cosmic game of transformation. They have helped a major portion of mankind to feel helpless and powerless against microbes and other disease-causing factors. The extreme denial of the infinite power of healing and rejuvenation that lies inherent in everyone is forcing the pendulum of time to swing back and allow the masses to gain complete and unrestricted access to this power within. Without the hazards of the old medicine, the new medicine could not come about.

The perfection of all this lies in the fact that no person can fall ill, regardless of whether it is through a microbe or a medical drug or treatment, without having (unconsciously) agreed to this. The Universal Law of Non-interference makes certain there are no victims and no victimizers. Each person's Higher Self knows exactly what lessons are needed to move on and evolve toward greater wisdom, love and empowerment, however hard and painful the learning process may appear to be. The final lesson of each individual is to *discover* and *produce* the New Medicine, the medicine of one's Higher Self.

The New Medicine

The return of old diseases and the emergence of chronic illness divided mankind into two camps: one that continues to uphold the trust and confidence in modern medicine, and one that takes recourse to natural methods of healing. Although alternative (complementary) medicine is still battling to make its approaches available to the masses, in some countries of the world such as Australia, Germany, England, New Zealand and now even in the United States, it is becoming more and more common sense to try the natural route, either along with or without conventional medicine. Now both approaches are well represented in the overall scheme of things and can be accessed by almost anyone. Medical doctors still risk prosecution and loss of their license to practice medicine if they dare speak out in favor of alternative health modalities or even apply these in their practice. But before long we will find that both approaches of medicine will intermix or merge together. Indications for merger are already subtly there; when it happens in a more obvious way, a New Medicine will be born, one that will be entirely different from that which existed before. It will work according to the principle 'the whole is more than the sum of its parts'.

The New Medicine will be less concerned about what is wrong with the body or mind; it won't need to be. Instead, it will focus on unleashing the creative power of the individual as the principle source of health and youthfulness. The New Medicine will recognize that disease is ultimately the result of disconnection from our Source intelligence and Source energy. It will give healthcare back to the people. Miracles will take place as frequently as operations take place today. Reconnecting with our spirit Source will be the most important thing that can be done to improve one's health. It's like switching on the light that dispels darkness. Mankind as a whole will realize that trying to find out everything about the symptoms of disease is like trying to investigate all the possible problems that darkness could cause to a person who has no light to see the path along which he is walking. Although switching on the light is a very simple act, it can solve some of the most complex problems arising from being in the dark. Imagine if there was no light. What could you possibly do in your life except sit and think? Fixing diseases is similar to fixing darkness; there is no end to the fixing.

Both the alternative/complementary and conventional systems of medicine are incapable of eliminating disease on this planet. Both of these systems are expressions of duality, therefore their scope of influence remains very limited and incomplete. They each have their value in upholding their particular expression of duality; some of it is effective, and some of it is not. To find the eternal fountain of youth and healing, however, we must return to the origin of both these streams i.e. human consciousness. Now is the time to move collectively into the Divine moment where the consciousness of spirit and the physical matter of the body meet, and are recognized as one. It is in the gap of the moment where the two spirals of duality find their common origin. Of the two approaches, neither is better or more important than the other. Both are capable of taking us to the desired place of wholeness. Here in this gap of simple existence we activate our creative intelligence, the intention of desire that becomes instant manifestation. The power surge emanating from the Divine moment of being within our own awareness creates the instant and automatic healing of that which is without.

In The Gap of Non-Judgment

Healing does not need to take long. In fact, if it does it is likely to be incomplete. According to Japanese research studies, spontaneous remission and complete cure of cancer occurs when those afflicted with the disease move into the gap of non-judgment or non-duality, i.e. when they relinquish all needs or desires to have it one way or the other. This cannot be accomplished by will or by use of the rational mind. It may occur when someone faces death and, oddly, loses all hope for survival. *Giving in to* death may take someone into the gap of their eternal spirit self, provided this is in the person's highest interest. Thus, consciously losing the fear of dying and stepping into one's essence may instantly stimulate the body's immune system into a powerful response that can dismantle egg-sized malignant tumors in the brain, bladder, intestines, etc. within less than 24 hours, and in some instances within as little as 15 seconds. There are thousands of documented cases like these.

What is most interesting in these cases of spontaneous remission is that the healing merely (if that is not enough) consisted of gaining freedom from judgment, of accepting one's situation *at that moment*. Fighting for life doesn't get you to this magical place of the Divine moment, for effort and struggle are born out of fear. Giving up one's desire to live, on the other hand, is born out of resignation or frustration and merely represents the other end of duality awareness. However, accepting death without trying to avoid or enforce it moves you into the Divine moment where miracles take place.

Of course, we don't all have to face death, either our own or someone else's, in order to find the opening to slip into the Divine moment. Life provides us with plenty of other opportunities that can serve in the same way. Reading this book and looking at the Double Spiral symbol from time to time are just a few of the many ways of creating gap awareness. Ener-chi Art™, which helps to activate the New Medicine within one's body, mind and soul through light-encoded artwork, is perhaps one of the fastest and most thorough methods to unite spirit with matter. It prepares the cellular structures of the body to be able to hold a higher vibration and more Chi, which bridges the otherwise insurmountable gap that exists between the two.[6] In due time, our polarized duality consciousness becomes anchored in the singularity of Self. The body simply follows suit. Once we lose our polarity thinking i.e. our mode of reference to what we believe is right and wrong or good and bad, the DNA of our body begins to lose its polarity mode as well. As soon as we are able to accept whatever *is*, which means all our strong and weak sides, our successes and failures, fears, anger, and guilt, etc., our body will move, automatically and spontaneously, out of its polarity mode.

---

[6] For more information on Ener-Chi Art™ please refer to the section **Ener-Chi Art™ - Timeless Medicine** at the end of the book or visit the web site: www.ener-chi.com

You Can Make Your Body Do Anything

When you are under the strong emotional influences of fear, anger, or even excessive joy, your body is out of balance, too. The stress of sudden joy can cause a heart attack just as easily as the stress of sudden rage. Being 'good' is no antidote to disease. We need to remember here that being or expressing one quality also means that its opposite is not far away; in fact, it lurks in the invisible shadow part of our consciousness known as the subconscious mind. True healing begins when we can be both qualities and have no judgment about which one is better or worse. Shadow and light serve each other well and co-exist all the time. The reason we have 'weak' spots in our attitudes and behavior is to bring out and develop their opposite, 'strong' counterparts. Accepting both creates oneness or balance, and balance is the key to healing. Preferring one quality to another generates discord in the body and mind. For example, even if we choose happiness over sadness, it counts as an imbalance. Consequently, the body has no other choice but to develop a physical imbalance, too.

Everything in life is valuable and once we see that, we then become graced with the perception of oneness. Since the body does nothing of its own accord but simply follows instructions, the new perception of oneness and acceptance of whatever *is* becomes the new blueprint reference for DNA. The genetic codes in your body's DNA adjust to the 'new you' and copy that information into a new RNA which subsequently alters the functioning of your body, making complete rejuvenation not just possible but unavoidable. When the adjustment is complete, the DNA structure will go off like a time bomb in order to accommodate the light of oneness. The time for genetic detonation is now.

Our body is nothing but soft clay, shaped and molded on a minute-by-minute and day-by-day basis. If you tell your body that something is good for you, it believes you. It has no other choice but to serve one master, *you*. If you tell your body it cannot heal itself and requires help from outside it will believe this too and you will find yourself in need of a doctor, a drug or surgery.

On the other hand, your body can walk on fire if you can convince it that it can. You can even pierce your body with knives and needles and suffer no injuries if you can make it believe that this won't hurt it. If you persuade your body that it can live without air for several days while being buried under the earth, then it can even do that for you. Levitating in mid air or walking on water are other so called impossible feats the

206

body can accomplish if it trusts its instructor enough. Sri Chinmoy, the well-known peacemaker and musician from India living in the United States, repeatedly lifts 1,000 pounds of weights in front of camera crews. He claims that the power comes from his mind. Numerous 'miracle performers' have been scientifically studied and show that the above abilities have actually nothing to do with the body but come from the power of the mind. Likewise, your body can remove a tumor that has metastasized (spread) everywhere. But for this to happen you need to step outside the awareness of the body (duality) and move into the awareness of the spirit (oneness).

Going Beyond the Shackles of Memory

Our true physical/mental abilities far exceed those controlled by the programs and memories we have stored in the brain. As long as we only resort to what we learned and experienced in the past we cannot create a future that is much different from the past. Only a new seed can yield a new crop. Using past judgments of situations to create our future, in fact, prevents us from tapping into the present moment. The present moment, where past and future merge, is the only place of transformation in life where impossible things are made possible. Models of science or medicine tell us what is possible and what is not. However, in the sacred place of the now, limitations are non-existent. Imagination is all that counts here.

When disciple Peter walked across the raging waves of the Sea of Galilee to meet his beloved master Jesus, he was in the Divine moment of complete faith or connectedness with his radiant Higher Self. Naturally, his physical form immediately assumed the form of light (his light-body) making it as easy for him to walk upon the sea as upon dry land. But as soon as Peter slipped into his duality mode of thinking, which was a recall of the memory that walking on water isn't possible, the faith (in his own divinity) crumbled. "Swimming across, yes, but walking on water, no way!" Peter entered a human fear vibration, which immediately lowered his body's density and frequency and caused it to sink.

We face a similar dilemma in our lives. We know instinctively that we can heal ourselves from cancer, diabetes, or lupus; otherwise, we would not be capable of having feelings of hope. The hope might even be so strong as to expect a miracle and to wake up in the morning fully recovered. Yet, the vast majority of us doubt that we can do this, perhaps because we feel unworthy of a miracle or because our past memories do not allow for something that unusual. The faith in healing is entirely negated by the doubt that healing is possible. Such is our power. Understand this: *the power behind doubt is no less strong than the power that supports faith.* Even the faintest of doubts can sabotage the healing process.

You Are Your Own Healer

During the early 1990s, researchers once again reviewed all the major heart disease studies in order to determine what the greatest risk factors were for the biggest killer disease in the Western hemisphere. Much to their surprise they found that the greatest risk factors for heart disease weren't obesity, cigarette smoking, cholesterol or high blood pressure, etc. but the happiness rating and job satisfaction. In other words, if you don't like your job and if you are not getting along with your spouse, you are living dangerously. Being in a disharmonious relationship not only affects the emotional heart but also the physical heart. Having heart disease means that the whole body is sick. You cannot have a poorly performing heart and expect it to pump enough oxygen and nutrients to the cells of the body - a prerequisite for even the most basic physiological processes such as digestion and metabolism.

Brain and heart researcher Dr. Glen Rein has shed some light on why the happiness of the heart is so essential to our health. He discovered that it is a matter of the heart as to whether you get ill or not. Using Fast Fournier Transformation (FFT), he converted a conventional EKG of the heart into a frequency diagram, like the ones normally made only to map brain wave frequencies. It is well known that the heart generates its own electricity and, as he points out, is much more powerful electrically than the brain. But what Dr. Rein went on to discover was simply amazing.

Negative emotions such as unhappiness, frustration, anger, hatred, and the like generate chaotic, weak and high frequency heart wave graphs. Positive emotions, on the other heart, such as lovingness, appreciation and gratitude produce very orderly, low frequency, but very powerful waves on the graph. Dr. Rein showed that only when the heart shows coherent wave patterns, as in feelings of love and connectedness, could its energy be transmitted properly throughout the body. This may explain why lovers seem so healthy and energized.

Like a dynamo, the heart is capable of feeding healthful energy into the body. Chronically negative people, those who are angry, depressed, guilt-ridden, anxious or hateful, prevent their own healing *by disordering and blocking their heart waves*. This greatly reduces the heart's energy

208

production and distribution; sickness follows eventually. As the heart is the seat of the soul, we are in charge of whatever happens in the body. Truly happy people (not those who pretend to be happy) are those that have love in their hearts, and they are the healthiest people. They are their own healers. They trust that they are capable of healing from any illness.

This statement, illustrated by the work of David Hawkins is beautiful. Hawkins conducted a 29-year long study that showed that the health of the human body improves or deteriorates depending on a person's mental state. He created a scale from 1-1,000 which measured human consciousness in response to emotional frequency. He found that any state that caused a person to vibrate at a frequency below 200 (or 20,000 cycles per second) weakens the body. On the other hand, a frequency condition from 200 to 1000 makes the body stronger. Hawkins discovered that the experience of shame had the lowest frequency effect on the body. This means, basically, if you have thoughts of shame, you become very weak, and thereby susceptible to illness. Guilt turned out to be the next most weakening emotion, followed by apathy, grief, fear and anxiety, craving, anger and hate.

Higher on the scale was trust, vibrating at a frequency of 250 (or 25,000 cycles per second). Trust turned out to have a strengthening effect on the body. If you trust in yourself, you naturally trust that all is well with you and with the world, even if it doesn't seem that way.

Then going up the scale are willingness, optimism, acceptance and forgiveness, reason and understanding. Love, reverence, joy and serenity had particularly high frequencies. They were surpassed only by peace and bliss. Unity consciousness - the experience of you and the world as Spirit - is the highest calibration at a scale of 1000. This is the frequency of absolute power.

By bringing the higher frequencies of love, joy or faith into the lower frequencies of what we call problems or fragmentation, enables these difficulties to reveal their true purpose to us. Hence, they become opportunities for change and healing. To heal means to become whole, which means, this is the end of fragmentation.

Faith Heals

The 'placebo effect' is the occurrence of spontaneous healing among patients who believe a particular drug or treatment is going to cure their illness. The placebo response ranges from 30%-70%. During research trials, a number of control subjects are given only a sugar pill and another group receives the drug to be tested. If the drug group comes up with better results than the placebo group, the drug is considered effective and ready to be marketed. Yet since none of the subjects of either group knows what they are taking, the placebo effect applies to both the drug and the dummy. Since human beings are not robots and run by the same program, there are bound to be varying degrees of faith or doubt in the different people who undergo such testing procedures. If there are more 'believers' or optimists in the drug group than in the placebo group; the drug wins. On the other hand, if there are more 'doubters' or pessimists in the drug group than in the placebo group, the placebo wins. This renders the much-acclaimed objectivity of scientific research virtually invalid.

If nobody had doubts in their own healing power, there would be no need for medicine. Everyone would enjoy 'placebo healing'. People would be cured from any illness simply by having faith in their own infinite healing powers. On the other hand, those who doubt that the medicine they are taking is going to work for them, even though it may be known to be 99% successful, sabotage their own healing abilities. This effect has been termed 'nocebo'. The placebo phenomenon leaves plenty of business opportunities for medications, therapies, charlatans and other bogus products that do absolutely nothing except act as a placebo. Any of these approaches will be considered 'highly successful' even if the placebo effect, (intrinsic to all these approaches regardless of whether they are real or bogus) is only 35%-45% efficient. Those who do not benefit from a placebo have their own reasons for not being able to heal; and they all have one thing in common - low self-worth or self-doubt.

In truth, medicine itself never cures or heals anything; suppressing or removing the symptoms of disease cannot be considered a cure, for this only transfers the problem elsewhere. Medicine can only ever serve as a trigger to awaken the sleeping healer within. People are first their own healers. Anyone who claims to be able to heal you has either no idea how healing occurs or they are simply lying to you. It is the conscious and subconscious acceptance of oneself and one's worthiness at the time of taking the medicine that translates into a healing response in the body. True healers merely assist the mind/body to heal itself. When Jesus healed the sick, he always pointed out that it was their own faith that did the healing. Laying his hands on them served as a trigger (like the medicine) to bring their faith to the surface of awareness. While being in his presence, trusting in a higher power was easy for them. Similarly, being in the presence of, or being treated by, a reputable and self-confident doctor or healer can make patients euphoric about their own healing chances.

Because Jesus acted from the state of oneness of duality where limitations do not exist, he never used such words as "It is not possible." He only saw possibilities, not impossibilities. So it wasn't astonishing to him to be able to restore someone's sight or make lame people walk again. Even raising people from the dead was not off limits to him, although the involved souls had to consent to return to their bodies beforehand. His awareness wasn't of the physical body although he used it as an instrument. Jesus was one with his 'father' i.e.his Higher Self. Thus, he was one with his Source and therefore one with everyone he met. Being in direct telepathic communication with their Higher Selves, he knew who was ready to be healed in body, mind, and soul and who wasn't. Referring to his higher nature, he spoke and acted with the authority of a king, but his kingdom was of the higher dimensions. Being a master of the consciousness of oneness while inhabiting a human body, he was able to direct the lower dimensions in any way appropriate and according to the highest good of everyone. We are here to become masters of consciousness, too.

The Creator of Your Life Lessons

The consciousness of oneness cannot be realized on the level of body awareness (ego), which perceives opposites and limitations as the dominating features of reality. Miracles cannot even be understood on this level and there are no natural laws supporting their occurrence. Hence, they remain elusive to the objective domain of scientific investigation. Albert Einstein believed that miracles are a subjective choice of every person. According to him, "There are two ways to live your life: one is as though nothing is a miracle; the other is as though everything is a miracle."

True healing of the body doesn't take place in the body, it occurs in the fabric of consciousness. It is a choice we make every day. If awareness is divided into the dualities of good and bad, right and wrong, etc., the body and spirit are divided, too. This impedes the lifeline energy supply from spirit to body. Aging and disease emerge as natural consequences of duality awareness. Duality always means conflict. The negative or destructive thought-forms that are part of duality awareness become internalized and cellular. Disease is equated to cells that have died or are dying for a number of different reasons. Other cells known as viruses may deliberately kill them.

When consciousness rises to the state of unity, however, the body moves into a unity mode, too. Because of this ascension, the cells that are viral in nature receive a new blueprint that is supportive instead of destructive to the overall health of the body. Cells that have died or are dying are resurrected. The body becomes invulnerable because it will have no more enemies, neither on the microscopic nor macroscopic level. This in turn becomes expressed as continued youthfulness for as long as one desires to be in physical embodiment. There are still people living in remote areas on this Earth who live youthful lives for 500 and more years. They haven't done anything to master the body as such except to keep it clean and pure. All they did was go beyond the reach of duality consciousness. They are masters of consciousness.

The most important thing to understand in this regard is that the body's limitations are only the ones *we* superimpose on it. This is true whether it concerns the healing of a simple infection, the achievement of physical bi-location or the attainment of eternal youthfulness. If you use your energy to accept illness in your life, you are destined to become ill. By focusing on your limitations and problems, you freeze them and lock them into your life, into every aspect of your body and mind. And by continually seeing the limitations you have created, you expect them to be there in the future. They become part of your personal reality because that is what you see over and over again. Your life will stay stuck according to the images fixed in your mind. If you were able to focus constantly on a different kind of expectation, such as perfect health, abundant energy and freedom, you would spontaneously manifest these in your life instead. There is no other influence on the body than the one you allow and/or create through your awareness.

If in your life you are moving through one of the spiral modes that lead you away from the center of oneness toward dispersion and dissolution (see cover picture), your access to power is limited, your faith and trust are constrained and your beliefs are restricted to what you see or perceive. Being in duality awareness also means being confused (ignorant) about what is right or wrong. The very fact that things appear to be right or wrong shows the dominating influence of duality in your awareness. Karmic influences from past deeds return to us as lessons and opportunities, which may require us to go through the experience of illness. Even children (and animals) may need to pass through these experiences, not realizing why it all happens. But when the confusion settles, clarity begins to dawn, shedding light on why things had to turn out the way they did. Although our Higher Selves have no need to learn the lessons of duality, they have organized life in such a way that our human selves will learn them. The more we understand that what is happening behind the scenes of appearance, our ability to make conscious choices in life begins to increase considerably. These choices can draw us closer and closer to the gap that unites the opposing spiral movements of duality. When children move into the gap they become master teachers, touching those around them to the core of their being so profoundly that their lives are changed forever.

The new children coming to this Earth now are among the first to live in alignment with their higher selves, their only difficulty is fitting into the world of duality. They are not understood, just as Jesus wasn't understood in his time. They and their bodies resist and rebel against being limited by the rules and regulations of modern society, its school systems, methods of learning, lifeless processed foods, and old ways of parenting. The brains and DNA of these so-called 'Indigo children' have new characteristics, and function in different ways to ours. Many of them are computer geniuses and game experts rarely found in older generations. This new generation will be instrumental in birthing the New Medicine, the New Economy, the New Politics, and the New Law. They will lead us to a greater level of understanding of ourselves and the Earth and they will set an example of how performing from the gap not only heals disease, but also every other area of life and even the planet as a whole.

Magic of the Gap

While in the gap of eternal consciousness - the Divine moment - you are the creator, fully united with the creative force that is God, the unified field of consciousness. Everything that has ever been created and will ever be created originated from this very same gap of consciousness that you are. Whatever wish you can possibly conceive of while you are one with the gap will find instant fulfillment. Even desiring won't be necessary in the gap of pure consciousness, because you are in alignment with your own purpose and that of the cosmos. The prayer 'Thy will be done' is nothing but the joyful surrender to one's Higher Self or the Divine moment. When the surrender occurs at every moment, living becomes spontaneous and effortless. Effortless living marks the end of medicine, as we know it.

For the time being, though, there is still a need for both the alternative and conventional forms of medicine. Gradually they will be infused with the New Medicine, which aims to make everyone self-sufficient regarding all aspects of life. Going through the lessons of duality, which

213

may include disease, will become less traumatic as time goes on and the planet's health will return to a balanced state. The so-called 'incurable' diseases will suddenly be curable and disappear by themselves. This, in turn, will improve the health and life expectancy of those eager to grow spiritually, but will make it more and more difficult for those on the planet who continue to live unhealthy lifestyles. Those with persistent self-destructive tendencies will not be able to sustain themselves and subsequently they will leave the planet altogether. Since they have not yet fully explored the world of duality, it is not in their best interests to move into the unity world of the fifth dimension. Besides, it would cause a tidal wave of energies if all human beings came rushing into the new world at the same time. There would be total chaos and confusion, which would serve no one.

The New Medicine, which will make us masters of the elements, lies within each of us. The old medicine was created externally to keep us dependent and restricted, according to the limited beliefs we have had about nature and ourselves. The New Medicine requires no intervention, just being in the moment of 'Divine grace', the oneness within. We have set up our own limitations and rules, our borders and our laws of 'truth' so that we could remove them again in order to learn what it means to be free and unbounded in body, mind, and soul. Duality medicine, which is mainly comprised of alternative and conventional methods of treating disease, is one of these man-made boundaries. The very idea that we may need either of them, for whatever reason, creates the reason for having them and thus becomes a self-fulfilling prophecy. Surrendering this idea of needing the assistance of a system of medicine makes us invulnerable and youthful for as long as we desire to be on this Earth plane.

In Sickness and In Health

If you accept that you are creating your own lessons in life, you must also acknowledge that there can be no coincidences. It is not a coincidence how and where you live, what people you meet in your life, how your parents treat or treated you, and what preferences you have. Your Higher Self arranges all the things that make up your life, which you may normally consider coincidental, and co-ordinates them with all the other things, people, circumstances, etc. that are required for the creation of every new moment. You are Your Higher Self; sometimes you are aware of *it*, sometimes you are not. When you are, you know inside that what happens is not by accident and you trust yourself 100%. The Higher Self is the *you* behind all the beliefs and defenses you have

214

created for yourself. It is the *you* that knows why you are here, what it is that you really need, and what it needs you to do to get it. *You* know for sure that there is a larger picture involved that unerringly steers your life stream towards fulfillment of your life purpose. When you are not aware of your Higher Self, you tend to look for answers elsewhere, you doubt, and you have difficulties making decisions. Even so, the choices you make remain overseen and arranged by your higher intelligence; the only difference is that you are not aware of it.

Likewise, if your favorite color is red, it is because you need this particular vibration either to stimulate a particular energy center in your body, to decrease a color deficiency you may be suffering from, or to facilitate the release of anger from your emotional body. Correspondingly, your choice of food is always accurately in alignment with an inner need of some sort, regardless of whether it is a positive or a negative one. A positive need would be to nourish and sustain your body. A negative need would be to suppress certain emotions, to unconsciously want to punish yourself, or to feel unworthy of being strong and healthy.

Food isn't just fuel for the body. Eating is perhaps the most intimate exchange we can have with the natural world. A great portion of what we eat becomes our cells and organs. The old saying "You are what you eat" is certainly true, but it is not limited to the body only. What you eat just as much affects your mind, your emotions, how you feel about yourself, and the genetic information that controls all the physiological and biochemical processes in the body. If this is so, why isn't everyone choosing to eat the most nourishing foods?

What and where we choose to eat is a reflection of our state of consciousness and its requirements to learn everything about duality. For example, there are foods that are of a very high frequency, such as most fruits, vegetables, some grains, almonds, and certain herbs. More and more people feel attracted to these foods because they need the high level of cellular vibration (of these foods) to move into the higher frequencies of their light bodies, a necessary step toward integrating with the higher dimensional realities of life.

On the other hand, the majority of people born in the developed world choose to eat low frequency foods in order to maintain the physical density of their bodies. To further their lessons of duality, which include enduring pain, they need compact, dense physiologies that keep them grounded. Both these choices are equally correct, for both serve the best interest of the individual eating the food.

Because different people have different needs with respect to their evolutionary process, their psycho-physiological types (body types) vary too. Each specific body type has specific preferences regarding diet, lifestyle and sensory enjoyment. Ayurveda has complete knowledge of these body types and their characteristics.[7] Each body type responds to food in a different way. One body type, for example, the *Vata* type, has no problem digesting and assimilating salted nuts, vinegar, and wheat products, whereas the *Kapha* type will become severely congested when eating the same foods. If we constantly eat foods that do not harmonize with our body type, we become sick. This is the situation with most people who suffer from an illness. Still, their food choices aren't wrong. They require foods that make them sick. Why? Because the sickness serves them as they go through major shifts in life. Illness can be life-altering and raise one's vibration. So whether you choose to eat foods that lower your body's frequency or raise it, you will end up in the same place. The only difference is how you get there. One is the path of sickness and suffering and the other is the path of joy and harmony. Neither path is better than the other. Whether in sickness or in health, you are always treading the right path for you.

Everyone Eats the Right Foods

Humankind has managed to produce two basic types of foods i.e. low vibration and high vibration foods. Low vibration foods are those which are processed, refined, preserved, genetically altered, enhanced, flavored, etc. They include all the dead foods (void of Chi or life force), such as meat, fish, chicken, pasteurized milk and dairy foods, canned, frozen, packaged and shelved products such as cold cereals, candy, soft drinks, and most of the other 20,000 or so food products that are on the market today. Very few foods that have gone through processing have enough life force in them to sustain health and vitality. Chemical additives, as well as added vitamins and minerals, further degrade the food's ability to maintain balance in the body. Only foods left the way nature created them can be considered high frequency, health-promoting foods.

Food derived from killed animals, birds or fish has the lowest vibration of all because it imbibes the death frequency. It is helping those who eat this type of food to experience the more crude opposites of life, to be grounded on the dense physical plane and to learn about death and destruction. Dead foods further the death experience, one of the most

---

[7] To learn more about body types and their specific dietary requirements refer to the book, *Timeless Secrets of Health and Rejuvenation* or any other book on Ayurveda.

216

important experiences of all. Isolation, endings, decay, deterioration, etc. all resonate with the fear of death, and these foods allow a person to manifest these qualities in order to live through them and to release them. In many cases, this means actually needing to die physically because of eating these foods. It is not surprising that these low frequency foods are now more and more recognized to be the cause of such killer diseases as heart disease, cancer, and diabetes.

In addition, every year, 5,000 deaths, 325,000 hospitalizations and 76 million illnesses are caused by food poisoning. That is 34% *above* what it was in 1948, despite (or rather, because of) all our technology aimed at better food handling. The amount of contaminated food on store shelves has reached its highest level in more than a decade. Parasites enter and thrive in those foods that are basically useless, and many of these creatures are also harmful to the human body. Nature has the tendency to get rid of what is no longer good for consumption; these organisms help to do just that. But since we don't get the message, we need to learn it the hard way. Fresh, high frequency plant foods that are *not* treated or grown with chemicals are rarely visited by disease-causing germs because the plants' immune system knows how to subdue the intruders naturally. If an organic food is potentially harmful, nature will destroy it before it can reach your mouth.

Just moments before you intend to ingest food, your body knows whether it is old, dead, or contaminated through special 'radar' called instinct. You can verify your body's natural instinct through Kinesiology muscle testing. Your body's muscles will suddenly turn weak when you look at the food or hold it in you hand. I personally feel moisture appearing on my fingertips when I touch something that doesn't harmonize with my body, for example, medical drugs. Most people have subdued their natural instinct or simply choose to ignore it. What eludes the perception of what is happening with our bodies, though, is the real reason *why* we choose to eat what we eat.

You Know When It's Time to Make Changes

Being the creator of your own destiny, you (your ego self in coordination with your Higher Self) organize your life in such a way that all circumstances and situations allow you to eat the type of food you need in order to go through your cycles of experiences that eventually take you home to the awareness of who you really are. Remember, it is not a coincidence what foods enter your mouth or even how and when you eat them. The cycles of duality include health and sickness, joy and

217

pain, strength and weakness, and everything else that lies between birth and death.

When it is time to enter a new or different cycle of experience you will know when to make changes in your life. You will feel a sudden inclination to eat different foods, to wear different clothes, or to alter your lifestyle. You will literally stumble over the information you need to make these changes, either through meeting someone, a radio or television show, a book a friend wants you to read, or through intuitive insight. There comes a time when you will choose the purest of foods to take you out of the duality cycles altogether. Consequently, the density of your body will lessen and you will move into your high frequency body, which is no longer influenced by disease or ageing. When this occurs, you, that is, consciousness, will know you are immortal; you have always been, and now you will experience it. The New Medicine has been birthed to assist you in this process.

It is with sovereign mind that we speak the Truth, almighty and together we can mine the niches of the depths of our beings. We can assume solemn and wholehearted righteousness to these acts, for they come from God, the Godhead within each of us. And so we say, forget the past sins and troubles. Accept what there is without doubt or duty. For this is yours, your lesson to reap—life upon life, life after life. Take it fully within thyself. And never doubt for a day, or a moment, that it is without a plan. For every thing— every thread and fiber of your existence—is woven into the tapestry of time, by sheer and pure design. It is ordained, by you, in truth and beauty.

Edgar Cayce Group Mind
Channeled on April 16, 2001

Chapter Thirteen

Healing the Natural World

May your days be bright with the spirit house.
May you see the birds flock around.
May your heart rejoice in the moment,
For every song will resound.
We will weep in stages as they come for us.
We will reap the harvest of delight.
While our guides and children wait afar from
us,
We will grieve no more by your side.
May we find the pleasure in the sorrow that
we've known,
For the teachings have sprouted from these
times.
To think that sorrow can beget a noble day
Is but one of the lessons of our time.

Choir of Wellblies (type of fairy)
Channeled on December 26, 2000

We are NOT Superior to Animals

None of the species on this Earth is meant to act in a superior manner toward any other. Exploitation in any form may bring short-term benefits but result in long-term losses. Exploiting humans or animals reflects loss of power and freedom for both the exploiter and the exploited. We have entered a time when every action not serving the highest interest of all involved, and that includes every person and animal on this planet, is

220

backfiring immediately. Those who exploit animals to reap financial benefit and those who eat them or what they produce, are now treading the path of self-annihilation (of their physical bodies) through disease. This is not to say that eating flesh foods is wrong, just as it is not wrong to say that driving our cars with fossil fuels is wrong. What I am saying is that we may need to watch out for the opportunities for change, opportunities that correspond to a new level of energy waiting to be discovered and utilized for the betterment of all living creatures on Earth. Perhaps the most complex of human relationships with the animal kingdom exists between humans and cows.

Our societies are basically mute and deaf with regard to their relationship with cows. It is purely one-sided. Cows have become 'food machines' that provide us with our 'daily bread'. We have concluded that this must be the reason why they exist. In truth, though, they are here to symbolize and manifest the frequencies of unconditional love and care, the feminine principles of our innermost giving nature. They also reflect to us how weak and vulnerable we have become by making ourselves so dependent on them for our livelihood and survival.

The exploitation of billions of farm animals for their meat and milk has become such a lucrative and accepted business on Earth that even the cutting down of the Earth's rain forests to make room for cattle pastures is legalized and sanctified by governments. Yet the governments are only mirrors of the collective consciousness of the people. The rapid destruction of the planet and her species are part of what we do to ourselves, and although it seems so meaningless and wasteful, it serves as a last-minute wakeup call for every one of us to choose love over fear.

Cows are very much our equals. Just because we do not share the same language does not mean that they are non-conscious beings. Can we really be so arrogant as to believe that animals don't think or have feelings of their own? Their Higher Selves are no less developed than are ours. In actual fact, their connection to the higher dimensions usually is much more open than ours because they have little choice but to accept who they are in each moment. Because of their high state of consciousness, out of love for humankind and the Earth, cows have even accepted centuries of abuse and exploitation for meat and milk by humans. Now it is no longer acceptable for any species, including the cows, to be used against their will.

The Milk is Turning Sour

Cows were never meant to provide milk for anyone but their own offspring. After a certain length of time, a cow's child (that is what it is) naturally begins to forfeit milk and instead relies on solid foods. Like human babies, calves are weaned off milk and the cow's breasts or udders become 'dry' until once again they fill in response to the birthing of new children. Today, cows are forced to give many times more milk in a day than is natural for them. Cows are forcefully kept pregnant to keep milk production high. The constant overuse of their reproductive organs results in disease. They receive antibiotics and growth hormones to accelerate further growth and milk output, stressing all their organs and systems beyond endurance. When they give birth, their children are often taken away from them and raised for meat and slaughtered before they even have a chance to experience the world. Humans rarely, if ever, notice the emotional trauma mother and child experience because of all this.

Cow's milk is meant for cows and only cows, just as human milk is meant for humans only. The quality of mother's milk is different in different species of animals. Each type of milk was specifically designed during the course of millions of years of evolution for exactly that kind of animal. For example, cow's milk consists of relatively large amounts of protein and crude calcium, whereas human milk has hardly any protein and very little calcium. If you give human milk to a calf, it will die quickly from lack of protein and weak bones. If you give cow's milk to a human baby, it may develop colitis, bloating, allergies, ear and throat infections, etc. in the early stages of development, and protein buildup in blood vessel walls, calcified and brittle bones, obesity, arthritis and diabetes, cancer, heart disease, etc. in the later stages of life.

Before cows were used for commercial reasons their milk was less poisonous than it is today. In some countries, cows were considered sacred animals and their milk was used for sacramental purposes only. The cows were traditionally honored and cared for. They were brushed, cleaned and adorned. Those who kept cows knew that in order for their milk to be nourishing they had to really care for them. When the cows felt loved and cherished, they produced milk that was even suitable for human consumption in small quantities.

Energy and information are the sole components of everything in the universe. Whatever energy and information goes into something, that is the energy and information that is going to emerge from it again. The way our cows are being treated today and the reason behind keeping them as farm animals has turned cow's milk from being a source of joy, inspiration and nourishment to a source of destruction. There is no more sacred bond left between humans and cows. The connection has been severed. Because of this, the milk we force cows to produce is charged with the destructive elements of human collective consciousness.

Isn't it ironic that milk, which used to be a symbol of love and nourishment, has become one of the principle causes of illness on the planet?[8] The milk has become poisonous for us not because cows want to kill us. They merely pass on to the milk the destructive energies they receive from the human species. Highly evolved species, ones that have a flawless connection with the higher realms, never complain or hit back when they are hurt or tortured. They do not judge us when we destroy them, because they know we are only destroying ourselves. You may kick a rock because you feel angry about something, but the rock does not kick you in return; it knows that you are only hurting yourself by this action. Most of nature is like that. The poor and harmful quality of the milk produced by our cows merely reflects how we treat ourselves. Today's milk is not just filled with synthetic hormones, pus, antibiotics, and added chemicals but with the grief and fear hormones made by the cows due to the lack of love and care they suffer and the loss of their children. When we ingest the milk, these vibrations of grief, fear and anguish become part of our body, mind and soul.

All Life is Sacred

All creatures that inhabit this planet are here to evolve, to learn, to grow and to love. If you stand in front of an animal and hold a knife in one hand and a piece of food in the other, is the animal going to run into the knife and kill itself or grab the food from your hand? The answer is obvious. No living creature wants to be killed or be eaten. Each one seeks happiness and freedom from fear. However, there needs to be an overseeing agency that makes sure life on the planet, as a whole, remains balanced. Nature has its own self-regulating system of controlling growth and it is not for us to disturb it by intentionally or unintentionally decimating or increasing the populations of different species. But we

---

[8] It is left to the reader to look up the overwhelming amount of scientific research conducted on the adverse effects of milk and its products. The author has comprehensively dealt with the subject in his book, *Timeless Secrets of Health and Rejuvenation.* Many other sources can be found on the Internet.

223

have disturbed the ecological balance so severely that pests and killer microbes now fight to restore it, at the cost of human lives.

Under normal circumstances, the natural cycles of birth and death keep the populations of the various species in check and in balance with one another. Our body follows a similar system. Each day there are 30 billion old cells giving up their lives to make room for 30 billion new ones. Life continues, only because these cycles harmonize with each other. The cells that are left behind do not suffer or mourn because they 'lose' their companions. The old and dying cells leave willingly because serving the whole is their chosen contract. But when we attack ourselves emotionally, for example, by suppressing anger and fear, we force at least some of these cells to defend themselves against the assault. These cells do everything they can to survive as long as possible and through genetic mutation manage to live longer than they ought to. Naturally, these cancer cells upset the normal balance of cell replacement and create severe chaos in the body. Eventually their greed of wanting to live longer lives, causes their own and the host's death. Many humans on Earth are acting like cancer cells in the body. Their actions have caused severe chaos on the planet, even though this is chaos with a purpose.

The numerous species that have lived and still live on Earth are playing their part in serving the whole and bringing forth a new world, out of compassion and love for all. If humans had left them in peace, the planet would already be a paradise today. The human race, however, has chosen the path of greed, excess and illness to arrive at the same goal. The detour became necessary because of our lost connection to the Source of all life, a connection that most wild animals and other species still maintain. Although doing it the hard way has been, and still is, a very painful process for many of us, we are learning greatly from this lesson.

We are learning that physical existence is not the only reality in life. We have regressed into this dense state of physical existence by overindulging in the physical pleasures of life, including sex, eating and drinking. Still, we keep longing for something more until we realize that what we really want lies both within and beyond the field of material existence. Yes, physical nourishment is important but so is exposure to the beauty of nature. Eating from the fruits and vegetables of the Earth not only gives great pleasure to the stomach but also to the eyes and other senses. It reconnects us with nature, its spirit beings and its intended purpose. The plant kingdom reaps great benefit from the joy and gratitude we feel when we eat of its produce. In fact, being eaten is their preferred way of spreading and continuing their existence. The animals that eat plant foods excrete the seeds through their fertilizing excrements, thereby giving the plant species a better chance of survival. Plants thrive with happiness when they know that they sustain life on the planet. They are naturally at peace with the planet.

Make Peace by Being Peace

We cannot really move forward individually and collectively without first making our peace with the planet and all its life forms. It is time to cherish and honor *everything* that is given to us. Taking the lives of animals and eating them is not their choice. We have put ourselves above other beings that share their presences with us on this Earth. But such superior behavior is backfiring now. Chief Seattle rightly said: "All things are connected. Whatever befalls the Earth befalls the sons of the Earth. Man does not weave the web of life; he is merely a strand in it. Whatever he does to the web, he does to himself."

This also applies to the creatures of the Earth. Cows in particular exhibit the qualities of contentedness, gentleness and motherliness. Humans greatly benefit from seeing cows in their natural settings. The cows, which embody the Divine Feminine, instill sacred imagery in our heart and thereby strengthen our feminine qualities of love and tenderness. But we have distanced ourselves so far from our own Divine qualities that we are unable to even conceive of the Divine qualities that all the other creatures living on the Earth represent.

The human race at large has denied its Divine Feminine for a long time. As a result of suppressing these nourishing and giving qualities, the aggressive and hostile masculine qualities became the rule of life on Earth. The exploitation of cows, pigs, sheep, horses, chicken, sea creatures and natural resources has been an exploitation of the Divine Feminine in all these creatures and Mother Earth; it reflects the exploitation of our own feminine essence. We have dishonored and disrespected nature and its creatures because we dishonored and disrespected the Divine Feminine within ourselves. It is the lack of connection with our Divine Feminine that makes it possible for us to kill and eat animals and to destroy our natural world.

There are basically two ways to save our environment from further destruction, both of which are already being enacted. The first and most preferable one is to enliven our inner Divine nature, which naturally translates into a harmonious and caring relationship with the natural world. This may not be easy because it involves the experience of pain that we ourselves have inflicted upon the creatures of Earth, and thereby ourselves, during the eons of abuse and exploitation. This pain is reflected in the current public outcry of large numbers of people who feel they are being called to save the environment from further degradation. Animal protection groups, Greenpeace, 'Save the Planet' organizations, etc, are desperately trying to avert the danger that has already come. The more people who start to feel the pain that we all have directly or indirectly 'caused' to the humans and other creatures sharing our space, and to the Earth herself, the more quickly will we all transform into a harmonious organism of oneness, love and power. Feeling the pain allows us to become peace and to make peace with life.

Disease Starts in the Minds of Men

The second and even more painful solution to heal the imbalanced and wounded relationship between humans and their planet is through disease. The famous words "Wars start in the minds of men" can also be applied to human health. Diseases start in our minds too. They originate in the imbalanced perception of who we are. The new diseases brought to us through animals, such as Mad Cow Disease, merely reflect our own distorted (mad) thinking. The cows are driven mad because we have no respect for them and for their offspring. We even feed them with animal flesh, which completely goes against their bodies' natural design. Apart from harboring multiple numbers of worms and parasites, their dead flesh contains dozens of poisonous chemicals, hormones, and drugs. They do not mean to harm us, but our actions and passiveness have enslaved them to participate in another human holocaust. The list of diseases caused by eating meat and dairy foods is nearly endless, diseases that are virtually non-existent in places where people do not eat such foods. It drives the cows 'insane' to be a part of this massive decimation of the human population. If we are in our hearts, we must be feeling their pain now, as they are slaughtered in their millions at the hands of those who act as butchers on behalf of much of humanity.

Although diseases like Foot and Mouth Disease are no longer a threat to either animal or humans, an outdated post-war law demands the destruction of all farm animals if even only one becomes infected. Foot and Mouth Disease is as dangerous for animals as a cold is for us; the ulcerating sores that form around the mouth and feet heal within two weeks and in nearly all cases the animals recover completely, even leaving it immune against future infection. The disease doesn't affect the quality of the milk or meat. It is then ironic that those who have profited from exploiting large numbers of farm animals are now experiencing

226

untold hardship and suffering due to an outdated law that forces them to kill their animals and shut down their businesses.

Outbreaks of animal diseases force us to deal with our abusiveness and lack of respect for life and the natural environment. We are collectively participating in the trauma that the animal kingdom has been subjected to for a long time. The animals (through their diseases) show us that feeding them their brethren's flesh and bones is similar to feeding blood to a human baby. They let us know that the 'inhuman' ways with which we are raising, treating and killing them in order to make greater profits bear no fruit in the long term. So the real reason behind the unnecessary destruction of hundreds of thousands of farm animals is a wakeup call for humanity to make peace with all animals, and respect and honor their lives as we respect and honor our own loved ones. As so often in the past, we have chosen to learn this the hard way.

Living With an Open Heart

A considerable part of the collective consciousness is already becoming aware of the boomerang effect that now returns to us the 'harm' we have done to each other and to the Earth's creatures, trees, plants and auric field (atmosphere). Disease, natural disasters, and destruction of the beauty of nature all play an important part of this awakening process. This is not meant as punishment; sometimes we just need a thorn to pull out another thorn, or a little push to move forward in life. As in everything apparently destructive, there is a hidden constructive and life supportive element. For example, devastating tropical storms add to the richness of rainforests. Research on rainforests in Nicaragua has revealed that the number of tree species doubled and tripled in eight storm-affected areas, compared with nearby ones in an intact forest.

Likewise, animals that are dying 'as a result' of our greediness or ignorance are not victims. They have guided themselves to be at the right place at the right time, to learn and grow and become the teachers and guides to help the rest of us find our truth. Their Higher Selves are only grateful for serving the whole. True healing is a matter of taking self-responsibility for all our thoughts and actions. This not only brings us closer to selfhood, to coming into alignment with our soul purpose, but also prevents us from feeling superior to anything or anyone. When oneness takes over and we move into our true power, the need for these duality-based judgments naturally ends.

227

Oneness begins when we open our hearts to the simple beauties of life: the land, the plants, the animals, the sun, the moon and the stars. Being in nature and breathing its breath nourishes your soul. You begin to see and feel that all things have consciousness and they deserve your respect and gratitude for being here. In time, you become 'addicted' to their charm and beauty. Yet this addiction doesn't leave you empty, it fills you up more and more. In the beginning, this may bring up the pain and sadness that you have endured in the past but this is part of the healing action of nature. It stimulates the impulses of oneness in our hearts, and with the onset of oneness, separateness leaves. Our Divine Feminine becomes One with our Divine Masculine. This is the end of Duality Awareness.

Of course, as always, the choice is yours and you can make it at every moment. Each moment carries the entire you and offers you a brand new start in life. Start giving your loving attention to nature and you cannot imagine how much love you will receive back. Earth is ready to give abundance to those who love and respect her. If you feel you can, live your life with much more simplicity and with as much contact with the natural world as possible. You will find that nature is your extended self and a true and lasting source of pleasure here on Earth.

The short-lived pleasure you derive from consuming more than you really need is only a fraction of the lasting happiness you will get from sharing your essence with the creatures and things of this Earth. When enough of us start treating one another and everything in the natural world with the same respect and honor we ask to receive ourselves, all the conflicts, sickness and problems that plague us will subside. We are at the point in time where whatever we chose will be executed almost immediately, that is, liberation or devastation. Such is our power.

May the gods shine upon you like a lamplight.
May you see the earth from afar.
May you rejoice in the heavens as they hold
you,
for you come to us from afar.
We are here to joyfully unite with you.
We are ever at your sword's command.
May you reap the benefits surrounding you,
for we all can do what e'er we can.
Let us sing the hymns of the centuries,

228

joining forces of the land above.
May our love alight the world around you,
for no one can see that far.

Chorus of Angels
Channeled on January 7, 2001

Chapter Fourteen

Wondrous Times Ahead

Be mindful of the times for we are heading into a no man's land of thought, wisdom and conjecture. It is of paramount importance to be clear in one's thinking, observant in one's daily ruminations and compassionate in one's heart and in all the endeavors of one's soul. We are on the verge of a great cataclysm of thought, and thinking will see a great fork in the road. We are on a plateau of grand opportunity and great scale. Be prepared to leap across the crevasse of logical thought processes and make way for a new visionary future.

Aristotle
Channeled on December 21, 2000

The Final Days of Clearing

We are now being filled with a constantly increasing power to manifest whatever we are holding in our attention. As never before, we are now capable of manifesting our deepest desires and dreams, but we are also confronted with deep-seated frustrations, doubts and fears that have been part of our lives for a long time. All 'unfinished business', including personal issues that have never been resolved or are buried beneath our conscious awareness, are now making themselves known to us, ready to be accepted, allowed, and released. Returning karma, when dealt with in this way is no longer perceived as negative and hurtful and is thus transformed into a constant stream of opportunities. This gives each of us a chance for a grand new beginning in life, one new chance for each new moment.

The reason we are offered the opportunity to deal with our unfinished business now lies in the ascension process of the Earth, and that includes every natural thing that exists on her. Earth, as a conscious being, is evolving just as we are. By entering the frequencies of the fourth and fifth dimensions, she is rising above the thought-forms of right and wrong, victim and victimizer, abuser and abused. Earth is letting go of duality consciousness. In so doing, everything on Earth must rise above such thought forms, too, or else perish. Each human is now being given the final opportunity to choose to evolve and to alter his or her thought forms, beliefs and physical bodies in order to facilitate their own ascension into higher consciousness. Those who choose not to take responsibility for themselves and their actions, on the other hand, are likely to suffer greatly and die in due course. This is a natural cosmic event and is in the best interest of all involved. There is no good or bad in this situation, only learning.

The vibration of Earth is quickening. Whatever does not quicken with her is becoming a drag to the whole and needs discarding. Those creatures and human beings that resist the energy shift find that there is more energy running through their forms than their forms were designed to handle. All emotional or mental resistance manifests as physical blockages or congestion in the body. With the increasing Earth vibration, more life force energy, or Chi, flows through the subtle energy body (Etheric body); it worsens the blockages, which in turn causes disease to manifest more rapidly than before. The higher the Earth vibration goes, the more rapidly those who resist the changes will become diseased. This natural sorting process will guarantee that only those who are ascending to the Oneness of All are going to inhabit the new Earth 'Terra', which will be a planet of love. Duality and its master, the law of karma, will be absent from the New World.

As we are finally freeing ourselves from our karmic 'baggage', we are reaping such precious gifts as freedom, abundance, perfect health, and youthfulness. At the same time, our present world, which is comprised of numerous political, social, educational, economic, ecological, and religious systems, seems to be falling apart, giving rise to tremendous confusion

231

over what is happening. It almost feels like we are all trapped on a sinking ship and there is no way to escape the tragedy of dissolution. Yet there is intelligent order behind the chaos. Similar to the pain that a mother experiences during the birth process, we are passing through very challenging and often-painful periods with only one reason: to raise ourselves to the perfection we are within. By raising our own vibration, we transform the dysfunctional patterns that exist in our surroundings and the world. Although we may not recall the agreement we made with Earth to assist in her birthing process into the light, we have willingly taken on the heavy burden of denying our true self, our purpose and our power - a prerequisite for the ascension. Within each new moment now, we are capable of learning and mastering lessons that until not so long ago would have taken many lifetimes to learn. The speed with which all this is taking place may be exciting for some but very unsettling for others. The following are some of the symptoms of discomfort that you may be experiencing during this time of inner and outer transformation:

Confusion, depression, feelings of emptiness, frequent headaches, sinus trouble, breathing difficulties, blurry vision, ringing in the ears, flu-like symptoms but not the flu, nausea, vertigo, dizziness or spinning feelings, ear trouble, weird fever that is not from illness, pressure or pain in the heart, aches in back, spine, and shoulders, or unusual fatigue.

If you have been troubled by any of these or similar symptoms in recent weeks and months, you may be in the process of clearing deep emotional imbalances, mental stress and physical waste, freeing yourself from all sorts of limitations. The new energies, which you are receiving now, help you 'upgrade' your physical body and its genetic makeup to a new level of frequency and efficiency. Your physical body's metabolism is undergoing great stress because of these alterations. This turmoil inside you is equivalent to a massive war. Monumental changes are occurring that are quickly unleashing old, suppressed thought-forms, dormant genetic errors, and possibly dysfunctions in the major organs. The medical profession is unable to make sense of all these occurrences. Many people are hospitalized for problems doctors have never observed and treated before. Yet the real phenomenon behind these changes is the integration of the physical body with its mental, emotional, and spiritual bodies. Most people, however, only experience some of the above listed symptoms.

Cellular transmutation is necessary to accommodate your evolutionary leap into Light. This of course means that your biology and senses are becoming much more acute, refined, and sensitive. There will probably be moments of exaltation followed by sudden crashes of energy - crashes that can be felt by the body. There may be emotional upheaval as you temporarily swing back into your old reality. You are actually becoming more sensitive to things around you that are of an invisible nature, such as the thoughts and feelings of others. When there are groups around you this sensitivity becomes even more amplified. You feel also more sensitive to external imbalances in the environment. You react to these by developing flu-like or allergy-like symptoms. Do not stop this process even if it involves some aches and pains or emotional discomfort. It does you no harm. The best advice is to be kind to yourself. When you complete most of these alterations, you will feel whole and healthy once again, and even more so.

This clearing prepares you to sustain an entirely different state of consciousness, which is unlike the one known as ordinary waking. You will start seeing things you never saw before and hear things you never heard before. The gap between the invisible and visible world is closing fast. We are in the final stages of reclaiming our basic 'soul right' to become a multidimensional being of love and light living in a multidimensional world of love and light. As we change, our world changes, too. By accepting that the current chaos occurring within and around us is only a side effect of the tearing down of our old world in order to build a new one, we make this process gentle, easy and exciting. Our lesson in this is to trust that all is well that ends well, as it always does.

Every Moment is a Precious Opportunity

Since we are in the midst of the most profound period of transformation that humankind has ever been involved in, each moment is now loaded with priceless significance. If it comes disguised as a negative event, you can take it for granted that it will reveal itself as a precious opportunity, provided of course that you see it that way. Rinaldo S. Brutoco once said: "There is no such thing as a negative occurrence....It's all just useful information." Thomas Edison had an extraordinary ability to see great value in disaster. He knew from within that nothing happens in God's world by mistake. What follows is a description of the experiences he had during a destructive fire, taken from *Good Tidings*.

Fire virtually destroyed Thomas Edison's laboratory in December 1914. Although the damage exceeded $2 million, the buildings were only insured for $238,000 because they were made of concrete and were thought to be fireproof. Much of Edison's life's work went up in

233

spectacular flames that December night. At the height of the fire, Edison's 24-year old son Charles frantically searched for his father among the smoke and debris. He finally found him, calmly watching the scene, his face glowing in the reflection, his white hair blowing in the wind.

"My heart ached for him," said Charles. "He was 67 - no longer a young man - and everything was going up in flames. When he saw me, he shouted, "Charles, where's your mother?" When I told him I didn't know, he said, "Find her. Bring her here. She will never see anything like this as long as she lives."

The next morning, Edison looked at the ruins and said, "There is great value in disaster. All our mistakes are burned up. Thank God we can start anew." Three weeks after the fire, Edison managed to deliver his first phonograph.

Similar to the pieces of the jigsaw puzzle where each seemingly meaningless piece is needed to form a meaningful picture, all life experiences are important for completing the picture of life; yet we so often fail to recognize their true value.

Several years ago, I spent a very joyful week in Eilat, Israel, diving with and being around a group of dolphins. Before and after this delightful experience I became involved in four extensive security checks (up to an hour and a half each) at two Israeli airports. My first reaction was: "What a nuisance and waste of time", but then accepted the view that the Israelis did not want to take any risks. During my second encounter with the tough-looking security staff, I started to feel somewhat intimidated and became quite annoyed after they broke a very expensive electric appliance of mine. I wondered what possible good could there be in all this. The answer to my question was certainly not what I had expected.

My reward for going through this 'inconvenience' was the discovery of a simple method to neutralize harmful energies instantly. Since I was going to stay in a hotel apartment, I had taken several food items, fruits, and a bottle of water with me. After each item had been X-rayed (about three times during the first security check alone), I felt these goods were highly polluted and incompatible with my body's energy and digestive system. When I tested them with a dowsing instrument called 'oekotensor', they all emitted strong negative energies and were no longer fit for human consumption.

As 'coincidence' would have it, I carried a small, clear quartz crystal with me (which I had never done before). Just before going on this trip, I had cleansed it and programmed it for the purpose of neutralizing harmful energies and amplifying good ones (which again I never had done before). I rotated my crystal above the contaminated (irradiated) foods and drinks a few times in a clockwise direction (something I never thought of doing before, either). When I checked their energy output and compatibility with my body, the goods were all clear of harmful effects and once again useful to me.

Soon I discovered that all natural foods and beverages that are treated with chemical fertilizers, or have been in contact with electromagnetic fields produced by electric cookers, stoves, mixers, juicers, toasters, refrigerators, food processing machines, trucks, airplanes, or that contain chemical additives, etc., produce a strong distorted, negative energy. Since the human cells cannot utilize this kind of energy, such processed foods are 'dead' and very difficult to digest and assimilate and can therefore become a major cause for food intolerance, allergies, and disease. Yet after applying the above crystal method, they lose their harmful features and become 'alive' again. Even bottled water, which is lifeless, can be brought back to life in this way. There are only a few foods that a quartz crystal cannot make wholesome again. They include heavily sprayed foods such as grapes and tomatoes, refined oils, and most junk foods. You may try the above method and see for yourself how it can change the digestibility of foods and even their taste.

About a year later, my partner Lillian and I received the ability to facilitate the creation of what we call 'Ionized Stones.' The stones are an integral part of the 'New Medicine' that is helping mankind and the Earth in the transition to the higher dimensions. The stones are capable of cleansing foods and drinks, instantly balancing all chakras (energy centers) in the body, clearing any kind of unsuitable energies in the auric field, house or environment - doing what quartz crystals do but on a much more intensified scale - protecting against electromagnetic fields from computers, TV, electric wires, re-energizing water that comes out of faucets, and much more. Without the 'annoying' security checks at the Israeli airports, I would not have discovered or understood the value of crystals and ionized stones.

What I learned from this and other similar incidences is that *all difficulties in life are encoded with hidden messages*; it is up to us to decipher and use them for the enhancement of our personal growth and our service to humankind and to our planetary home. As always, our difficulties are also our opportunities. Stepping back and taking a moment to see why something 'inconvenient' or 'unfortunate' happens to us can change our attitude towards it and turn it into something entirely different. Every instance in life is a non-coincidental occurrence and is marked with a unique opportunity of some kind. To benefit from our problems, whether their nature is physical, emotional, interpersonal, social, environmental, etc., we must see them from a new perspective. The proverb: "All's well that ends well" best sums up the following simple lesson of life, given to us by an unknown author:

A farmer's horse ran away. In response, a neighbor said, "What a shame, your horse ran away!"

"We'll see," said the farmer.

One day, the farmer's son spotted the horse and broke his leg running after it to try to catch it. "How sad that your horse ran off and your son broke his leg," sympathized the neighbor.

"We'll see," said the farmer.

War was declared and the farmer's son was drafted, but, due to his wounded leg, he couldn't pass the physical. Many young men were lost, but the farmer's son was spared. *Blessings often come masked as disaster.* In fact, I discovered in my own life that if you hold such an expectation in your heart and perceive the larger picture of things, a great disaster always is always followed by a great blessing.

We Are Awakening

If a particular problem such as a persisting financial difficulty or a physical weakness brings up fear in you, rather than immediately pushing for a quick solution you may need to allow yourself to be afraid or insecure for a while. You cannot experience fearlessness unless you have experienced fear first. You may be afraid that you cannot fulfill other people's expectations of you, or that you will make mistakes and be judged for it. The fear centers on your state of health or the prospect of having to die one day.

Acknowledging and accepting whatever fear comes up in you is the first and most important step to going beyond it. "Okay, I am afraid to speak up for myself," is an example of how you can bring fear from the subconscious realm to the conscious realm. **Dare to make the mistakes you are so afraid of making and let others know that you made them.** This quickly removes any fear of disappointing others or yourself. Taking tranquilizers or antidepressants, drinking alcoholic beverages, watching TV, reading a magazine, etc. when feeling anxious or fearful, on the other hand, only pushes the fear back into the unconscious realm of the mind. And, as with everything else that is suppressed, the fear will resurface with greater intensity some time in the future. Simply being conscious of fear lessens it until it becomes fearlessness. Once the grip of fear has lessened, you will be ready to recognize that it is only the fear that causes the discomfort. You will learn that there is nothing to fear because in reality, there is nothing that can be against you or do you harm. Behind the mask of fear is hidden an opportunity. When it emerges, perfectly timed, it may trigger an avalanche of events that can turn a seemingly insignificant incident into a powerful event of cosmic importance.

Each one of us is an enormously precious instrument for the God-presence within us. We are here to create a world characterized by love, prosperity, wisdom and harmony. A beggar in the street may make his or her own contribution to a better world by developing the rare quality of humility and at the same time offering to teach the rest of us about compassion. Each lesson learned and every bit of karma gone through and understood causes an exuberant applause by the angels in heaven, for it raises the overall vibration of the Earth and brings it closer to that of Heaven.

One of the more significant events of restoring oneness in our personal lives and on the planet as a whole was the September 11 attack on America in 2001. Those who perished in the attack had volunteered to be at the right place at the right time. Their Higher Selves had agreed to leave the Earth plane in this way, and, although it took a few days for the departing souls to let go of their previous existence, very few had difficulties with their transition. By leaving in this dramatic and painful manner, the so-called 'victims of terrorism' accomplished within moments a magnificent feat that otherwise would have taken many years. When someone dies, a portal or vortex is created, which permits the soul of the person to transit to the other side of the veil (spirit world). In most cases, the process of dying helps to transmute much of the negative energies from that person and their immediate environment.

Throughout the ages, mankind as a whole has accumulated an immense amount of disharmonious and destructive energies in its collective consciousnesses. Major waves of hatred and violence and also constant smaller waves of tension have circulated through world consciousness. Almost every individual who has ever lived on this planet has contributed to the collective stress and tension in thousands of small and mindless ways. We all have added to this buildup through our individual thoughts, behaviors and actions. From time to time, it became necessary to let off some of the 'steam' in order to avoid a bigger eruption, like another World War. Group death is one of the ways to avoid major calamities and allow collective consciousness to take major leaps of evolution. When thousands leave their bodies at once, a huge portal is generated. This occurred, for example, during the holocaust in World War II and any natural disaster in human history, or whenever hundreds or thousands of people have lost their lives. Recently, a powerful wave of violent energy needed grounding

237

and it had to land somewhere. America turned out to be a suitable place because of her capacity to receive and transmute a vast amount of tension and hatred.

During the collapse of the World Trade Center, the departing souls opened a portal or a vortex that allowed much of the remaining dark energies of Earth to be siphoned off. Those whose souls volunteered to be trapped in the Twin Towers and the Pentagon building at the time of the collapse, deliberately took a large portion of the world's hatred and suffering and transmuted it through the process of their collective, simultaneous physical death. By opening the portal, they 'pierced' the veil that exists between the lower and higher dimensions of reality. This created the final bridge for humanity to 'walk across.' When these heroes of the Light will become reunited with their families in the not too distant future, all the pain and suffering that was created by this event and similar ones will dissolve into bliss and exuberance. The opening or tear in the veil is not only sucking the remaining dark energy off the planet (like a vacuum cleaner), it also permits massive amounts of spiritual Light to enter the Earth plane. As the darkness is leaving the planet and Light is streaming in, all that has blinded mankind throughout the ages is transformed into wisdom, power and love.

How much light energy comes through and is put to use depends entirely on us. Each of us has to choose love, light, compassion and truth over anger, hatred, aggression and violence for the transition to be smooth. It is our job to replace the darkness of division with the Divine Light of Oneness. Each one of us counts in this mighty task and no one is more important than another. There may be more events like the ones that occurred in September 2001 but it is important for us to remember that they will all be part of a bigger picture that serves the whole. Dwelling on the dark side of the picture is a choice that some of us will make. Mistaking the release of negative patterns for an increase of fear, hatred and aggression, they will believe that things are getting worse in their lives and in the world. This will cause them to latch on to the negative patterns that are coming up for healing Dwelling on the negative sides of these events or situations will take them into the lower vibrations of fear and anger, sowing new seeds of violence and retaliation. On the other hand, more and more of us will choose to see beyond the appearance and locate the profound purpose in these events. This will greatly multiply their beneficial effects (of cleansing and healing) and enhance the power of love, unity and freedom for all mankind.

We are collectively in the process of moving out of the purely second and third dimensional experience, which has kept us in darkness, sickness and suffering throughout the ages. At the same time, we are raising ourselves into the fourth and fifth dimensions of reality, where heavenly life will be the *only* reality. Freedom from limitations, instant realization of desires, and continuous youthfulness are a few of the ancient dreams bound to come true once we have entered the new state of higher dimensional awareness. The switch to higher consciousness will be like waking up from a bad dream. Our new channel of perception will only allow us to see perfection everywhere and to experience unconditional love, continuous growth, and unlimited potential.

There won't be a place for sickness, fear, anger, abuse, jealously, intolerance, greed, egotism, lack of forgiveness, etc. in the New World, which is the main reason we are now being challenged to let go of all our limitations. We are indeed given the choice of whether we want to proceed into Heaven on Earth or to continue on the path of physical density (somewhere other than Earth). The current strong influx of cosmic energy pouring into the Earth brings old personal problems related to health of body and mind, emotional trauma, relationships, work, economics, politics, religious beliefs, etc. to our attention. This allows us to deal with them and to free us from their limiting effects. The old world's systems are in great turmoil and about to collapse because their motivators - fear and greed - are being phased out on this planet and relocated to another planet where its subdivisions are still useful and welcome.

At the same time, attitudes of acceptance and willingness to make favorable changes in one's life are receiving a major boost. But since time is moving so much faster now than ever before, hours, days, weeks, months and even years seem to pass so quickly that we almost feel time is running out. This dramatically accelerates all changes and events. The new energies give us the opportunity to find lasting solutions to our problems and to draw great love and harmony to our lives. We are in the process of awakening to the realization that we actually deserve the very best of everything because we are one with everything. The path to finding our way 'home' may be pleasant and easy for some but difficult and rough for others, yet at the end it doesn't matter *how* we get there, only that we do.

Creating a Temple of God

Although humankind at large is still stricken with much poverty, disease, and confusion, those who have made their choice to proceed to the next dimensions will now quickly find their way to the light of solutions, opportunities and freedom. We have been allocated a little more time for this transitory phase of adjustment and decision-making. To safely make it through the phase transition, we need to listen to and honor our body, for it is a temple of the Highest Spirit - God, the ultimate state of Self.

If your body gives you any problems now, try to attend to its needs as much as is possible and allow yourself to feel whatever is coming up. The clearing of old mental, physical, and emotional waste causes most of the discomfort. Supporting the body through cleansing and nourishing it well will greatly speed up the process. In fact, with the influx of stronger energies on the planet, having a healthy body is more important now than ever before. A congested body is likely to suffer and fail to make the ascension to higher consciousness smooth and comfortable.

Suppressing the symptoms of *dis-ease* through drugs, operations or stimulants is synonymous with denial or fear, which may make you feel lethargic or numb and even more uncomfortable. Know that the body is helping you in any way it can to facilitate the clearing. Ask your body (out aloud) why and where it doesn't feel good. If it is in the eyes, what is it you are resisting to see or wanting to see too much? If it is in the throat/thyroid, (infection, dysfunction, etc.) what are you scared to express? If it is in the liver, what or who are you really resenting? If the *dis-ease* is in the colon, stomach or bladder, what are you afraid of resolving or releasing? Do you have loss of use in your legs? Then ask yourself whether you are afraid of promotion, taking greater responsibility, or moving forward in life. Always 'feel' the answers; there is no need to understand them intellectually.

This form of self-diagnosis is also one of the most profound forms of self-healing. Just stay with this feeling even if it gets stronger and stronger as you are doing this. Let it build up until it becomes almost unbearable. This is the point where you can let it go, where it actually goes by itself, where you no longer feel like having to fight or reject it.

Find out what part of your body evokes shame or self-loathing. Are you embarrassed about having too big a stomach, too large a nose or too pale a face? What areas of your body do you try to cover up or hide with cleverly designed clothes, make-up, and coloring, skin lifting, etc.? Society has a very narrow definition of glamour. Its notion of beauty leaves very little room for the majority of us to think of ourselves as beautiful. Yet each part of us is wonderful and gorgeous. Why, for example, should we hide our tears? Having tears is one of the most powerful ways for the body to release pent-up feelings and to heal old emotional wounds. Others who see people in tears spontaneously open their hearts to love, forgiveness and compassion. Tears have a magical way of melting down barriers between people.

Having menstrual blood is nothing abhorrent; it is part of the cycle of preparation for creating new life and for releasing waste products from the body and helping to remain youthful and balanced. Many people see their excretions, such as feces, urine and sweat as a nuisance, whereas in fact they are the most essential functions keeping the body healthy and strong. Those who suffer constipation never feel quite right or comfortable in themselves. Ask a woman who suffers cystitis how *she* feels about life. The body holds on to waste because there is still 'unfinished business' that requires one's (loving) attention.

Find out what is devalued or unmentionable about your body. Which part/parts of your body do you not like to look at or seen by your spouse or friends? Whenever you consciously or unconsciously resist, deny or abhor an aspect of your anatomy or physiology you deprive it of energy and love. Without loving attention to every part of your body, you are destined to create or sustain difficulties there. It is in your best interest that physical problems persist for as long as you have not fully accepted yourself as a lovable being.

Illness is but a cry of the body to let you know that you are sending it fear, anger, hate, shame or guilt. Saying things like: "My heart is giving me trouble" or "My aching joints are making my life miserable" are self-fulfilling prophecies that are hard to combat. Being afraid of your own heart, kidneys, stomach, liver, brain, ovaries, prostate, blood, bones, etc. short-circuits the energy and nutrient supply to these parts of the body and sabotages self-healing. Your love energy is the essential fuel for healing and rejuvenation. Accept and appreciate whatever you do not like or resist in your body and it will transform itself miraculously. Your new vision of your physical self will greatly facilitate and ease the way you are able to handle the new energies that are pouring into us right now.

If you feel confused or have problems in a close relationship, this may be because you are not able to relate to your Higher Self. External sources of negative information and influence can strongly interfere with your inner dialogue. You may greatly benefit from cutting out watching television and reading newspapers; learn to listen to your internal messages instead. A few minutes spent in meditation or in nature each day helps to recognize them. New light and energy is pouring into each one of us, and we need to be prepared to handle it in a way that does not wreak havoc in the body. The body needs to become a true Temple of God before it can accept, work with and sustain these higher energies.

Every time we receive a stepped-up vibration, the body needs to deal with the heightened frequencies, which is not too difficult if it is relatively pure and free of toxicity. If the body hasn't been working well in the past or is not nourished properly in terms of giving it pure food, clean air, fresh water, and love, it is now persistently demanding our attention. When the body is not in alignment with Spirit it becomes unbalanced and asks for assistance. That is when we usually look for help.

Taking Self-Responsibility

We can change our personal reality if we recognize that we are powerful enough to change it. The power to bring our individual self into alignment with our cosmic self and Divine purpose is now freely available to us; all we need to do is to be still, to ask for it and to listen to our inner wisdom. This also applies to most physical ailments. The common methods of medical intervention, i.e. drugs, medical tests, surgery, etc., unless they are used for an emergency, are far too crude and are no longer sufficient to effectively deal with physical problems and to bring lasting relief. In fact, they cause more problems now than they can resolve, hence the rising number of doctor/drug/diagnosis-caused diseases and fatalities. Since all our personal problems (which in reality are our solutions) result from our previous own doings (including those from past lives), our active participation in the healing process is our best way of clearing from us all physical, emotional, or mental difficulties.

To help the body accept and sustain the ever-increasing amount of light and energy pouring into all aspects of our being, we need to purify it. It certainly is not a coincidence that such basic health and rejuvenation methods as the liver cleanse, colonic irrigation, kidney cleanse, tissue cleanse and many other approaches of clearing and rejuvenation are being brought to our attention at this time. Also, day by day, an increasing number of people recognize the great importance of a balanced diet and lifestyle.[9] This is part of the Divine Plan, which provides us with every possible assistance to go through the current phase of transition without experiencing too much hardship.

The Choice is Yours

All teachings come from within. Each person, depending on his/her personal karmic background and unique purpose in life, will receive whatever is necessary to proceed on his/her journey. Therefore, all

---

[9] The author's books, *The Amazing Liver & Gallbladder Flush* and *Timeless Secrets of Health and Rejuvenation* offer a complete package of information on how to cleanse, nourish and rejuvenate the body.

circumstances and all people are perfect just the way they are. If we feel the need to change them, it reflects our fear of not being good enough and is motivated by the false hope that by fixing the situation or someone else's problems, our own problems will also be resolved. It further implies a lack of confidence and knowledge that each one of us can only create or receive what is in our current highest interest, nothing more and nothing less. Trying to make things 'better' for someone who doesn't ask for it will deprive them of a self-empowering opportunity to grow stronger in an area of weakness, and as such, has little to do with love. On the other hand, being there for someone who is in need, *and asks for help,* can open the hearts of all involved and alter any stuck patterns of behavior that they may have.

Disastrous events such as 9/11, hurricanes in the U.S. and tsunami waves in Indonesia occur to bring human hearts closer together and to bridge the deep gap that exists between the rich and the poor, the fortunate and the less fortunate. We are being challenged to be there for one another, to develop the great powers of love and compassion within us, for without these, the world would surely self-destruct. Being now on the threshold of even more drastic Earth changes, we need to take care of every aspect of our personal lives as well as be prepared to provide whatever service we can give to others who choose to be ready and willing to accept it. It is a time when we all depend on each other and can help each other, but we must understand that the real changes only occur when we each, individually and consciously, decide that they do. Now is the time to make our choice. Collectively we can make this final part of our journey into the higher dimensions of our own Self as comfortable and wonderful as possible. Together we can make our oldest dream come true - Heaven on Earth.

At any given moment, you can make multiple choices in your life. Each one leads to a different set of consequences. For example, while driving your car through a town you can choose to drive into various streets, and each one will take you to a different destination. Even if you decide to go only to one specific place, you will still have the choice to go to any of the other places. If you chose to go to your hairdresser, you would create entirely different future events than if you had decided to go to the airport and fly to another country. Each new moment provides you with the opportunity to make a multiple number of choices.

The wonderful thing about making choices is that you never can make wrong ones. In truth, every single choice you could conceivably make through your thoughts, actions and deeds is pursued and fulfilled, and if not on the human sphere of 3D reality, then certainly on a higher

243

dimensional level. Your Higher Self lives out every potential event that has not been manifested in your physical life. Sometimes in your dreams, some of these other potential choices are recognized in symbolic form. The choice is always yours, which potentials you prefer to manifest in your human form and which ones you wish to realize in your Divine form. Yet, none of them can ever get lost. You always make all possible choices simultaneously and all of them are perfect for the entire You. Using the above example, if you decided to go to the hairdresser, the other potential reality of driving to the airport would be experienced by your Higher Self.

Here is another example. If you decided today to divorce your spouse and quit your job, on the level of your Higher Self you would continue to pursue all the other possibilities, such as reconciling with your spouse and keeping your job. Whatever you decide to do, you can never go wrong. The choices that you make in your life are the ones that take substance here in the 3D world. All the other potential choices also take form, yet only as higher dimensional elements of energy. No potential experience is ever lost. Your Higher Self keeps track of all the numerous alternative possibilities while you are acting out the chosen one.

The thinner the veil between our human self and our Higher Self, the more we become aware of the parallel realities or potentials that our Higher Self is living out. Each decision we have ever made in life has helped us get a little closer to this precise moment in time as we lift the veil of illusion from our awareness. Life is not a crooked path. The trials and errors, the immense challenges and suffering that each one of us had to endure on this long journey of awakening were not in vain. Our human selves chose the bumpy road in order to bring the light of love into the darkness and density of lower existence, whereas our Higher Self was left with the task of acting out the easy and joyful potentials.

Fortunately, our difficult (human) journey is ending now. Our Divine and human paths are crossing and merging as one. This is how we are creating Heaven on Earth. The final choice we are making now is to honor all the choices we have ever made (and the ones we will still be making), as being the most appropriate, sacred and purposeful, no matter how wrong or harmful they may seem to be. This will end the era of conflict, civil strive and suffering on Earth. Living free of judgment will be the principle force behind creating and sustaining a world of love, peace and prosperity. This freedom from judgment is the eternal message waiting within you. Simply lift the veil of duality to receive it.

We see before us a great civil strife. No one understands this better or is wiser than the almighty savior within. Trust your instincts. Unlock the promises held within. Seek out your eternal message. Breathe deeply from the ocean and mountain air. Allah has spoken.

Allah
Channeled on April 14, 2001

Methods for
Living without Judgment to be a Master of Life

Eight Lessons

By reading through the pages of this book, you have taken the first steps on your journey to Freedom and Mastery. The following eight lessons summarize the material and can serve as signposts along your way. Refer to them often and allow their wisdom to come to your attention on a daily basis. You will then find that *living without judgment*, the resulting mastery of life will become more and more you as you journey on.

1. *Consciously give meaning to and bless whatever happens to you.* Whatever meaning you attach to an event or situation literally forms your reality. Free will or freedom of choice is your greatest gift. It even allows you to give new meanings to things that have already passed, thereby altering your present and your future reality. Being the ultimate master of your destiny, consciously create the attitude that every moment in your life is a Divine moment, blessed with momentous opportunities for growth and learning. There may be days when you feel depressed or ill and you don't understand why. Allow these changes to occur and give them the meanings that you like the most. Realize that *all* changes are helping you to learn and grow and are so good for you. If you are suffering from 'battle fatigue', know that there is no need for you to battle anymore. Let go of the old, for it only tires you. This creates the space for the new to emerge. If the Divine moment brings you uncertainty and confusion, then allow it to be, and wait until clarity dawns. There is perfect timing in everything.

2. *Know that there are no negative or positive events, people, or situations in life.* They only come disguised as such. All of them are there to assist you in reaching your full integration with your Higher Self. There is no real separation or distinction in the universe, only change of form for the best of all. Know yourself to be loved beyond limitation, for everything that you are represents a piece of the giant jigsaw puzzle of life. The struggles and polarities you need to go through to help build this larger picture matter very little. What matters is that you are always an essential

246

part of it, no matter how happy or sad life may appear to you. You are precious in every respect. Outer appearances are deceptive and do not reveal your Divine nature. Feel this in your heart, for knowing this within is your doorway to freedom, happiness and all possibilities.

3. *Welcome, accept, celebrate and express gratitude for everything that occurs in your life.* There is nothing more perfect than what each current moment brings into your life, so why judge and lament over what already is in your best interest? See through the illusion of appearances and recognize that you are orchestrating your life for your own highest good, regardless of how useful or useless something may appear to be. Insist that all is well and know that very often the best things in life come disguised as misfortunes. Look at all your resistances in life and bless them until they dissipate. Avoid limitations in your heart that allow it to flow only in one or two directions, otherwise your heart can never be open and free. Be a blessing to all and insist that all is well. And if, for the time being, you cannot see the larger picture, trust that your Higher Self is mighty enough to take care of everything in the best possible way.

4. *Be encouraged when things don't move in accordance with your wishes.* Not having the things your ego desires can serve you well and bring you closer to your essence self, which has no attachment to anything. Freedom will dawn when you desire nothing but gain everything. Having no more expectations (offshoots of fear) liberates your soul and brings you the greatest treasures imaginable. Trust there is a larger picture for everything you do. You have designed it for yourself and with others. In this larger picture, you are always protected and never alone, even if you go through 'the dark night of the soul'. Losing everything you believe you cannot be without helps you 'find' yourself, which is the greatest discovery you could ever make. So be grateful for all the losses in your life, for they have brought you closer to knowing who you are.

5. *Consciously allow yourself to be judgmental.* This puts you in touch with the fears and beliefs that urge you to pass judgments. Judgment has been your tool to grow in the world of duality; it has brought you the most important lessons in your life. Bless it with

your love and gratitude and accept it for the role it has played for you. It has had its purpose but you no longer need it now. Fighting, struggling against or resisting anything or anyone only sustains the prison of duality and the need for further judgment. Whatever you deny others or do not like in them, give yourself permission to do yourself and you will no longer see it to be a reason for concern or annoyance. Dare to make mistakes. Release the fear of creating something new in your life and release it out with your breath. Give up the idea that you need to struggle against the odds of life. Instead, just give in to everything you resist and the need for judgment will leave you in the same way a feather is carried away by the wind.

6. *Look at the double spiral symbol to remind your soul of the larger picture of things.* The opposing spirals of duality are eternally united in the brilliant gap of pure being - the Self. Whether you consider events to be positive or negative, right or wrong, good or bad, etc., they all come from and lead back to the eternal gap of the Divine moment, which is the connection to your Higher Self. It matters not which route you take. You need not try to be a good person to deserve enlightenment. Duality is your friend whose only purpose is to take you home where you belong, to *be* your true Self and to be *true* to your Self. Learn from all your experiences even if they seem unfavorable and harsh, and know that you are safe, always. And remember, there is no one who truly judges you, except you.

7. *Treat your body as best as you can,* for it is your doorway to heaven, the temple of God within. You *are* God just as a wave of the sea *is* the sea. Everything you do to assist your body and increase its purity is considered a gift of love to the universe, your Higher Self. Cleanse your organs of impurities, feed your body well with natural foods and give it sufficient rest. Treat every part of your body with utmost respect and honor and it will reward you with joy, happiness and vitality for as long as you desire.

8. *Know that you are the master who has taken on the role of a student.* You have always been the executive director of your life, for the Universal Law of Non-interference prevents it from being any other way. This has steered your life to the point where it is now. Bless all of it because every breath you took and every

248

moment you perceived were all for your own highest good. Whatever meaning you have attached to an event or situation has become your reality. *Free Will* or freedom of choice has so far been your greatest gift. It served you as a tool to create things that weren't there before and it also allowed you to explore and learn from all the complexities and simplicities of life in duality. Free will even allowed you to give new meanings to things that are in your past now. Because of these new meanings, your changed attitude and understanding about your past has altered both your present and your future reality. Through all of this, you have learned that you are not a slave to destiny but its master. Being the master of your destiny you can now decree that every moment in your life is a Divine moment, blessed with momentous opportunities for growth and learning. All that is required from you now is to become *Divine Will,* which is the will of your Universal Self or God Self. The beautiful thing about being Divine Will is that nothing is required of you except to be who you already are. Breathe in your own Divinity and radiate it out wherever you go. You no longer need to seek guidance outside yourself to be safe and well. While free will helps you to navigate the field of duality, Divine Will allows you to step out of it and forever enjoy the personified freedom of Eternal Oneness. Above all, choose joy in everything you do, for joy is your anchor to the one and only Source of life.

Sacred Santémony – for Emotional Healing

Sacred Santémony is a unique healing system that uses sounds from specific words to balance deep emotional/spiritual imbalances. The powerful words produced in Sacred Santémony are made from whole-brain use of the letters of the *ancient language* - a language that is comprised of the basic sounds that underlie and bring forth all physical manifestation. The letters of the ancient language vibrate at a much higher level than our modern languages, and when combined to form whole words, they generate feelings of peace and harmony (Santémony) to calm the storms of unrest, violence, and turmoil, both internal and external.

In April, 2002 I spontaneously began to chant sounds that are meant to improve certain health conditions. These sounds resembled chants by Native Americans, Tibetan monks, Vedic pundits (Sanskrit), and languages from other star systems (not known on planet Earth). Within

249

two weeks, I was able to bring forth sounds that would instantly remove emotional blocks and resistance or aversion to certain situations and people, foods, chemicals, thought forms, beliefs, etc. The following are but a few examples of what Sacred Santémony is able to assist you with:

⇒ Reducing or removing fear that is related to death, disease, the body, foods, harmful chemicals, parents and other people, lack of abundance, impoverishment, phobias, environmental threats, the future and the past, unstable economic trends, political unrest, etc.

⇒ Clearing or reducing a recent or current hurt, disappointment, or anger resulting from past emotional trauma or negative experiences in life.

⇒ Cleansing of the *Akashic Records* (a recording of all experiences the soul has gathered throughout all life streams) from persistent fearful elements, including the idea and concept that we are separate from and not one with Spirit, God, or our Higher Self.

⇒ Setting the preconditions for you to resolve your karmic issues, not through pain and suffering, but through creativity and joy.

⇒ Improving or clearing up allergies and intolerances to foods, chemical substances, pesticides, herbicides, air pollutants, radiation, medical drugs, pharmaceutical byproducts, etc.

⇒ Undoing the psycho-emotional root causes of any chronic illness, including cancer, heart disease, MS, diabetes, arthritis, brain disorders, depression, etc.

⇒ Resolving other difficulties or barriers in life by 'converting' them into the useful blessings that they really are.

To arrange for a personal Sacred Santémony session with Andreas Moritz please visit www.ener-chi.com **.**

Ener-Chi Art—Timeless Medicine

Andreas Moritz has developed a new system of healing and rejuvenation designed to restore the basic life energy (Chi) of an organ or a system in the body within a matter of seconds. Simultaneously, it also helps balance the emotional causes of illness.

Eastern approaches to healing, such as acupuncture and Shiatsu, are intended to enhance well-being by stimulating and balancing the flow of Chi to the various organs and systems of the body. In a similar manner, the energetics of Ener-Chi Art is designed to restore a balanced flow of Chi throughout the body.

According to most ancient systems of health and healing, the balanced flow of Chi is the key determinant for a healthy body and mind. When Chi flows through the body unhindered, health and vitality are maintained. By contrast, if the flow of Chi is disrupted or reduced, health and vitality tend to decline.

A person can determine the degree to which the flow of Chi is balanced in the body's organs and systems by using a simple muscle testing procedure. To reveal the effectiveness of Ener-Chi Art, it is important to apply this test both before and after viewing each Ener-Chi Art picture.

To allow for easy application of this system, Andreas has created a number of healing paintings that have been 'activated' through a unique procedure that imbues each work of art with specific color rays (derived from the higher dimensions). To receive the full benefit of an Ener-Chi Art picture, all that is necessary is to look at it for less than a minute. During this time, the flow of Chi within the organ or system becomes fully restored. When applied to all the organs and systems of the body, Ener-Chi Art sets the precondition for the whole body to heal and rejuvenate itself.

Ener-Chi Ionized Stones

Ener-Chi Ionized Stones are stones and crystals that have been energized, activated, and imbued with life force through a special process introduced by Andreas Moritz, the founder of Ener-Chi Art.

Stone ionization has not been attempted before because stones and rocks have rarely been considered useful in the field of healing. Yet, stones have the inherent power to hold and release vast amounts of information and energy. Once ionized, they exert a balancing influence on everything with which they come into contact. The ionization of stones may be one of our keys to survival in a world that is experiencing high-level pollution and destruction of its eco-balancing systems.

In the early evolutionary stages of Earth, every particle of matter within the mantle of the planet contained within it the blueprint of the entire planet, just as every cell of our body contains within its DNA structure, the blueprint of our entire body. The blueprint information within every particle of matter is still there - it has simply fallen into a dormant state.

251

The ionization process 'reawakens' this original blueprint information and enables the associated energies to be released. In this sense, Ener-Chi Ionized Stones are alive and conscious, and are able to energize, purify and balance any natural substance with which they come into contact.

Potential Uses for Ionized Stones

Drinking Ionized Water
Placing an Ionized Stone next to a glass of water for about half a minute ionizes the water. Ionized water is a powerful cleanser that aids digestion and metabolism and energizes the entire body.

Eating Ionized Foods
Placing an Ionized Stone next to your food for about half a minute ionizes and balances it. Due to the pollution particles in our atmosphere and soil, even natural organic foods are usually somewhat polluted. Such foods are also impacted by ozone depletion and exposure to electro-magnetic radiation in our planetary environment. These negative effects tend to be neutralized through the specified use of Ionized Stones.

Ionized Foot Bath
By placing Ionized Stones (preferably pebbles with rounded surfaces) under the soles of the feet while the feet are immersed in water, the body begins to break down toxins and waste materials into harmless organic substances.

Enhancing Healing Therapies
Ionized Stones are ideal for enhancing the effects of any healing therapy. For example, 'LaStone Therapy' is a popular new therapy that is offered in some innovative health spas. This involves placing warm stones on key energy points of the body. If these stones were ionized prior to being placed on the body, the healing effects would be enhanced. In fact, placing Ionized Stones on any weak or painful part of the body, including the corresponding chakra, has healthful benefits. If crystals play a role in the therapy, ionizing them first greatly amplifies their positive effects.

Aura and Chakra Balancing
Holding an Ionized Stone or Ionized Crystal in the middle section of the spinal column for about one-half minute balances all of the chakras, or energy centers, and tends to keep them in balance for several weeks or even months. Since energy imbalances in the chakras and auric field are

one of the major causes of health problems, this balancing procedure is a powerful way to enhance health and well-being.

Attach to Main Water Pipe in Your Home
Attaching a stone to the main water pipe will ionize your water and make it more absorbable and energized.

Place in or near the Electrical Fuse Box in Your Home
By placing a larger Ionized Stone in, above, or below the fuse box in your house, the harmful effects of electromagnetic radiation become nullified. You can verify this by doing the muscle test (as shown on the instruction sheet for Ener-Chi Art) in front of a TV or computer, both before and after placing the stone on the fuse box. If you do not have a fuse box that is readily accessible, you can place a stone next to the electrical cable of your appliances or near their power sockets.

Use in Conjunction with Ener-Chi Art
Ionized Stones may be used to enhance the effects of Ener-Chi Art pictures. Simply place an Ionized Stone over the related area of the body while viewing an Ener-Chi Art picture. For example, if you are viewing the Ener-Chi Art picture related to the heart, hold an ionized stone over the heart area while viewing the picture. The nature of the energies involved in the pictures and the stones is similar. Accordingly, if the stones are used in combination with the pictures, a resonance is created which greatly enhances the overall effect.

Creating an Enhanced Environment
Placing an Ionized Stone near the various items that surround you for about half a minute helps to create a more energized and balanced environment. The Ionized Stones affect virtually all natural materials, such as wood floors, wood or metal furniture, stone walls, and brick or stone fireplaces. In work areas, especially near computers, it is a good idea to place one or more Ionized Stones in strategic locations. The same applies to sleeping areas, such as putting stones under your bed or pillow.

Improving Plant Growth
Placing Ionized Stones next to a plant or flowerpot may increase their health and beauty. This automatically ionizes the water they receive, whether they are indoor or outdoor plants. The same applies to vegetable plants and organic gardens.

Creating More Ionized Stones

Make any number of ionized stones by simply holding your "seed stone" against any other stones or crystals for 40-50 seconds. Your new stones will have the same effects as the seed stone.

Double Spiral Symbol
As Seen On the Cover of This Book

The double spiral, (two spirals with opposite spins, converging in a common point or gap) is a powerful, dynamic model that is intrinsic to every process of creation. Each thought, feeling and action, every movement of a wave or particle, and the activities of the entire universe, all follow the basic principles inherent in this symbol. The Devic realms use such geometry to create forms and proportions for all life forms in the universe, from tiny crystals, to the human being, to an entire planet. In fact, there is nothing that doesn't follow this same geometric pattern. Your brain, every process of growth and transformation in the body, the complex situations of life and the laws controlling the areas of politics, justice, education, economics, religion, etc., all use the mechanisms displayed by this geometric symbol.

The cover picture characterizes the very process of creation itself. From the oneness of the gap (zero point) emerges the destructive mode of duality in order to give rise to its constructive mode, converging back into the oneness of the gap. Whatever you feed into the gap will determine your new reality. Every thought, feeling, and emotion emerges from the 'gap of *Being*' that you are (one spiral) until it is fully expressed. It then collapses back to the gap, and disappears from the screen of the conscious mind. However, it also sows the seeds for the next moment of your reality to emerge. As you sow, so shall you reap. If you feed fearful thoughts into the gap, more fear becomes manifest. If you feed love into the gap, more love is generated. The gap materializes and amplifies everything you put into it. Yet whatever you create has to be deconstructed and come to an end again, for nothing can last forever.

The cycle of life is continuous because both modes occur simultaneously and are present at every moment. The gap represents the universal consciousness of your Higher Self; the opposing spirals are the creative and destructive aspects of individual consciousness experienced as the every changing facets of duality. Life is complete when we know ourselves as all three of them.

personal message from the author:

ar Reader,

I congratulate you and honor you for staying with this book and
ding through to the end.

You may have discovered that this is not an ordinary book that just
vides you with some insights or guidance. The book is encoded
th the blueprint of natural living that exists deep within you, and
reading the words enlivens it in the fabrics of your awareness. This
kes the book a practical tool for inner transformation.

If you have found this book interesting - maybe even challenging in
places - I recommend you put it aside for a little while and then
d it again. I promise you will find it to be so much clearer the
ond time around and your soul growth will benefit enormously.
Another way to help yourself and the environment you live in is to
ommend this book to your friends. We are so close now to the time
transition/ascension to oneness that the more we do to help each
ier, the easier and more delightful this process will be.

Blessings to you and thank you,

Andreas

Let hatred come not between men. In oneness, there is greatness, power, unity of brotherhood. Let it rise within you. Feel the power and the glory united. We cannot be split apart, you and me, for we are part of the greater whole of life. We are One.

Malcom X
Channeled on April 16, 2001

ABOUT THE AUTHOR

Andreas Moritz is a medical intuitive; a practitioner of Ayurveda, iridology, shiatsu, and vibrational medicine, a writer, and an artist. Born in southwest Germany in 1954, Andreas had to deal with several severe illnesses from an early age, which compelled him to study diet, nutrition and various methods of natural healing while still a child.

By age 20, he had completed his training in both iridology - the diagnostic science of eye interpretation - and dietetics. In 1981, Andreas began studying Ayurvedic medicine in India and finished his training as a qualified practitioner of Ayurveda in New Zealand in 1991. Rather than being satisfied with merely treating the symptoms of illness, Andreas has dedicated his life's work to understanding and treating the root causes of illness. Because of this holistic approach, he has had great success with cases of terminal disease where conventional methods of healing proved futile.

Since 1988, he has practiced the Japanese healing art of shiatsu, which has given him insights into the energy system of the body. In addition, he has devoted eight years of research into consciousness and its important role in the field of mind/body medicine.

Andreas Moritz is also the author of *Timeless Secrets of Health and Rejuvenation, The Amazing Liver and Gallbladder Flush, Cancer Is Not a Disease! — It's A Survival Mechanism, Feel Great, Lose Weight; It's Time to Come Alive, Heart Disease No More!, Simple Steps to Total Health, Diabetes - No More!, Ending the AIDS Myth, Heal Yourself with Sunlight* and *Hear The Whispers, Live Your Dream.*

During his extensive travels throughout the world, Andreas has consulted with heads of state and members of government in Europe, Asia and Africa, and has lectured widely on the subjects of health, mind/body medicine, and spirituality. His popular *Timeless Secrets of Health and Rejuvenation* workshops have assisted people in taking responsibility for their own health and well-being. Andreas has had a free forum '*Ask Andreas Moritz*' on the large health website, curezone.com (five million readers and increasing). Although he has stopped writing for the forum, it contains an extensive archive of his answers to thousands of questions on a variety of health-related topics.

Since taking up residence in the United States in 1998, Andreas has been involved in developing a new and innovative system of healing called Ener-Chi Art that targets the root causes of many chronic illnesses. Ener-Chi Art consists of a series of light ray-encoded oil paintings that can

257

instantly restore vital energy flow (Chi) in the organs and systems of the body. Andreas is also the founder of Sacred Santémony - Divine Chanting for Every Occasion, a powerful system of specially generated frequencies of sound that can transform deep-seated fears, allergies, traumas, and mental or emotional blocks into useful opportunities for growth and inspiration within a matter of moments.

About Lillian Maresch, Ph.D.
(The person who channeled the messages before and after each chapter)

At a very early age, Lillian became aware of her spiritual gifts, which include a heightened sense of intuition. While she has always relied upon these abilities in her own life and professional career, in recent years Lillian has expanded her focus, using these skills to help others gain insights into their personal life situations. She has been sought after by people in the US and around the globe for her keen insights, astute intuitive guidance, sensitivity and understanding. Her counseling sessions focus on:

- Helping people identify their life's purpose and mission
- Getting in touch with one's inner wisdom and intuitive abilities
- Inspiring the emergence and expansion of one's creative abilities
- Assisting individuals to gain insights and heal after the loss of a loved one
- Delving into an individual's past, and understanding how "unfinished business" may be affecting the person today
- Helping people work through stress, insecurity, anxiety or depression with compassionate and insightful coaching, augmented by related spiritual perspectives

Lillian's background is anchored in psychology and the business world. She received a Doctorate in Personality-Social Psychology from New York University at age 25. With that strong educational foundation, she has gone on to enjoy a successful professional career, spanning both the corporate and advertising agency worlds. Early in her career, *Advertising Age* named her among the nation's 100 Best & Brightest individuals.

In 1989, she co-founded Generation Insights, a consulting firm specializing in understanding the consumer mindset. Lillian is adept at uncovering consumers' driving needs, attitudes, values and purchase motivations. Her work has taken her from Los Angeles to Minneapolis, and most recently to Greenville, South Carolina where she founded GPS for Changing Times.

The media has sought Lillian's insights and viewpoints about the Baby Boom generation. She has been widely quoted by *The Wall Street Journal* and other major newspapers and magazines around the country. She has also co-authored spiritual articles for several regional publications.

Additionally, Lillian has served as a workshop leader at the Creative Problem-Solving Institute and as a member of the Board of Directors of WE International, a global organization supporting individuals experiencing profound shifts in consciousness. She also co-founded Ener-Chi Resources, a company specializing in innovative wellness products.

Scheduling an appointment with Lillian

You may schedule a session with Lillian over the phone or in person. For more information, or to reserve an appointment, please contact her at:

By phone 1.864.895.1857
By email lily@acrossdimensions.com
Web Site: www.acrossdimensions.com

Gift Certificates are also available.

The Amazing Liver and Gallbladder Flush
A Powerful Do-It-Yourself Tool
to Optimize Your Health and Wellbeing

In this revised edition of his bestselling book, *The Amazing Liver Cleanse,* Andreas Moritz addresses the most common but rarely recognized cause of illness—gallstones congesting the liver. Although those who suffer an excruciatingly painful gallbladder attack are clearly aware of the stones congesting this vital organ, few people realize that hundreds if not thousands of gallstones (mainly clumps of hardened bile) have accumulated in their liver, often causing no pain or symptoms for decades.

Most adults living in the industrialized world, and especially those suffering a chronic illness such as heart disease, arthritis, MS, cancer, or diabetes, have gallstones blocking the bile ducts of their liver. Furthermore, 20 million Americans suffer from gallbladder attacks every year. In many cases, treatment consists merely of removing the gallbladder, at the cost of $5 billion a year. This purely symptom-oriented approach, however, does not eliminate the cause of the illness, and in many cases, sets the stage for even more serious conditions.

This book provides a thorough understanding of what causes gallstones in both the liver and gallbladder and explains why these stones can be held responsible for the most common diseases so prevalent in the world today. It provides the reader with the knowledge needed to recognize the stones and gives the necessary, do-it-yourself instructions to remove them painlessly in the comfort of one's own home. The book also shares practical guidelines on how to prevent new gallstones from forming. The widespread success of *The Amazing Liver & Gallbladder Flush* stands as a testimony to the strength and effectiveness of the cleanse itself. This powerful yet simple cleanse has led to extraordinary improvements in health and wellness among thousands of people who have already given themselves the precious gift of a strong, clean, revitalized liver.

Timeless Secrets of
Health and Rejuvenation
Breakthrough Medicine for the 21st Century
(550 pages, 8 ½ x 11 inches)

This book meets the increasing demand for a clear and comprehensive guide that can helps people to become self-sufficient regarding their health and wellbeing. It answers some of the most pressing questions of our time: How does illness arise? Who heals, and who doesn't? Are we destined to be sick? What causes aging? Is it reversible? What are the major causes of disease, and how can we eliminate them? What simple and effective practices can I incorporate into my daily routine that will dramatically improve my health?

Topics include: The placebo effect and the mind/body mystery; the laws of illness and health; the four most common risk factors for disease; digestive disorders and their effects on the rest of the body; the wonders of our biological rhythms and how to restore them if disrupted; how to create a life of balance; why to choose a vegetarian diet; cleansing the liver gallbladder, kidneys and colon; removing allergies; giving up smoking, naturally; using sunlight as medicine; the "new" causes of heart disease, cancer, diabetes, and AIDS; and a scrutinizing look at antibiotics, blood transfusions, ultrasound scans, and immunization programs.

Timeless Secrets of Health and Rejuvenation sheds light on all major issues of healthcare and reveals that most medical treatments, including surgery, blood transfusions, and pharmaceutical drugs, are avoidable when certain key functions in the body are restored through the natural methods described in the book. The reader also learns about the potential dangers of medical diagnosis and treatment, as well as the reasons vitamin supplements, "health foods," low-fat products, "wholesome" breakfast cereals, diet foods, and diet programs may have contributed to the current health crisis rather than helped to resolve it. The book includes a complete program of healthcare, which is primarily based on the ancient medical system of Ayurveda and the vast amount of experience Andreas Moritz has gained in the field of health restoration during the past 30 years.

Cancer is Not a Disease!
It's A Survival Mechanism
Discover Cancer's Hidden Purpose, Heal its Root Causes, and be Healthier than Ever!

In *Cancer is Not a Disease,* Andreas Moritz proves the point that cancer is the physical symptom that reflects our body's final attempt to deal with life-threatening cell congestion and toxins. He claims that removing the underlying conditions that force the body to produce cancerous cells, sets the preconditions for complete healing of our body, mind, and emotions.

This book confronts you with a radically new understanding of cancer - one that revolutionized the current cancer model. On the average, today's conventional "treatments" of killing, cutting out, or burning cancerous cells offer most patients a remission rate of a mere 7%, and the majority of these survivors are "cured" for just five years or fewer. Prominent cancer researcher and professor at the University of California at Berkeley, Dr. Hardin Jones, stated: "Patients are as well, or better off, untreated..." Any published success figures in cancer survival statistics are offset by equal or better scores among those receiving no treatment at all. More people are killed by cancer treatments than are saved by them.

Cancer is Not a Disease shows you why traditional cancer treatments are often fatal, what actually causes cancer, and how you can remove the obstacles that prevent the body from healing itself. Cancer is not an attempt on your life; on the contrary, this "dread disease" is the body's final, desperate effort to save your life. Unless we change our perception of what cancer really is, it will continue to threaten the life of nearly one out of every two people. This book opens a door for those who wish to turn feelings of victimhood into empowerment and self-mastery, and disease into health.

Topics of the book include:

- Reasons the body is forced to develop cancer cells
- How to identify and remove the causes of cancer
- Why most cancers disappear by themselves, without medical intervention
- Why radiation, chemotherapy, and surgery never cure cancer
- Why some people survive cancer despite undergoing dangerously radical treatments
- The roles of fear, frustration, low self-worth, and repressed anger in the

262

origination of cancer

How to turn self-destructive emotions into energies that promote health and vitality

Spiritual lessons behind cancer

It's Time to Come Alive!
Start Using the Amazing Healing Powers of Your Body, Mind, and Spirit Today!

In this book, the author brings to light man's deep inner need for spiritual wisdom in life and helps the reader develop a new sense of reality that is based on love, power, and compassion. He describes our relationship with the natural world in detail and discusses how we can harness its tremendous powers for our personal and humanity's benefit. *It's Time to Come Alive* challenges some of our most commonly held beliefs and offers a way out of the emotional restrictions and physical limitations we have created in our lives.

Topics include: What shapes our destiny; using the power of intention; secrets of defying the aging process; doubting - the cause of failure; opening the heart; material wealth and spiritual wealth; fatigue - the major cause of stress; methods of emotional transformation; techniques of primordial healing; how to increase the health of the five senses; developing spiritual wisdom; the major causes of today's earth changes; entry into the new world; 12 gateways to heaven on earth; and many more.

Feel Great, Lose Weight
Stop Dieting and Start Living

No rigorous workouts. No surgery. In this book, celebrated author Andreas Moritz suggests a gentle – and permanent – route to losing weight. In this ground-breaking book, he says that once we stop blaming our genes and take control of our own life, weight-loss is a natural consequence.

"You need to make that critical mental shift. You need to experience the willingness to shed your physical and emotional baggage, not by counting calories but by embracing your mind, body and spirit. Once you start looking at yourself differently, 80 per cent of the work is done."

In Feel Great, Lose Weight, Andreas Moritz tells us why conventional weight-loss programs don't work and how weight-loss 'experts' make sure we keep going back. He also tells us why food manufacturers, pharmaceutical companies and health regulators conspire to keep America toxically overweight.

But we can refuse to buy into the Big Fat Lie. Choosing the mind-body approach triggers powerful biochemical changes that set us on a safe and irreversible path to losing weight, without resorting to crash diets, heavy workouts or dangerous surgical procedures.

If you've done every diet, taken every pill and read every book, you're probably wondering if there's any point giving it one more shot. But you've possibly been seduced by conventional propaganda that places your health and weight in the hands of weight-loss experts, the gymnasium, medical doctors and the pharmaceutical industry. There's a very definite payoff - for them - in getting vulnerable individuals to believe their self-serving promotional spiel.

But what the universal weight-watcher's guide won't tell you is that losing weight - yes, a considerable amount of weight - is about healing. Despite the notion we've grown up with, that we cannot heal without prescriptions, pills and surgery, conventional wisdom says something else.

In this book, we'll discuss the natural way to losing weight - no pill popping, no crash or fad diets, no calorie counting or rigorous aerobic exercise. The human body is a wonderful precision machine that is constantly seeking a state of equilibrium or homeostasis.

An overweight or obese body is a body in distress. But the human body is also amazingly resilient. So despite the abuse it has been subjected to, it is possible to reverse the processes that led to this state and rebalance the body's biochemistry to achieve its normal, optimal weight.

Simple Steps to Total Health!
Andreas Moritz with co-author John Hornecker

By nature, your physical body is designed to be healthy and vital throughout life. Unhealthy eating habits and lifestyle choices, however, lead to numerous health conditions that prevent you from enjoying life to the fullest. In Simple Steps to Total Health, the authors bring to light the most common cause of disease, which is the build-up of toxins and residues from improperly digested foods that inhibit various organs and

264

systems from performing their normal functions. This guidebook for total health provides you with simple but highly effective approaches for internal cleansing, hydration, nutrition, and living habits.

The book's three parts cover the essentials of total health - Good Internal Hygiene, Healthy Nutrition, and Balanced Lifestyle. Learn about the most common disease-causing foods, dietary habits and influences responsible for the occurrence of chronic illnesses, including those affecting the blood vessels, heart, liver, intestinal organs, lungs, kidneys, joints, bones, nervous system, and sense organs.

To be able to live a healthy life, you must align your internal biological rhythms with the larger rhythms of nature. Find out more about this and many other important topics in *Simple Steps to Total Health.* This is a "must-have" book for anyone who is interested in using a natural, drug-free approach to restore total health.

Heart Disease No More!
Make Peace with Your Heart and Heal Yourself
(Excerpted from Timeless Secrets of
Health and Rejuvenation)

Less than one hundred years ago, heart disease was an extremely rare illness. Today it kills more people in the developed world than all other causes of death combined. Despite the vast quantity of financial resources spent on finding a cure for heart disease, the current medical approaches remain mainly symptom-oriented and do not address the underlying causes.

Even worse, overwhelming evidence shows that the treatment of heart disease or its presumed precursors, such as high blood pressure, hardening of the arteries, and high cholesterol, not only prevents a real cure, but also can easily lead to chronic heart failure. The patient's heart may still beat, but not strongly enough for him to feel vital and alive.

Without removing the underlying causes of heart disease and its precursors, the average person has little, if any, protection against it. Heart attacks can strike whether you have undergone a coronary bypass or had stents placed inside your arteries. According to research, these procedures fail to prevent heart attacks and do nothing to reduce mortality rates.

Heart Disease No More, excerpted from the author's bestselling book, *Timeless Secrets of Health and Rejuvenation*, puts the responsibility for healing where it belongs, on the heart, mind, and body of each individual. It provides the reader with practical insights about the development and causes of heart disease. Even better, it explains simple steps you can take to prevent and reverse heart disease for good, regardless of a possible genetic predisposition.

Diabetes--No More!
Discover and Heal Its True Causes
(Excerpted from Timeless Secrets of
Health and Rejuvenation)

According to this bestselling author, diabetes is not a disease; in the vast majority of cases, it is a complex mechanism of protection or survival that the body chooses to avoid the possibly fatal consequences of an unhealthful diet and lifestyle.

Despite the body's ceaseless self-preservation efforts (which we call diseases), millions of people suffer or die unnecessarily from these consequences. The imbalanced blood sugar level in diabetes is but a symptom of illness, not the illness itself. By developing diabetes, the body is neither doing something wrong, nor is it trying to commit suicide. The current diabetes epidemic is man-made, or rather, factory-made, and, therefore, can be halted and reversed through simple but effective changes in diet and lifestyle. *Diabetes—No More* provides you with essential information on the various causes of diabetes and how anyone can avoid them.

To stop the diabetes epidemic you need to create the right circumstances that allow your body to heal. Just as there is a mechanism to become diabetic, there is also a mechanism to reverse it. Find out how!

This book was excerpted from the bestselling book, *Timeless Secrets of Health and Rejuvenation.*

Ending The AIDS Myth
It's Time to Heal the TRUE Causes!
(Excerpted from Timeless Secrets of
Health and Rejuvenation)

Contrary to common belief, no scientific evidence exists to this day to prove that AIDS is a contagious disease. The current AIDS theory falls short in predicting the kind of AIDS disease an infected person may be manifesting, and no accurate system is in place to determine how long it will take for the disease to develop. In addition, the current HIV/AIDS theory contains no reliable information that can help identify those who are at risk for developing AIDS.

On the other hand, published research actually proves that HIV only spreads heterosexually in extremely rare cases and cannot be responsible for an epidemic that involves millions of AIDS victims around the world. Furthermore, it is an established fact that the retrovirus HIV, which is composed of human gene fragments, is incapable of destroying human cells. However, cell destruction is the main characteristic of every AIDS disease.

Even the principal discoverer of HIV, Luc Montagnier, no longer believes that HIV is solely responsible for causing AIDS. In fact, he showed that HIV alone could not cause AIDS. Increasing evidence indicates that AIDS may be a toxicity syndrome or metabolic disorder that is caused by immunity risk factors, including heroin, sex-enhancement drugs, antibiotics, commonly prescribed AIDS drugs, rectal intercourse, starvation, malnutrition, and dehydration

Dozens of prominent scientists working at the forefront of AIDS research now openly question the virus hypothesis of AIDS. Find out why! *Ending the AIDS Myth* also shows you what really causes the shutdown of the immune system and what you can do to avoid this.

Heal Yourself with Sunlight
Use Its Secret Medicinal Powers to Help Cure Cancer, Heart Disease, Hypertension, Diabetes Arthritis, Infectious Diseases, and much more. (NEW edition 206 pages)

This book by Andreas Moritz provides scientific evidence that sunlight is essential for good health, and that a lack of sun exposure can be held responsible for many of today's diseases.

On the other hand, most people now believe that the sun is the main culprit for causing skin cancer, certain cataracts leading to blindness, and aging. Only those who take the risk of exposing themselves to the sunlight, find that the sun makes them feel and look better, provided they don't use sunscreens or burn their skin. The UV-rays in sunlight actually stimulate the thyroid gland to increase hormone production, which in turn increases the body's basal metabolic rate. This assists both in weight loss and improved muscle development.

It has been known for several decades that those living mostly in the outdoors, at high altitudes, or near the equator, have the lowest incidence of skin cancers. In addition, Studies revealed that exposing patients to controlled amounts of sunlight dramatically lowered elevated blood pressure (up to 40 mm Hg drop), decreased cholesterol in the blood stream, lowered abnormally high blood sugars among diabetics, and increased the number of white blood cells which we need to help resist disease. Patients suffering from gout, rheumatoid arthritis, colitis, arteriosclerosis, anemia, cystitis, eczema, acne, psoriasis, herpes, lupus, sciatica, kidney problems, asthma, as well as burns, have all shown to receive great benefit from the healing rays of the sun.

Hear the Whispers, Live Your Dream
A Fanfare of Inspiration

Listening to the whispers of your heart will set you free. The beauty and bliss of your knowingness and love center are what we are here to capture, take in and swim with. You are like a dolphin sailing in a sea of joy. Allow yourself to open to the wondrous fullness of your selfhood, without reservation and without judgment.

Judgment stands in the way, like a boulder trespassing on your journey to the higher reaches of your destiny. Slide these boulders aside and feel the joy of your inner truth sprout forth. Do not allow another's thoughts or directions for you to supersede your inner knowingness, for you relinquish being the full, radiant star that you are.

It is with an open heart, a receptive mind, and a reaching for the stars of wisdom that lie within you, that you reap the bountiful goodness of mother Earth and the universal I AM. For you are a benevolent being of light and there is no course that can truly stop you, except your own thoughts, or allowing another's beliefs to override your own.

May these aphorisms of love, joy and wisdom inspire you to be the wondrous being that you were born to be!

**All books are available paperback and as electronic books
through the Ener-Chi Wellness Center**

Website: http://www.ener-chi.com
Email: support@ener-chi.com
Toll free 1(866) 258–4006 (USA)
Local: 1(709) 570–7401 (Canada)

For a Sacred Santémony phone session with Andreas Moritz,
please use the above methods of contact.

INDEX

271

273

274